CREATING
CONNECTICUT

CREATING
CONNECTICUT

Critical
Moments That
Shaped
a Great State

WALTER W. WOODWARD

Globe
Pequot

GUILFORD, CONNECTICUT

Globe
Pequot

An imprint of The Rowman & Littlefield Publishing Group, Inc.
4501 Forbes Blvd., Ste. 200
Lanham, MD 20706
www.rowman.com

Distributed by NATIONAL BOOK NETWORK

British Library Cataloguing in Publication Information available
Library of Congress Control Number: 2020932487

ISBN 978-1-4930-4702-4 (cloth : alk. paper)
ISBN 978-1-4930-4703-1 (electronic)

♾™ The paper used in this publication meets the minimum requirements of American National Standard for Information Sciences—Permanence of Paper for Printed Library Materials, ANSI/NISO Z39.48-1992.

TABLE OF CONTENTS

INTRODUCTION

As Connecticut's state historian, I've had the good fortune to spend my career focusing my historical research on this state, its people, and their stories. *Creating Connecticut* is a product of that effort. It's a collection of 24 stories—12 shorter, 12 longer—each of which tells us something important about Connecticut's past; something that still, in one way or another, affects our lives as Connecticans today. Some of these stories are adaptations or expansions of the most popular public talks and lectures I have given around Connecticut and elsewhere. Others (the shorter entries) are based on the "From the State Historian" column I have written for many years now in *Connecticut Explored*, the magazine of Connecticut history. All of them are revised for presentation in print, and designed to be readable, engaging and informative introductions to aspects of our state's history that will be new, or nearly so, to most readers.

Some of the stories in *Creating Connecticut* show people we thought we knew—Mark Twain, Nathan Hale—in new and surprising ways. Some tell us about people many of us *don't* know about—Eleazar Wheelock, Samson Occom, Adriaen Block—but ought to. Many are about events, movements, and periods of change—the Pequot War, the Hartford witch hunt, outmigration to Connecticut's Western Reserve, Irish immigration into the state—crucial moments when Connecticans were tested and called on by circumstance to change their minds, values, approaches, and even lives. And some are about the uniqueness of our state, and the ways in which Connecticans have celebrated their past, in the past.

This is not a comprehensive history, nor does it touch on all things that have shaped Connecticut today. The focus here is on individual stories, but stories that both interest and matter. You can read them from front to back—they are arranged more or less in chronological order—or you can scan the Table of Contents and jump in with the story that seems most interesting to you.

My hope is that you will read them all and come away with a desire to know more about Connecticut history.

Walter W. Woodward
Connecticut State Historian

RESTLESS BEGINNINGS

When the Dutchman Adriaen Block sailed the "Restlessness" up the Connecticut River in 1614, he launched an era of restless change and transformation.

In the spring of 1614 Adriaen Block sailed the little ship he had built and named *Onrust—Restlessness*—into the river the Algonquians called Quinnetukut or the "place of the long water." The forty-seven-year-old Dutchman was as restless as his vessel and anxious to make up the losses he had experienced the previous winter when his ship *Tyger* had accidentally burned to the water line at Manhattan. The trader and explorer was anxious too—to secure the Dutch government's recent promise of a trading monopoly over any new countries or harbors discovered by Dutch explorers.

Restless to turn his fortunes around, Block came up a river that was itself restless, running fresh, and full of upriver snowmelt and spring rain. He named the river the *Versche,* meaning fresh (as in fast-running) and, as the first known European to probe its courses and seek its opportunities, he launched an era of restlessness that would change this river and its people forever.

Then as now, restless had many meanings, and all would apply to the world the arrival of this little boat would create. A generation of restless Europeans, both Dutch and English, constantly in motion, never ceasing or pausing, would come to the Quinnetukut, the "place of the long water," first in search of trade with the indigenous people, and soon after, in quest of those peoples' lands and resources. Some of them were spiritually restless, troubled in mind and spirit, and seeking a place to serve their God as their consciences demanded.

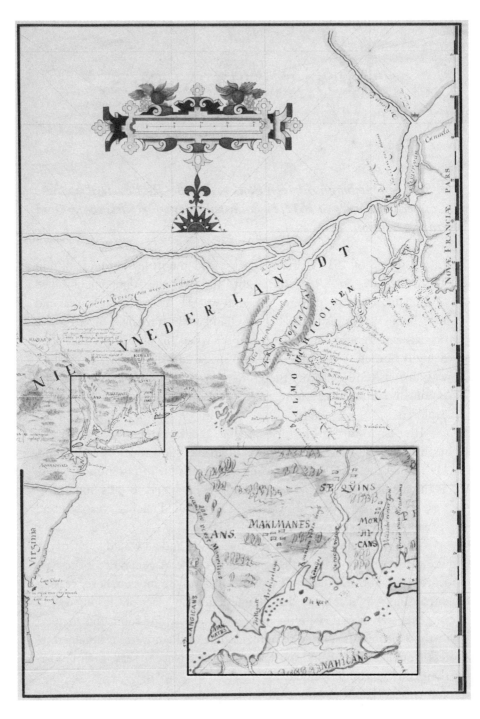

The figurative map of Adriaen Block. NEW YORK PUBLIC LIBRARY DIGITAL COLLECTIONS

For the Native Americans already here, the arrival of the *Onrust* heralded a new restlessness—first, as they jostled to control distribution of European trade goods, and later, as they fought the incoming insurgents' efforts to take their lands and control their lives. For Connecticut's First Peoples, the arrival of the *Onrust* brought centuries of restlessness—literal unrest, sleepless worry, sickness, turmoil, and death.

Block, an experienced navigator with a trader's eye for land and resources, created a map during his voyage that detailed the region he surveyed and the people he encountered. He was the first to name the region "New Nederlandt" and his map helped create the New Netherland Company that received the Dutch government's promised three-year monopoly over the newly discovered colony's trade in 1615.

In the detail of Block's figurative map, the Versche (Connecticut) River is the long river near the center of the image. Present-day Hartford is near the tribal name "Sequins."

While Block was creating his map, another man, not far away, was creating a different map. Captain John Smith, best known for his role in the Virginia Company's settlement of the colony at Jamestown, was also exploring the coast of New England in 1614, and he was completely captivated by the country and its potential. He returned to England fully committed to establishing new plantations there. Dubbing the region New England, just as Block had called it New Netherland, Smith spent years working to convince the English people that northeast North America was virtually an extension of Old England, but with unlimited possibilities. Key to that effort was the map Smith produced in 1616, which was subsequently distributed by the thousands.

Although Smith's map of New England and Block's map of New Netherland were created within a year of each other, and both laid claim to the same geographic region, the differences between them are striking and important. They reflect the different English and Dutch orientations to North America and foreshadow the inevitable conflict that would divide these two seventeenth-century European powers.

Block's map was a trader's map. It focused on rivers as highways to the interior and its fur trade, as well as the people on the ground who could facilitate access to those furs. He concentrated details on the longest rivers, such as the North (left side of map detail above Manhattan

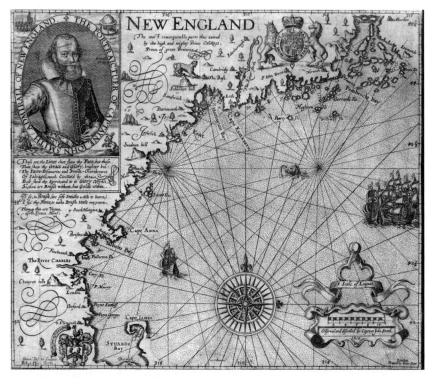

John Smith, Map of New Engand. MAP REPRODUCTION COURTESY OF THE NORMAN B.
LEVENTHAL MAP & EDUCATION CENTER AT THE BOSTON PUBLIC LIBRARY.

[Manhates] Island) and the Fresh—the Hudson and the Connecticut
Rivers—taking care to name the tribes along those rivers and indicate
their relative strength with clusters of dwellings.

Smith's map was a colonizer's map and took an opposite tack from
Block's. It hugged the coastline, paying scant attention to riverine detail,
and ignored indigenous tribes all together. This was a promoter's map.
Although the first English colonists would not arrive for four more years,
Smith's New England was full of English towns, with names such as Cambridge, Oxford, London, and Ipswich, that he anticipated would soon be
filled by the English ships he placed just appearing on the horizon.

Traders versus colonists. New Netherlanders versus New Englanders.
A half-century of future conflict outlined in the very first maps. Caught

right in the middle of this conflict, often at the very epicenter, would be the people along the Versche River, which the English called the Great River, and which the Indians called Quinnetukut.

Time is the acid rain of historical memory. Slowly, often over generations stretching into centuries, important details of the past can fade one by one until what once was crucial to the life of a time and people is all but forgotten. So it has been with the Dutch history of Connecticut.

Most school children are still taught that the first European to come to Connecticut was Adriaen Block. And many students of Hartford history know the Dutch had a trading house there, somewhere close to the later site of Samuel Colt's onion-domed arms manufacturing complex. But for the average Connectican, that's the sum of it. The English arrived, and the Dutch faded to black. The rest of the colonial story as they remember it is a simplistic tale of English versus Indians that quickly morphs into one about Patriots versus Tories.

But that is not how it was. For its first fifty years Connecticut was a restless, seething site of constant competition, pitting nation against nation, tribe against tribe, and colonies against colonies in a Rubik's Cube of combinations that always involved the Dutch. Nothing was done by the English at Connecticut without first calculating the Dutch response in New Netherland or at the States General, the seat of government, in The Hague. No English settlement was expanded, no tribal alliance contracted, no trading venture launched without calculating the Dutch reaction. From the arrival of Jacob van Curler, who established a Dutch trading house called the House of Hope (Huys de Hoop) at the site of present day Hartford in June of 1633, to the occupation of New Amsterdam/New York by the English in September of 1664, to the final surrender of all Dutch claims in the region a decade later, the Dutch-Connecticut story was a deeply conflicted, sometimes harrowing experience. Those who lived in that time knew their lives depended on knowing it in detail.

It is not a story that can be told quickly or that follows a simple narrative. But here is a sample of the issues over which Connecticut, Saybrook, New Haven, Plimoth, and Massachusetts Colonies (yes, at first they were all separate and independent colonies), Long Island and the border towns of Greenwich, Stamford, and Fairfield, plus the Mohawk, Narragansett,

Munsee, Mohican, Pequot, Nipmuck, Montauk, Shinnecock, Mahican, and other tribes contended during the first fifty years of European occupation. Each entity had its own particular interests and sought its own advantages. This produced a shifting landscape of loyalties and alliances as complicated as any you'll find in today's most Balkanized battlegrounds, and it made Connecticut's first fifty years of colonial settlement a time of confusion and anxiety for everyone involved.

At the foundation of Anglo-Dutch contention was the question of who could claim rightful ownership of the land between the forty-first and forty-fifth parallels of latitude, roughly the area from Maine to the Delaware Bay. Both the English and the Dutch claimed the entire region by sovereign or legislative grant and by right of discovery. But for practical purposes, settlement patterns that placed the greatest concentration of English settlers in Massachusetts and the greatest concentration of Dutch settlers and traders along the Hudson Valley also limited the truly contested lands to the area between those two settlement centers. These were sites of both the greatest Anglo-Dutch interaction and the greatest conflict: the colonies of Connecticut, Saybrook, and New Haven; the English-speaking towns of eastern Long Island; the Anglo-Dutch border towns of Stamford, Fairfield and Greenwich; and, because the Dutch trading house there was such a burr under the Puritan saddle, the upriver town of Hartford. Life in and around those places was one of nearly continuous Anglo-Dutch contention, in which native groups figured, importantly and often unpredictably, as allies, opponents, go-betweens, and at times enemies aligned with a foreign power. The Anglo-Dutch struggle for authority in Connecticut and its border regions was expressed through claims, threats, demands, assaults, thefts, secret alliances, rumors, negotiations, beatings, fines, guerilla tactics, wildcat range wars, and repeatedly at the end, international war fought on domestic soil. The one thing usually missing among the members of each of the three major competing groups—Dutch, English, and Native American—was unity of purpose. Each group was so fragmented that its members were almost never able to act together as a cohesive entity.

Between the founding of the trading fort at Hartford in 1633 and the Dutch surrender at New Amsterdam in 1665, the following incidents, now all but forgotten, occurred. These are not a comprehensive list; rather, they are just a sample of Connecticut's sustained inter-colonial struggle with the Dutch.

In 1633, just four months after they built the garrisoned trading fort Huys de Hoop at Hartford, the Dutch troops there threatened to blow Plimoth trader William Holmes—who was coming to establish an English trading house north of the Dutch post at present day Windsor—out of the Connecticut River with cannon fire if he sailed past their fort. Holmes, correctly sensing it was a bluff on the part of the Dutch, ignored the threats and kept sailing. After he set up his trading house at Windsor, Dutch Governor Wouter Van Twiller sent seventy armed men to again threaten the Plimoth trader out of the area. This proved to be a second bluff, and was faced down successfully, but it set the stage for the long series of contentious and more serious Anglo-Dutch interactions that followed.

Almost from the moment Reverend Thomas Hooker and his group of one hundred Massachusetts émigrés settled the place they called Hartford in 1636, they and the House of Hope Dutch engaged in continuous mutual harassment. The English assaulted Dutch farm workers in their fields, stole Dutch cattle, and ruined Dutch crops. The Dutch harbored and gave sanctuary to English lawbreakers, encouraged disgruntled English servants to run away to their fort, and conducted a black-market trade in buying and selling stolen English goods. This back-and-forth harassment continued at varying degrees of intensity for seventeen years, until the English finally seized control of the Dutch fort in 1653.

Nearer to the Dutch stronghold of New Amsterdam, New Netherland's Governor Willem Kieft sent troops to break up English settlements on Long Island in 1641 and imprisoned the English planters there. Connecticut leaders believed these attacks were a prelude to a combined Dutch and Native American assault on their colony and urged all English colonies to unite in a preemptive war against the Dutch, but Massachusetts—far from the conflicts—politely declined to participate.

Shortly after the English settlement of Greenwich had been founded by former Massachusetts colonists as part of New Haven Colony in 1640, they were visited by armed troops from New Netherland, sent by Kieft to warn them to submit to New Netherland's authority or face the consequences. The settlers may have verbally submitted to the Dutch at that time, but in 1642, after Kieft's assaults on the Long Island towns, they agreed in writing to reject English claims to jurisdiction and formally become part of New Netherland. A key factor in that decision, over and above the Dutch threats, was the English settlers' need for protection from the nearby and warring Munsees, which had not been forthcoming from New Haven. Groenwits, as the Dutch called the settlement, remained a New Netherland border town with a mixed English and Dutch population for the next sixteen years.

In 1647, mocking New Haven colony's pretensions to security, the Dutch smuggled troops aboard a New Haven–bound vessel who, upon arrival there, took advantage of the Puritan colony's Sunday proscriptions against all forms of work to seize the merchant ship *Saint Benonio*. They sailed it to New Amsterdam where both ship and cargo were confiscated. A heated war of words ensued between the two colonies which, coupled with a widespread belief that Dutch traders were actively selling indigenous warriors guns for use against the English, dramatically escalated fears of an imminent intercolonial war. Negotiations followed, but despite a temporary accord reached through the 1650 Treaty of Hartford in which the Dutch agreed to move their territorial claims from the Connecticut River to a line fifty miles west, and to limit their Long Island claims to lands west and south of Oyster Bay, Anglo-Dutch relations continued to spiral downward. Despite the treaty, New Haven and Connecticut remained on continuous war footing for the next two years, certain the Dutch governor had enticed the Narragansett sachem Ninigret to lead a pan–Indian and Dutch assault against the English. Fears were further amplified when news reached the colonies that war had broken out between England and the Netherlands in July of 1652, an act that triggered a series of naval confrontations in the North Sea, English Channel, and the Mediterranean.

In 1653, believing a Dutch-Indian attack on southern New England was imminent, all the English colonies but Massachusetts declared war on Ninigret and the Dutch. A defense force was sent to Stamford and a Connecticut frigate of twelve guns was sent to guard the English towns on Long Island. The arrival of a Dutch fleet was expected to trigger the Indian and Dutch assault. Stamford and Fairfield raised their own army to oppose the Dutch, prepared to fight alone if necessary. Connecticut troops seized the House of Hope at Hartford.

To galvanize support from London, a pamphlet appeared that summer, part of whose title was (titles were much longer then) ". . . A True Relation of a Most Bloody, Treacherous and Cruel Design of the Dutch in the New-Netherlands in America for the Total Ruining and Murdering of the English Colonies in New-England." The pamphlet was based, it said, upon letters sent in haste from the English colonies, and described in detail a Dutch plot that had begun in March 1653 to arm indigenous warriors and join with them to attack all the Puritan colonies together in a coordinated surprise Sunday attack. The French in Canada had apparently signed on to this anti-English alliance, and the English colonies were thus "environed"—that is surrounded—by enemies. The pamphlet, short and urgent, was convincing. Oliver Cromwell, the new Puritan Lord Protector of England, wrote New England's leaders saying he was sending a four-frigate fleet and an army to Boston to help launch an offensive against New Netherlands.

Cromwell's attack squadron departed England in February of 1654, and by the time the storm-delayed fleet and army reached Boston in June, all the colonies were on a war footing busily preparing to attack the Dutch. Just as the English fleet and combined colonial and English army of nine hundred infantry and one troop of cavalry were about to embark from Boston for the assault on New Amsterdam, a ship arrived from London carrying news that a peace treaty had been concluded and the Anglo-Dutch war was over. The attack on New Amsterdam was called off.

That did not, however, end colonial Anglo–Dutch–Native American tensions. The same charges and counter charges, threats and war rumors that had provoked the military mobilization remained a constant feature of the Connecticut–New Netherland relationship right up to 1664, when, during the second European Anglo–Dutch War, an English force assisted by Connecticut Governor John Winthrop, Jr. forced a peaceful capitulation of New Amsterdam, instantly creating the town and colony of New York. This was a fitting non-end to the story, as the Dutch regained control of their former colony briefly in 1673 during the third Anglo-Dutch War, only to surrender it back to the English permanently the following year. So ended four decades of Anglo-Dutch colonial conflict, much of it focused in and around Connecticut.

Almost none of this history, however, remains in the stories this state tells about its colonial past. The restless, conflicted tale of Dutch-Connecticut relations has faded through time into a bare-bones, simplistic tale of hopeful discovery and instant displacement. And that is not a good thing. Fully understanding and appreciating the richness of our state today depends, I believe, on getting back in touch with our real past, and that includes knowing about the years when, for all Connecticut colonists, New Netherland was central, and nothing happened here without restlessly wondering and worrying about the Dutch next door.

FURTHER READING

For an excellent account from the Dutch perspective of New Netherland, as well as the Anglo Dutch Wars and their effects in the English colonies read Russell Shorto's *The Island in the Center of the World* (New York: Doubleday, 2004) 260–65.

For the Anglo-Dutch history of today's Fairfield County region, see Missy Wolfe's Insubordinate Spirit (Globe Pequot Press, 2012) and *Hidden History of Colonial Greenwich* (Charleston, SC: History Press, 2018).

For more about John Smith's 1614 trip to North America and his subsequent efforts to promote New England, see Walter W. Woodward's "Captain John Smith and the Campaign for New England: A study in Early Modern Identity and Promotion," (*New England Quarterly*, 2008, vol 81(1) 91–125).

A thorough treatment of Connecticut's complicated relations with the Dutch colony in New Netherland remains to be written, though earlier histories tell the story in part. See for example, Richard S. Dunn's *Puritans and Yankees: The Winthrop Dynasty of New England* (Princeton, NJ, 1962, 2015), William DeLoss Love's *The Colonial History of Hartford: gathered from the original records* (Hartford, 1914), Harry M Ward's, *The United Colonies of New England–1643-90* (New York, 1961), and Isabel MacBeath Calder's *The New Haven Colony* (New Haven, 1934).

WHAT'S A PURITAN, AND WHY DIDN'T THEY STAY IN MASSACHUSETTS?

How do we in the twenty-first century come to an honest under-standing of the Puritans, those influential culture shapers from the 1600s? Answering two questions helps us not only get at the heart of Puritan beliefs but also helps us to understand why Puritanism in Connecticut differed in at least one important way from its ideological cousin in the Bay Colony.

WHAT WAS A PURITAN, ANYWAY?

The word Puritan usually conjures up a host of associations, mostly unpleasant ones these days. Puritans have been cast as mean-spirited (Nathaniel Hawthorne), priggish (H. L. Mencken), sexually repressed (Arthur Miller), pathologically superstitious (Marion Starkey) folk who liked nothing better than to mind other people's business and to hang their neighbors (especially women) for no apparent reason.

To be sure, a few seventeenth-century painters helped reinforce these images by depicting their subjects as dark-fashioned, arched-eyed, pursed-lipped people you wouldn't want to meet at a cocktail party or, worse still, in an alley off of Gold Street in Hartford.

But the frosty forebear image of the prudish Puritan competes with other, more appealing images: bold builders of Ronald Reagan's (well, actually John Winthrop's) "City on a Hill"; persecuted refugees who risked their all to find religious freedom; rugged egalitarians whose founding documents (the Mayflower Compact and Connecticut's Fundamental

Orders) laid the foundation for American democracy. These images, usually hauled out in civics classes or commemorated with scissors and construction paper at Thanksgiving, are generally no more accurate than the negative stereotypes.

In truth, a Puritan was someone for whom religion was the most important single aspect of life. It was more important than the self, family, friends, wealth, and status. Moreover, Puritans saw the hand of God's providence permeating every aspect of daily living and sought to read divine instruction in ordinary occurrences. Did it rain on the garden? A sign of God's blessing. Were there worms in the cheese? A warning to avoid Satan's snares. The most important thing a Puritan could do was get religion right; this was a lifetime pursuit, engaged in while milking the cow as well as while reading the Bible.

Puritans believed the reforms of the Church of England initiated by Henry VIII in 1533 had not gone nearly far enough. To their minds, the Anglican Church remained encumbered with liturgies and rituals that cast a Catholic shadow over God's Protestant glory. Puritans rejected these practices and pushed hard for further English reformation.

This stance complicated their tenure in England. The monarch, as head of the English church, was naturally prone to view the Puritan push for reform as an expression of disloyalty. James I, upon ascending the throne, said of the Puritans, "I will make them conform [to Church of England rituals] or I will harry them out of the land." Which, gradually, he and his son Charles I did.

Royal and ecclesiastical persecution led to what has been called The Great Migration, which saw some 20,000 Puritans leave England for New England between 1620 and 1640. Most of them landed in Massachusetts.

Did they come seeking religious freedom? For themselves, yes. But for Catholics, Jews, or even Anglicans, not in the least. *Now that we've finally perfected Christian practice, most Puritan migrants reasoned, why should we allow others to blaspheme in our presence?* That hardline stance led to problems among the godly in America almost from the beginning.

Few things unite people more than a common opponent. As long as the Puritans stayed in England, their focus was on what was wrong with the Anglican Church. But having risked their lives to come to New

England, far from the reach of king or archbishop, the émigrés could now concentrate on perfecting their own religious practices. This led to almost immediate internal conflict over a range of issues. How did one know if he or she was one of Christ's chosen people? How did others know if a professed "saint" really was a saint? Who should be admitted to the congregation, and on what grounds? These were fundamentals about which many New England Puritans disagreed, and, since getting religion right was the most important thing in the world, they disagreed with vigor.

WHY DIDN'T THEY STAY IN MASSACHUSETTS?

One person caught in the crossfire of this religious controversy was the Reverend Thomas Hooker, the celebrated English minister who arrived in Boston in 1633 with the equally celebrated minister John Cotton. Almost immediately both men were called upon to help resolve a number of religious conflicts that had arisen in the new colony. But Hooker and Cotton frequently had opposing views, which led to increased factionalism. One issue over which they strongly clashed involved the standards for admission into the church: Hooker argued for more inclusive membership, Cotton for more restrictive. Hooker believed that assurance that one was a Puritan saint came through a long and arduous process of living a Christian life, and that people should be admitted as church members as soon as they had achieved "some hope" of their salvation. Cotton disagreed. He believed membership should be open only to those who were convinced and could also persuade the membership that they had fully received God's grace.

Over time these disagreements, combined with other factors such as scarcity of good pasture land near Boston and fear of royal intervention in that colony's affairs (because of a widely trumpeted incident in which a Puritan zealot had cut the cross of Saint George out of the Bay Colony's royal flag), helped convince Hooker to remove to Connecticut. The early New England historian William Hubbard wrote, "Two such eminent stars, such as were Mr. Cotton and Mr. Hooker, both of the first magnitude, though of differing influence, could not well continue in one and the same orb."

On May 1, 1636, Hooker and his assistant, the Reverend Samuel Stone, left Newtown (later Cambridge), Massachusetts, with about 100 members of their congregation and 160 head of cattle on an overland journey to a place the Indians called Suckiaug. Stone, who had originally ministered in Hertford, England, had led an advance contingent to the area the year before. There, by the banks of the Little (later Hog) River, the company founded Hartford. Hooker's and Stone's new church was to follow the congregational model established in Massachusetts (in which the congregation selects its own ministers), but under Hooker's leadership, the people of Hartford proved more tolerant in terms of church admissions than their coastal peers.

This bent toward tolerance among Connecticut Puritans was later expressed in Connecticut's more lenient treatment of Quakers (whom Bostonians occasionally executed), the state's acceptance of the oath of religious tolerance imposed on New England colonies by Charles II in the 1660s, and Connecticut's cessation of witchcraft executions a full generation before the trials at Salem. These relatively progressive positions were further mirrored in Hooker's sermon on May 1, 1638, wherein he expressed the view, remarkable for the time, that the foundation of governmental authority rested in "the free consent of the people."

This is not to imply, however, that the Puritans of Connecticut were advocates of religious freedom for all. Far from it. Quakers, though allowed to live, were still run out of the colony, and in the early 1660s Hartford hanged more than its fair share of witches. And as Connecticut grew, people still managed to squabble over the details of Puritan practice with almost as much fervor as their cousins to the north and east. Ultimately, even Hartford's first church was torn by controversy. But the fact remains that Hartford in 1636 was founded by a minister who thought the Bay's practice of Puritanism was harsher than it ought to be. And he thought so with enough intensity that he and his congregation pulled up stakes and headed west for the promise of a kinder, gentler, and better, life.

WETHERSFIELD'S WAR: HUNGER, RUMOR, AND THE COST OF BATTLES NOT FOUGHT

Rumor was often the greatest enemy in the conflicts between English settlers and Connecticut's First People.

On June 8, 1771, the crusty Boston lawyer and future President of the United States John Adams took a horseback ride. Exhausted and ill from the stresses of defending the British soldiers who had participated in the previous December's Boston Massacre, Adams headed to the colony next door for a little rest and recreation. He left Hartford just after breakfast and headed south for his next destination. Here's what he wrote about what he saw:

> *Rode to Wethersfield four miles, on the West side of the River—Here is the finest ride in America, I believe. Nothing can exceed the Beauty, and Fertility of the Country. The Lands upon the River, the flatt low Lands, are loaded with rich, noble Crops of Grass, and Grain, and Corn. . . . They have in Wethersfield a large brick Meeting House, Lockwood the Minister. A Gentleman came in and told me that there was not such another Street in America as this at Weathersfield. . . . I have spent this Morning in riding through Paradise.*

Many Connecticans today share John Adams's view of Wethersfield. Contender with Hartford, Windsor, and Old Saybrook for bragging rights as Connecticut's oldest town, Wethersfield is now, as it was

in Adams's day, one of the nation's most beautiful places, rich in historical associations, with streets lined with lovingly preserved Revolutionary
War–period architecture. It still looks much like the town where General
George Washington met the French Comte de Rochambeau in May of
1781 to plan the campaign that led to the Revolutionary War's stunning
final victory at the Battle of Yorktown. But ironically a recent, and at first
seemingly non-descript, find in an archeological test pit in the yard of the
very home in which Washington and Rochambeau held their meetings—
now Wethersfield's Webb Deane Stevens Museum—has historians and
archaeologists around the country excited—not about Wethersfield's
Revolutionary War past, but rather its participation in a different, much
earlier, war.

The test pit was being dug at the museum in advance of construction
of a new education building. Museum officials needed to certify that the
new building would not impinge on any previously unknown but significant archeological remains. As expected, because of the length of time the
site had been occupied and its proximity to the Joseph Webb House, the
archaeologists first uncovered a nice assemblage of late-nineteenth- and
early-twentieth-century glassware, followed by numerous eighteenth-
century artifacts, including ceramic pieces, pipe stems, a shoe buckle, etc.

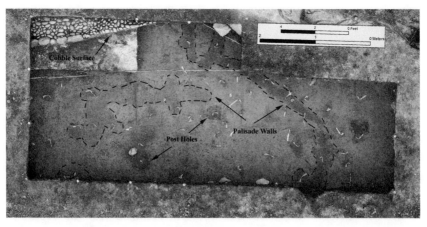

Earth stains that revealed a Pequot War-period palisade at the Webb Deane Stevens Museum in Wethersfield. PHOTO COURTESY OF PAST, INC.

16

But then, instead of reaching undisturbed soil, they began to find numerous artifacts from the seventeenth century, including a coin dating to the earliest days of Wethersfield's English occupation. This was exciting stuff. But the thing that created the stop-the-presses moment was the intersection of two long, uniformly wide, dark brown stains in the otherwise light brown, sandy soil. That was breathtaking, because what those two lines suggested—especially when considered in the context of the English and Native American artifacts found in close proximity—was that the archaeologists might be looking at a defensive wall or palisaded fort from New England's earliest Anglo-Indian war, the Pequot War, which had begun—at least as far as the English were concerned—in Wethersfield on an early spring day in late April 1637.

Right on the spot people associate with a colonial paradise, it looked like they had discovered the find of which we early-colonial-period historians heretofore had only dreamed: real and tangible evidence of the time when this area was—for a lot longer than people have ever imagined—a kind of living hell. This chapter is about the war those intersected stains in a pit brought back to life, and the time when life in Wethersfield was a relentless struggle with fear and the threat of danger.

Studies of war often seem to focus on a few essential themes: causation (why they fought), conflict (where and how they fought), and outcomes (who won and what happened because they did). Such considerations are essential, and each of them can be analyzed in a multitude of richly productive ways.

In the study of New England's seventeenth-century Anglo-Indian conflicts, especially the one that became a war in Wethersfield, there is one important aspect of war that a focus on cause, conflict, and outcomes usually causes historians to overlook. That is the high cost and widespread impact war has on people and resources far away from the scenes of conflict, the tremendous toll—economic, psychic, and physical—that a war footing takes on those who either never, or only rarely, experience any part of the actual fighting. The biblical prophecy "You will hear of wars and rumors of wars" (Matthew 24:6) has proven true in all times and places, yet historians almost always focus on the wars and not the rumors.

We will discuss a little bit of both, but focus on those rumors and how to incorporate their impact into our understanding of conflict. Often, the greatest expenditure of resources (human, material, and psychic) in conflicts is exerted by people defending themselves from things they fear will happen but never do. Yet these ancillary costs are frequently forgotten by historians, which makes war seem more concentrated and dramatic, and far less of a drain on capacities, than it actually is.

A good place to begin this look at the cost of wars *not* fought is with the start of one that was—the Connecticut Colony's May 1, 1637, order to launch an offensive war against the Pequot Indians. Tensions between the English settlers along the Connecticut River and the powerful Pequot Tribe had been escalating for well over a year, but an incident just eight days earlier that happened within an arrow or musket shot of the recent archeological discovery made war not just inevitable, but mandatory.

On April 23, 1637, a force of one hundred to two hundred Pequot and Wangunk warriors launched a surprise attack on Wethersfield. Six Englishmen and three women were killed. The two young daughters (the oldest was sixteen) of one of the town's most important men, William Swayne, were taken captive.

Why choose Wethersfield as the place to start a war? Geography was one reason. Wethersfield was the southernmost of the three English Connecticut River plantations, which made post-battle withdrawal an easy canoe-paddle for the warriors. Population, too, was a factor. Wethersfield was the smallest of the three river settlements, with an estimated population no greater than two hundred people, probably significantly less, most of them children. The biggest reason Wethersfield was targeted for attack, though, was that settlement's track record of cultural belligerence when dealing with the native Wangunk Tribe, upon whose land the English had settled.

The Wangunk sachem Sowheage, who lived at Pyquag (the site the English would rename Wethersfield when the English trader John Oldham and friends first arrived to scout the territory in 1633), initially welcomed and encouraged the English to settle in the region. He reasoned that they would be a useful ally in the Wangunk's competition with the aggressive Pequot Tribe, who had long sought domination over all the native bands along the Connecticut River. Sowheage made an arrangement whereby he would sell the English land near his village, and they would live side by side in a kind of mutual cooperation and defense alliance. No one knows the details behind what happened, but soon after Oldham and the ten original families took up residence, they forced Sowheage and his people, who were by then seriously weakened by decimating exposure to smallpox the year before, to leave Pyquag (which the English had already named Watertown, but that would soon change that to Wethersfield) and move to one of the other Wangunk villages at Mattabeeset (today's Middletown). Driven from his own home by people he had welcomed as friends and allies, Sowheage seethed with resentment.

The Wangunk, not about to relinquish their homeland without a fight, reversed course. This time, they allied with their former enemies the Pequots to take on the English. That led to the April 23 attack on Wethersfield, an assault that called for a whole-scale response. That response was Connecticut's May 1 declaration of war.

The colony's war orders reflected plans hurriedly arrived at in the days after the attack. Collectively, the Connecticans would put a force of ninety English militia into the field. Based on the relative size of each plantation, Hartford would provide forty-two men, Windsor thirty, and the still-reeling Wethersfield eighteen. The force would be commanded by Captain John Mason of Windsor, an experienced veteran of the early seventeenth-century Dutch wars, and Lieutenant Robert Seeley of Wethersfield, presumably a man with a score to settle. Twenty of the soldiers were to be fully armored, with the back and breast plate, neck gorget, and loin guards that rendered most vital body parts impervious to arrows. Every man was to bring from his personal stores a pound of gunpowder, four pounds of shot, twenty bullets, and a musket. Painfully aware that an army travels on its stomach, the colony ordered each town to provide two bushels of corn for each of its soldiers—half of it baked into biscuits, the rest ground into meal—and to do so quickly using "any meanes it can." Presumably that meant assigning most of the women in every town to biscuit-making as a contribution to the war effort. In addition to corn as the dietary staple, each town also had a specialized list of additional food requirements. Hartford was to furnish suet, butter, oatmeal, peas,

Statue of Captain John Mason, currently on the Palisado Green in Windsor.

five hundred fish, and salt; Windsor fifty pieces of pork, rice, and four cheeses; Wethersfield, again reflecting its straitened condition, one bushel of Indian beans. Good beer, sack (fortified wine), and strong waters were to be provided for the captain, Reverend John Stone, the army's chaplain; and sick or injured men.

It took ten days to prepare, gather, and stow provisions aboard the three vessels hastily requisitioned for the campaign. The English citizen-soldiers gathered to receive a war blessing from Hartford's minister Thomas Hooker, and sailed off for Saybrook accompanied by seventy-five Mohegan warrior allies under the sachem Uncas. Most historians of the Pequot War board those boats with them, and the resulting accounts of the conflict they tell are primarily tales of the battles that followed.

That story is, for the most part, clearly delineated. Within two weeks, a combined Massachusetts and Connecticut, Mohegan and Narragansett force killed some four hundred to seven hundred Pequot people in an early morning surprise attack on a palisaded Pequot village near present-day Mystic. Stunned by the wholesale carnage, the Pequots fled their homeland, but were defeated again in July in a swamp battle near Fairfield, Connecticut. The Pequot sachem Sassacus escaped the swamp but was found and executed by Mohawks and Mohegans at a cave known as Stone Church in today's Dover Plains, New York, just over the state line from Kent. By August 1, only two months after it was declared, the Pequot War was effectively over—at least for the historians.

But rather than follow those historians on their war paths, this account of the Pequot War stays at the water's edge in Hartford after the soldiers have sailed, to assess what had just happened and consider the effect the ensuing war had on the three English river towns, and others like them, far removed from the actual fighting. For them, the Pequot War lasted much longer, was much more uncertain, and far more terrifying than the historians' accounts show. Because these towns, even those far distant from any fighting, lived for more than a generation in fear of attacks that never came, and for which they felt terribly ill-prepared. Theirs is a story of unremitting vulnerability, caused by hunger, mistrust, history, and the persuasive power of rumor during war and its aftermath.

One thing easily overlooked in the battle-focused accounts is that the troops' departure left the river towns both hungry and virtually unmanned. The ninety men pressed into service represented nearly three-quarters of the new plantations' adult males, and every able-bodied one. This so concerned the mission commander John Mason that when a Massachusetts force of nineteen men showed up at Saybrook, he immediately sent twenty of the Connecticut men back home, where they were needed both for defense and the desperately important work of spring planting.

Hunger was a driving force behind the Pequot War. The two-year period leading up to it was a time of widespread food scarcity, of "dearth and desperation" in New England. "Plain hunger," one historian recently noted, "lay at the core of the frenzied English stumble into war."

"Our Commons were very short," wrote the English commander John Mason, "there being a general scarcity throughout the Colony of all sorts of provision, it being upon our first arrival at the place." The Pequots also faced pressure on their corn stocks, from the effects of devastating epidemics, destruction by English troops, and the loss of subject tribes who formerly paid the Pequots tribute in maize.

Given New England's extended food shortages, early spring was the worst possible time to put an army in the field. Spring was when families began counting heads and measuring provision barrels' contents to see how much they might have to ration to make it till first fruits. It was also time for men to bend their efforts to the plow and get the spring plantings in. A third year of poor harvests threatened to undermine the whole New England project. The Pequots and Wangunks understood this, which is why they planned their attack on Wethersfield during the late April planting. It also explains why eight of the nine people killed at Wethersfield were attacked while working in the fields. Significantly, the Indians also killed twenty cows and a mare, a clear sign the Pequot-Wangunk war strategy was to target the planters' already tenuous food security.

By factoring hunger into our strategic analysis, it becomes easy to see that the Connecticans' May 1 declaration of war was an act not only of retribution, but also of desperation. Hartford, Windsor, and Wethersfield used food they could not spare to send a critically needed labor and defense force off to fight a distant, though mobile, enemy. But it was also an enemy known to have large corn stores cached in underground granaries. Before sending the soldiers off, Reverend Hooker had told them, "The Pequots should be bread to us," a statement he meant literally as well as metaphorically. And it was a message not just for the troops, but for all those women who had worked to turn so much of their families' own remaining corn into soldiers' biscuits. Grain, without doubt, was the most important of the spoils John Mason hoped to acquire when he attacked the Pequot fort at Mystic. But that's a different story. Our story remains in Wethersfield. The army has departed, and in its absence there is hunger perhaps, and fear for certain.

The anxious settlers were living on edge. Hypervigilance led to daily alarms of impending attacks. All proved false, but they stretched the towns' human resources to the breaking point. "Our people are scarce able to stand upon their legs," Windsor's Roger Ludlow wrote. He used a harvest metaphor to describe Connecticut's straitened condition. "Our plantations are so gleaned by that small fleet we sent out, those that remain are scarce able to supply our watches, which are day and night." *Gleaned* meant to go into a field after it had been picked or harvested and scrape up what was left, which in terms of both available men and sustenance was a painfully accurate description.

Fear kept settlers away from their fields, close to home, and not just in Wethersfield but all over New England. "What we plant," Ludlow reported, "is before our doors, little anywhere else." Asked to send men up the river to Springfield to help defend the threatened settlement there, Ludlow regretfully declined, saying, "If the case be never so dangerous, we can neither help you, nor you us."

Faced with the likelihood of having to defend themselves with only the few and feeble men and military resources left, Wethersfield settlers used vital planting time to construct fortifications instead. Early Wethersfield historian Henry Stiles believed that at least one palisaded fort or garrison house (a home specially reinforced to resist attack) was built in the northern part of the village, along what today is Wethersfield's State Street, once called Fort Street. But a fort built to defend settlers in the northern part of the settlement would have left those in the southern part, people with even more potential exposure to attack from the Wangunks farther to the south, all but undefended. So logic would suggest, and the intersecting stains in the archeological test pit seem to confirm, that a second fort or garrison house was built in the southern section of the village, too. This supposition gains more credibility from the fact that the archeological feature is located on the former homesite of Clement Chaplin, one of early Wethersfield's most important men. If this working hypothesis is confirmed by the more extensive site excavations currently (Summer 2019) in the planning stages, these palisade stains merit the excitement they have generated. They take us back to the very beginnings of Wethersfield, of Connecticut, and of America, and one of the most important moments in Anglo- and Native American history. A very dark moment, when everyone slept with one eye open, and listened to every sound on the night air. Not just in Wethersfield, but in every village and town in New England.

One reason the Wethersfield attack spread fear so quickly to all places is that no one—native or English—knew for sure whom they could trust. One piece of advice Roger Ludlow gave to a leader of Springfield to whom he could not send assistance was, "I would desire you to be careful and watchful that you not be betrayed by friendships." Anglo-Indian alliances were confusing, fluid, and tenuous to all parties, subject to unilateral revision or termination, and based on agreements almost always

Early 1900s Postcard Image "Pilgrims Going to Church." NEW YORK PUBLIC LIBRARY DIGITAL COLLECTION

subject to conflicting interpretations. The very agreement Wethersfield's settlers made with the sachem Sowheage, which the English repudiated as soon as they arrived, was a textbook example of this. Such actions, which occurred on both sides of the cultural divide, made any Anglo-Indian alliance a source of anxiety for all involved.

This tenuous nature of alliances fed a historic specter too, which gave any report of an Indian attack region-wide significance. That specter was the 1622 attack of the Powhatan Confederation on English settlements up and down the James River of Virginia, which had left a quarter of that colony's population dead in a single morning. That event was seared into the consciousness of all New England planters, who feared nothing as much as a pan-Indian alliance against them. Any Indian attack was seen as a potential harbinger of coordinated multi-tribal assaults to come.

For all these reasons, news of the Wethersfield attack spread fear like wildfire among the English. And as it spread, it generated additional, even more fearful rumors. In Boston word of the raid was augmented by another report—subsequently proved false—that sixty men had been killed in an Indian attack on Springfield. After a subsequent rumor surfaced that the Narragansetts—southern New England's largest indigenous group—were being actively courted by the Pequots to join an anti-English confederation, fear gripped the Bay Colony as firmly as it held Connecticut.

Towns were put on the highest alert. The Massachusetts Governor's Council ordered that "none should go to work, nor travel, no, not so much as to church without arms." A guard of fourteen or fifteen soldiers was appointed to watch every night, and sentinels were set in convenient places about the plantations. Plymouth ordered a guard of twelve musketeers to accompany and protect the governor everywhere he went. The Bay Colony and Plymouth joined Connecticut's river towns, waiting anxiously for attacks that never came.

These fears of attacks were reinforced and amplified by the rumors that flew like projectiles across New England that year, and for many years thereafter.

The social psychologist Robert H. Knapp, who was in charge of rumor control for the Massachusetts Committee of Safety during World War II, theorized the influence of rumors in that war in ways that are useful when thinking about the Pequot War. War conditions are especially productive of rumors, Knapp argued, because military secrecy makes reliable information both intensely valued and extraordinarily scarce. Rumors fill war's information gaps, even as they give voice to the emotional insecurities or aggressive feelings of the rumor spreaders. Rumored information beats no information at all, and most rumors, though spread by word of mouth, are imbued with trappings, such as attribution to a high-ranking source, that make them seem highly credible. At the same time, they also clearly reflect and reinforce the anxiety, aggressive feelings, or wishful thinking of the rumor mongers. Some rumors are primarily informational, others primarily expressive, but most, though succinct enough to travel by word of mouth, contain both information and an emotionally charged interpretive slant.

Knapp posited the usefulness of three classifications of rumors: 1) anxiety or fear-producing rumors; 2) pipe-dream or wishful-thinking rumors; and 3) wedge-driving or aggression rumors, that express latent hostility and cause disunity. All three types of rumors figured prominently in the whirlwind of misinformation that accompanied the Pequot War and its aftermath, and none of the war's victors—Connecticut, Massachusetts, the Narragansetts or the Mohegans—were immune from rumor-mongering.

Roger Williams, the Massachusetts exile at Providence plantation, was a frequent reporter of Pequot War rumors. Between May of 1637 and the summer of 1638, Williams passed along thirty-five rumors he gathered from English leaders, native sachems, and a cast of characters in transit. Eight of those rumors were the kind that fed colonists' darkest fears and reinforced their expectations of attack, including a false report that there had been a far greater slaughter than the Wethersfield attack at one of the other Connecticut plantations, and that "the Pequots have entered into a league with the Man-Eating Mohawks." Considering that Williams was only one among thousands of conduits for rumors, the climate of fear created by these rumors was intense, and the resources expended in responding to that fear proved extremely costly in both material expense and diverted agricultural labor. Knapp found that such fear-inducing rumors are the most powerful of the three classifications of rumor, because of the potential dangers involved in ignoring them. In the climate of continuous fear rumors that swept New England in 1637 and 1638, colonial towns *and* Indian villages had little choice but to remain on highest alert.

Williams was aware of the value of rumors as propaganda, and on at least two occasions he deployed rumor to serve English goals. In one instance, he deliberately passed along a fear rumor that "the Mohawks and Pequots had slain many English and natives at Connecticut" to Massachusetts Governor John Winthrop. He did so because he knew Winthrop could use such news to mobilize additional defensive resources in the Bay Colony. On another occasion, Williams simply manufactured a wishful-thinking rumor and told it to Narragansett leaders to calm their fears in response to a rumored English defeat. A large English force in the field had not been heard from for some time, and a rumor had circulated that the English had been ambushed by a Pequot War party. Though Williams had no idea what had happened to the English troops, he confidently told the Narragansetts that the English force had returned to Connecticut for provisions.

If fear rumors help explain the prolonged war-footing of the colonists during the Pequot War, the even more numerous and persistent wedge-driving rumors help explain the chronic states of military mobilization that characterized the post-war years. Wedge driving, or aggression, rumors divide groups by calling into question the loyalty of allies. Their essential motivation, according to Knapp, is aggression against or hatred of the group targeted by the rumor. Roger Williams passed along wedge-driving rumors more than twice as often as fear rumors. Twenty-one of his thirty-five rumor reports contained information reflecting negatively on one or another of the Pequot War's allies, compared to the eight merely fear-inducing reports he transmitted. The disproportionate degree of wedge-driving rumors is an indicator of just how deeply the supposed allies in the Pequot War disliked and distrusted each other.

Conditions specific to the Pequot War made it fertile ground for the fabrication of wedge-driving rumors. Though the English sought in the wake of their victory to capture all Pequot combatants, blood bonds linked many Pequots to other regional tribes, including the Wangunks. So it was not unusual for a Pequot fighter to seek temporary shelter with family members from another tribe to avoid English detection, especially since the English had pre-sentenced all Pequots who had participated in the fighting to death. In this fluid environment, it was not easy for the English to determine *where* the enemy was, or at times, even *who* the enemy was. Native groups used this English confusion to undermine tribes with whom they were in conflict by suggesting those tribes—even if they claimed to be English allies—were actually aiding and abetting the Pequots by offering them shelter and concealing their identities.

Williams reported sixteen wedge-driving rumors asserting that various tribes were secretly giving sanctuary to Pequots. The largest number of these aggression rumors were lodged by the Narragansetts against the Mohegans and their sachem Uncas, whom the Narragansetts hated.

Although the Narragansetts and Mohegans had worked together as allies to defeat the Pequots in the war's initial conflict, once that tribe was brought down, they competed fiercely with each other to assume the Pequots' former regional dominance. Similarly, Connecticut and Massachusetts had allied together against the Pequots, but they too, like the Narragansetts and Mohegans, competed fiercely for control over the former Pequot lands in the war's aftermath. This produced a four-way power struggle involving two distinct cultures. In this power play, each party recognized that there was value in having close relations with a cross-cultural partner and used wedge-driving rumors to try to create such alliances for themselves or break them apart for others.

The Narragansetts sought to advance their status with Massachusetts through wedge-driving rumors intended to undermine positive English perceptions of the Mohegans and their leader Uncas. Such rumors claimed, for example, that Uncas was offering protection to three hundred Pequots and their allies, or that "Uncas himself took part in killing English men at Saybrook." Several of the aggression rumors delivered to Massachusetts authorities cast doubt on Connecticut's actions as well. Williams reported, among other things, that Connecticut officials were accepting "mighty bribes" of wampum from Uncas, and that Connecticut knowingly allowed him to harbor a Pequot warrior who had killed and tortured Englishmen.

While Williams and the Narragansetts were disseminating negative rumors about Uncas and the Mohegans to Massachusetts, Connecticut and the Mohegans were spreading the same kind of rumors against the Narragansetts. Reports from Connecticut claimed that the Narragansetts had offered sanctuary to a large number of refugee Pequots, and that the Narragansett sachem was personally plotting to kill Connecticut's most important native language interpreter Thomas Stanton.

Massachusetts was not immune from spreading wedge-driving rumors either. The Bay Colony's rumor-mongering, however, seems not to have been targeted at Indian tribes as much as at Connecticut. In a blistering letter John Winthrop received in late 1638, an outraged Reverend Thomas Hooker accused Massachusetts of having waged an aggressive, concerted rumor campaign to discourage new settlers from going to Connecticut. Massachusetts had told potential Connecticut emigrants, among other equally slanderous things according to Hooker, to "Goe any whither, be anywhere, choose any place, any patent, Narragansett, Plymouth, only goe not to Connecticut. . . . Their upland will bear no corn, their meadows nothing but weeds, and the people are almost starved." Hooker's outraged letter (it went on for many pages) reveals and underscores the intensity of the distrust and competition between the two English colonies that was an often overlooked consequence of the Pequot War and its aftermath.

How did such a climate of fear and rumor-mongering affect the people who built, or *may* have built, the palisade in Wethersfield? Very directly, and with lasting consequences. Throughout the war, tensions between the Wethersfield settlers and the Wangunk people under their sachem Sowheage remained deeply conflicted, with "divers injuries offered by some of the said English to Sowheage and likewise diverse outrages and wrongs committed by Sowheage and his men upon the English." Predictably, Sowheage became the focus of the same kind of fear-mongering and wedge-driving rumors as the Mohegans and Narragansetts. There were rumors that he was harboring many of the warriors who had killed settlers in the Wethersfield attack, and later, he was said to be allying with the Narragansetts to launch a coordinated multi-tribal regional war. Given his continued fury at the double-dealing he had experienced at the hands of the incoming settlers, few believed his protestations of innocence. English reports noted that Sowheage and his people continued to commit repeated "insolencies" against the English well after the Pequot War's supposed conclusion at the 1638 Treaty of Hartford, and in September 1639, because of Sowheage's continued refusal to turn warriors suspected of participating in the Wethersfield attack over to the English for execution, the Connecticut General Court voted to raise an army even larger than the one sent against the Pequots to force him to comply. Only the refusal of New Haven colony to join in the planned English assault kept a second war from breaking out, and though that war never happened, a continuous brink-of-war state of affairs characterized English-Indian relations in Wethersfield and across New England right up until 1675, when that long-dreaded pan-Indian alliance to drive the English out of the land finally occurred and became known as King Philip's War.

These troubled decades between the Pequot War and King Philip's War were as fearful and difficult for the indigenous tribes as they were for the English; probably more so. In addition to the ever-present threat of hostility from both the English and other tribes, a continuously shrinking land base, and declining resources, native people also experienced the unremitting toll inflicted through their exposure to European diseases for which they had no immunity. Yet through it all, native people and English people continued to find ways to meet, trade, and interact on something other than a hostile basis. We know they were doing this because the written records of the English tell us they did, and such reports are confirmed by the combination of English and native artifacts found in Connecticut's seventeenth-century archeological sites. Was this an effort to find a peaceable middle ground between cultures? Was it simply trade exchanges between people who didn't like each other but needed each other's resources? Or was it, perhaps, the effort of minority factions on both sides to go against a tide of increasing division and hostility to try and create a path forward together? We don't know yet, but the most exciting thing about those intersecting brown stains in Wethersfield is that with time and effort, the discoveries made there may well give us answers to a time about which we have so many questions, and right now, so relatively few answers.

Here is the great colonial irony. Though the outcome of the Pequot War was decided decisively in the summer of 1637, there was to be no real peace in New England for two more generations. Wethersfield felt the effects of this simmering rumor-fueled hostility more than most. Its population lagged behind that of the other river towns for decades. And many who came here to settle did not stay. After Connecticut's failed effort to field an army against Sowheage and the Wangunk people in 1639, two groups of early settlers abandoned Wethersfield and went off to start the towns of Stamford in 1641 and Branford in 1644.

The son of Reverend Henry Smith, whose father came to Wethersfield in 1637, fought in the Pequot War and became the minister who built the town's meeting house, wrote a description of life in Wethersfield during the years he grew up. Only a fragment of his original account survived when it was transcribed in the early 1900s, but that fragment is revealing, for it shows how rumors, distrust, and continuous intercultural friction made life during those decades most historians record as peaceful, anything but peaceful. Consider as you read, too, that the only full-scale Indian attack on Wethersfield ever recorded took place on April 23, 1637, the first day of the Pequot War.

Concerning the early days [in Wethersfield] I can remember but little save hardship. My honored Father . . . did help to reare both our owne house and the First Meeting House of Wethersfield, wherein he preached. . . . [It] was solid made, to withstand the wicked onslaughts of ye red skins. Its foundations was laid in the Fear of the Lord, but its walls was truly laid in fear of the Indians for many and grate was the terrors of them. All the able-bodied men did work therat and the old and feeble did watch in turns to espie if any salvages was in hiding neare, and every Man kept his musket nighe to his hand.

I do not myself remember any of the Attacks mayde by large bodyes of Indians whilst we did remayne in Wethersfield but did often times heare of them." Several families which did live back a ways from the river was either Murdered or Captivated in my Boyhood we all did live in constant feare of the like.

31

There is so much we do not know about those early colonial Connecticans. We know their lives were hard, and we know they lived in a steady state of anxiety, caused by fears of things that almost always did not happen, the very real and very high cost of battles not fought. What we don't know is how those anxious people actually dealt with their hardships, handled their fears, and how these same survivors of an embattled and fear-burdened land went on to become the builders of the town John Adams would a century later call "paradise." The real story of Wethersfield and of early America, in all its complexity, confusion, wonder, and inspiration, may be waiting for us to discover in the ground around an archeological test pit at the Webb Deane Stevens Museum.

FURTHER READING

The following recent scholarly works include significant discussion of the Pequot War and its aftermath.

Julie A. Fisher and David J. Silverman's *Ninigret, Sachem of the Niantics and Narragansetts* (Ithaca, NY Cornell University Press, 2014)

Katherine Grandjean's *American Passage* (Cambridge, MA, Harvard University Press, 2015)

Andrew Lipman's *The Saltwater Frontier* (New Haven, Yale University Press, 2015)

James A. Warren's, *God, War, and Providence* (New York, Simon & Schuster, 2018)

Walter W. Woodward's Prospero's America (Chapel Hill, Omohundro Institutute and University of North Carolina Press, 2010).

An older but more detailed account of the war is Alfred A. Cave's *The Pequot War* (Amherst, University of Massachusetts Press, 1996).

The key primary source narratives of the Pequot War by English participants are assembled in Charles Orr's *History of the Pequot War* (Amazon.com, 2018).

An excellent primary and secondary teaching resource of the Pequot War can be found on the Connecticut Humanities connecticuthistory.org website.

CONTROVERSIAL STATUES
STANDING . . . AT LEAST FOR NOW

The monuments to John Mason and Henry Daniel Cogswell remind us that histories, like fashions, can change.

With all the talk in recent years about removing offensive statues from public view, it is instructive to realize this is not the first time the topic has occupied Connecticans' attention. More than one Connecticut statue has a long history of provoking heated controversy and demands for its removal.

Consider, for example, the statue of Major John Mason, which currently resides on Windsor's historic Palisado Green (see page 20). Mason, who commanded Connecticut's troops in the 1637 Pequot War, was venerated for centuries as a Connecticut hero. His statue was commissioned by the state on the 250th anniversary of the Pequot War and installed in 1889 at the site of a surprise attack led by Mason near present day Groton, in which some four hundred to seven hundred Pequot people died. More than a century later, in 1992, a coalition of Native American groups petitioned to have the statue removed from what they consider sacred ground. Windsor, Mason's colonial hometown, agreed to take custody of the statue and moved it to the town's historic green in 1996. Recently, though, Windsor has reconsidered Mason's role in the surprise attack, now often called the Mystic Massacre. In December 2016 the town council voted to exclude the statue from a list of monuments worthy of restoration. They also discussed removing it from the green, but finding it was actually owned by the state, they decided to leave it on display—at least for now.

For all its mobility, the Mason statue barely compares with the now-you-see-it, now-you-don't history of the Cogswell Temperance Statue

Cogswell Temperance Statue, Central Park, Rockville, Connecticut. PHOTO COURTESY DAVID K. LEFF.

currently on display at Rockville's Central Park. Dr. Henry Daniel Cogswell, who donated the original statue to the town, was a native of Tolland who had risen from humble beginnings; gone west with the Gold Rush; and through dentistry, mercantile activity, and real estate development become one of San Francisco's first millionaires. A passionate temperance advocate, Cogswell believed the cure for alcoholism was abundant supplies of readily available fresh water, so he used his fortune to provide public fountains in cities across the country. Atop every Cogswell fountain was a sculpture of Cogswell himself, glass of water in one hand, temperance pledge in the other. The Rockville fountain, installed in 1883, was one of thirty-one such Cogswell installations, but its reception was not what the good dentist might have wanted.

A bustling mill town, Rockville had recently voted against going dry, and its thirty-three local saloons were, to say the least, well patronized establishments. Many of those patrons resented an outsider—from San Francisco no less—trying to tell them what to do, especially through a statue that seemed to many both egomaniacal and ugly. So, two years after its installation, someone decided to take Dr. Cogswell's statue out for a drink—in the bottom of Lake Shenipset. The local constables retrieved the good doctor and reinstated him atop the fountain, but he soon disappeared again. This time his statue remained missing until 1908, when it was found leaning against a downtown building with a sign around his neck saying, "I've come back for Old Home Week."

After participating in the town's Old Home Week parade—an annual festival held in many New England towns to encourage sons and daughters who had emigrated out of state to return to visit friends and relatives—Cogswell's statue was held in protective custody at the town poor farm until World War II, when it was melted down to help the war effort. The Cogswell Temperance statue was now well and truly gone, but it was certainly not forgotten. Some people even missed it.

In 2005, as plans to restore Rockville's Central Park were ramping up, philanthropist Rosetta Pikat donated $50,000 to have a New York studio create a replica of the 1883 statue. That same year, amid pomp and circumstance, Henry Cogswell returned to Rockville. Last time I drove through, he was still standing—at least for now.

CONNECTICUT: NEW ENGLAND'S FIERCEST WITCH HUNTER

A generation before Salem, Connecticut was the fiercest hunter of witches in all New England. Then one man ended the killing—forever.

Connecticut's record in handling witchcraft cases raises many questions. Some are unique to Connecticut; some apply to all witch hunts. Why, for example, in the early years of witch hunting (1647–1663), was Connecticut New England's fiercest prosecutor of witches? Why did it switch from being the region's greatest witch killer to the colony that ended executions permanently a generation before Salem? Why did people even believe in witchcraft? What exactly did people think witches could do and why did it scare them? Why were most witches women? What made someone who had been a neighbor for many years suddenly so dangerous that community safety made executing them mandatory? The answer to these questions begins not in Connecticut, but in Europe, where the witch culture that Puritans carried to New England originated.

One of the great ironies of history is that the Renaissance—that period we associate with a great flowering of art, literature, science, and creativity—also set the stage for the most horrific period of witch hunting ever recorded. In Europe, between 1300 and 1800, forty to sixty thousand people (some authorities say as many as one hundred thousand) were executed as witches. The toll by present-day country, especially considering their populations at the time, is staggering: Germany, twenty-six thousand; France, six thousand; Switzerland, five thousand; Poland, five thousand; Austria, three thousand. In Scotland, which entered into witch hunting a bit later than its continental counterparts, as many as two thousand people died as witches. England, which lagged behind Scotland in ramping up prosecutorial zeal, killed up to a thousand. Curiously, New England (thanks to curriculum classics such as Nathanial Hawthorne's *The Scarlet Letter* and Arthur Miller's play *The Crucible*) is for many people the icon of witch persecution. The total number of people executed as witches in New England? Thirty-six.

Witchcraft, loosely defined as the use of supernatural power by persons associated with evil spirits, has been a part of virtually all cultures in all times. Even today, in some countries, people are regularly killed because they are believed to be witches. But why did witch hunting take place on such a massive scale during this one particular period? Most historians agree that the pandemic of witch-fear that swept Europe in the sixteenth and seventeenth centuries was a consequence of the Protestant Reformation. The religious revolution that began when Martin Luther nailed his "95 Theses" to the door of the church in Wittenburg, Germany, in 1517 not only fractured the Catholic church, it destabilized society. Witch hunting became a tool not only of social control but also a source of competition between the new Protestant sects and the traditional Catholic churches. Through witch trials, witch hunters, both Protestant and Catholic, advertised and demonstrated their faith's power as well as a commitment to protect people from much-feared diabolical influences in worldly affairs.

But what *exactly* did the populace fear from the suspected witches in their midst? Witches—with the devil's help, of course—were believed to possess a battery of magical powers that were very strong and very dangerous. Through the use of love magic, for example, witches could make someone fall in or out of love. They could also foresee who that person was going to marry, and conjure whether they would be true or false to their vows.

It was believed that witches could use magic to alter the weather, brewing up storms, and causing floods or droughts. In the subsistence agrarian economies of early modern Europe, making it through the months of late winter and early spring without hunger—or even at all—could depend on the quality of the prior year's harvest, and that depended in large part on

Witches invoking weather magic. "TWO WITCHES PUTTING A SNAKE AND A ROOSTER INTO A CAULDRON." BY CEMIAKANO IS LICENSED UN CY BY-SA 2.0

the weather. In a world without scientific explanations for meteorological phenomena, the best explanation for what caused a drought or flood was often not *what*, but *who*, and the *who* was invariably a suspected witch.

Witches were believed to have the ability to alter other natural processes, too, from the ripening of cheese to the brewing of beer. So when unexpected problems occurred, maggots in the cheese wheel or a stuck fermentation, for example, the source of the problem was often sought not in the process but rather with the person of evil intent who caused it. Witches could also use magic to hurt animals, causing a perfectly healthy animal to founder, or sicken and die, having similar, sometimes even more dangerous consequences on a family's food or economic security.

Problematically, witches were believed to be able to change shape. Suspected witches were commonly reported to have appeared as a cat, or owl or other creature, or even in the shape of another person, which could present serious evidentiary problems in witchcraft trials. Moreover, this shape-shifting ability gave witches a particularly elusive quality that enhanced their ability to inspire fear. Any living being could be, under the right circumstances, the manifestation of a witch.

Another serious and very incriminating power attributed to witches was their ability to divine the future. Everyone believed that only God, the Alpha and Omega, knew what would happen from the beginning to the end of time, but they also believed that sometimes God, for reasons known only to Him, allowed Satan some knowledge of future events. If, then, a mere mortal had information about the future, and the source of that knowledge was not divine prophesy or revelation, then it had to have come from the Devil. Divining the future was perilous but powerful ground for a suspected witch to occupy.

The most problematic of all the magical powers, and the most common source of accusations, was a witch's ability to inflict harm on people through disease or injury. That's why many of the people accused of witchcraft were healers. All women in the early modern world were expected to practice household medicine and to make remedies for their families. When someone's healing abilities seemed unusually effective they became a healer for their neighborhood, and as their reputation increased, a healer for the community at large. But medicines that healed could sometimes

fail, and if they failed too often or were used on the wrong people—
say someone that healer was known to dislike—a great healer could very
quickly become a great suspect.

All these forms of harmful magic—love magic, weather magic, altering natural processes, harming animals, divining the future, inflicting
sickness or injury—were grouped together under the term *maleficia*, from
which we have derived the word *maleficent*. People were terribly afraid of
these kinds of magic powers and the people who were suspected of using
them, but why?

In the early modern world virtually every living person, to some
degree—and usually a very high degree—truly believed in magic. *Their*
universe was filled with *occult*, a word that literally means unseen or hidden, forces. These unseen forces emanated from the stars, planets, God and
angels, the Devil and demons, from stones, plants, and metals. A witch
was someone who, with the devil's help, became a master at harnessing
and focusing these occult forces to inflict *maleficia* in various ways on
various people. Witches' efforts, though not their goals or methods, were
not that different from those of the early modern alchemists who sought
prayerfully, and with God's and his angels' help, to use the rudimentary
scientific methods of the day and their own understandings of natural
magic to harness these same occult forces. The goal of these scientists was
not just to make gold, as most people believe, but also to achieve advances
in science, medicine, agriculture, and technology that would improve the
lives of all humankind. This was a prerequisite, they believed, for the onset
of the millennium, the moment when the resurrected Christ would return
to Earth to reign for a thousand years.

This kind of approach to scientific experiment, combining lab work,
prayer, and magic in the pursuit of goals that were both practical and religious, seems irrational today. But we live in a world that has established
solid firewalls that distinctly and markedly separate religion, science, and
magic. Each has its own isolated sphere of operation (if you believe in all
three) with virtually no overlap or interface among them. But this is the
exact opposite of how early modern people viewed that triad. For them,
religion, science, and magic were inseparable, woven together like a DNA
spiral helix, so interdependent you could not tease them apart or believe

in the influence of one without accepting the vitality of the others. Without magic there was no religion, without religion there was no science. And so, everyone in the world of the witch hunts believed in, and feared, the awesome power of diabolical magic to do evil.

The Puritans who came to New England in the early decades of the 1600s had drunk deeply at the well of this magical world view, and they carried their fear of the devil and his minions to New England along with their Bibles, clothing, and seed stock. Compared to their continental counterparts, the English came late to witch hunting. Witchcraft was not outlawed in England until 1542, but in the intervening years, English and Scottish authorities had put a particularly British stamp on their witch-hunting methods. James I, just prior to becoming the English monarch in 1603, had written a book titled *Daemonologie* in which he discussed the multiplicity of ways witches inflicted diabolical harm and outlined the procedures for trying and punishing them. Witches were not burned as heretics in England as they were elsewhere in Europe. Instead, witchcraft was a felony for which the punishment was mandatory hanging without benefit of clergy. Distinctively English also was the emphasis placed on witches' use of a familiar, a supernaturally empowered cat, dog, toad, rat, owl, hare, ferret, or even a human-like creature, who would help the witch inflict *maleficia* on victims. The 1604 witchcraft law that was passed the year after James I came to the English throne to "better restrain" and "more severely punish" witchcraft, made communing with a familiar a hanging offense. Because familiars were thought to feed on the blood of the witch they served, suspected witches were often forcibly strip-searched to see if they had a witch's teat (a mole, growth, or other nipple-like projection) somewhere on their body through which the familiar, and the devil, was thought to get nourishment.

These English variants on witch-hunting techniques figured significantly in English witch trials, which were at a peak during the period of early New England settlement. England's greatest witch hunt took place between 1644 and 1647 in the Puritan counties of East Anglia. There, a man named Matthew Hopkins, who styled himself England's Witch-Finder General, led a witch hunt that resulted in many executions (some sources claim three hundred). The East Anglian location of

Hopkin's witch hunt is significant; it is the place from which many of Connecticut's early settlers emigrated. They knew much about, and some had direct connections to, the Hopkin trials. Many must have feared that if the devil was assaulting the English Puritans this furiously in East Anglia, it was only a matter of time until he would find his way to New England. It is not surprising, therefore, that New England's first execution for witchcraft took place in 1647, just as the witch hunt in England was winding down.

Perhaps the most interesting thing about this first New England witch death is that we wouldn't know anything about it except for two sentences that appeared in two different documents produced one hundred miles away from each other and found some two hundred fifty years apart. Sometime between March and May of 1647, Massachusetts Governor John Winthrop, whose history journal of New England is one of our most important historical sources from this period, wrote, in that journal, the following sentence: "One _____ of Windsor arraigned and executed at Hartford for a witch." Winthrop left the blank space intending, no doubt, to add the witch's name once he had received further information. But for the next 257 years, that is all that was known. Some person who lived in Windsor was tried for witchcraft in Hartford and then executed. What was she charged with? Who conducted the trial? Who testified against her? What was her defense? Where was she hanged? None of this was known; in truth, historians did not even know whether New England's first convicted witch was a man or a woman. Then, in 1904, Annie Eliot Trumbull, daughter of Connecticut's first state librarian J. Hammond Trumbull, announced that she had come into possession of a "little old volume" with a "worn sheepskin binding" that contained the manuscript diary of Matthew Grant, a resident of Windsor from 1635 to 1681. In it, she reported, she had found a Grant-penned entry stating that on May 26, 1647, "Alse Young was hanged." Finally, after two and a half centuries, it was confirmed that New England's first executed witch *was,* as supposed, a woman, and that her name was Alice Young. That remains most of what is known for certain about her, though historian Richard Ross has recently argued that Alice emigrated to Windsor from London in 1640, which may have put her culturally at odds with her

Windsor neighbors, most of whom had emigrated from the English West Country. Those cultural differences made her an outsider, he speculates, which, combined with an epidemic of deadly influenza that hit Windsor the year of Young's execution, may have factored in her being singled out for prosecution.

In reviewing the historical record, it almost seems that because Governor John Winthrop knew so little about the first person executed for witchcraft in New England, when the second person was executed in Massachusetts a year later, he made sure to record all the reasons Margaret Jones was proven to be a witch, and why she deserved to die. He catalogued four different ways in which she demonstrated *maleficia*, and two additional confirmations of her collusion with diabolical forces.

A Malignant Touch. "She was found to have a malignant touch," *Winthrop wrote, "as many persons (men, women, and children) whom she stroked or touched with any affection or displeasure, were taken with deafness, or vomiting, or other violent pains or sickness."*

Interfering with Natural Processes. "She, practicing physic [medicine] and her medicines being such things as (by her own confession) were harmless, as aniseed, liquors, etc., yet had extraordinary violent effects.*

Altering & Predicting the Course of Illness. "She would use to tell such as would not make use of her physic, that they would never be healed, and accordingly their diseases and hurts continued, with relapse against the ordinary course [of nature], and beyond the apprehension of all physicians and surgeons."*

Divining the Future. "Some things which she foretold came to pass accordingly; other things she could tell of (as secret speeches, etc.) which she had no ordinary means to come to the knowledge of. "*

As if the evidence of her varied supernaturally inflicted harms were not enough, Winthrop reported that a search of Jones's body revealed she had a witch's teat. "She had (upon search) an apparent teat in her secret parts as fresh as if it had been newly sucked, and after it had been scanned, upon a forced search, that was withered, and another began on the opposite side."

Evidence of the witch's teat put her guards on alert for a familiar, who, needing nourishment, could be expected at some point, to visit her in gaol. This Winthrop confirmed, is exactly what happened. "In the prison, in the clear day-light, there was seen in her arms, she sitting in the floor, and her clothes up, etc., a little child, which ran from her into another room, and the officer following it, it was vanished."

The case for executing Margaret Jones was, by the standards of evidence then in use, beyond refute. To underscore, however, both the power and the danger a witch like Jones represented to the community, Winthrop reported yet another example of Jones's *maleficia*, triggered at the moment of her death.

Weather Magic. "The same day and hour she was executed, there was a very great tempest at Connecticut, which blew down many trees, &c."

There should be no doubt, Winthrop underscored, that the supernatural abilities of witches such as Jones were multifaceted, exercised across both space and time, and lasted right up to the instant of their death. Such was the nature of the witch fear that fed New England's long record of witch hunting.

There is one more thing Winthrop noted about Margaret Jones that helps us make sense from a present-day perspective of her being singled out as a suspected witch. Margaret Jones was a fiercely independent woman. "Her behavior at her trial was very intemperate, lying notoriously, and railing upon the jury and witnesses, etc., and in the like distemper she died," Winthrop recorded.

Although the entire power of the state was arrayed against her, and with the certainty, at some point, that she would die, Margaret Jones chose to yell and scream and fight her way to the gallows. That aggressive behavior, the rebellious streak that simply refused to be coerced into accepting others' authority, is an indicator of the kind of person that often became a target of witchcraft accusations. It also provides a partial explanation for why women in New England were singled out for accusations far more frequently than men. In New England, only one out of every seven witchcraft prosecutions involved a man, and not infrequently that man was a blood relative of a woman already suspected of or known to be a witch. Clearly, this reflects the misogynistic impulses deeply embedded in early modern Anglo culture, but there are other factors supporting these disproportionate accusations of women as well.

New England settlements were, especially in their early years, fragile entities in uncomfortable and dangerous surroundings. One historian has aptly characterized them as little islands of security in a sea of danger. English people did not know woodlands; they had little experience with forest environments. Such areas, home to indigenous bands that often had justifiably hostile attitudes toward the English interlopers, constituted the vast majority of New England's seventeenth-century landscape. Outside of their palisaded settlements, English emigrants felt, and often were, in a no-man's land filled with danger. They also lived in a world without safety nets—no police force, hospitals, or social service agencies. Each community and its families had to be, to a remarkable degree, self-sufficient, including being prepared to defend themselves against a sudden attack. New England experienced two major seventeenth-century Anglo-Indian conflicts, and the years between them were times of deep intercultural unrest and frequent military mobilization.

In such an atmosphere, towns needed effective mechanisms of command and control, which often meant having the ability to organize every family at a moment's notice to assist in community defense. The English approach to instituting the most responsive local chain of command possible was to treat every family as "a little commonwealth." Just like a monarchy, it had a ruler (the father or oldest male) to which the rest of the household had to be immediately subordinate without question. Anyone who resisted that command structure put the community in danger, and no one violated it more than a rebellious woman. Such women simply had to be controlled, as a matter of security, and witchcraft accusations were, in at least some instances, an extreme manifestation of that principle.

Another reason women were targeted as witches more often than men had to do with differing views of their innate moral impulses. Prevailing cultural attitudes held that men had naturally stronger morals, were better suited to self-discipline and restraint, and had an innate resistance to temptation. Women, as weaker vessels, were more easily tempted to the sins of the flesh, and to compacting with the devil. Proof of this attitude came from the biblical Book of Genesis's story of the Garden of Eden. The serpent's decision to tempt Eve instead of Adam was not arbitrary. It was based on her inherent susceptibility to temptation. One historian has argued that the reason so many women confessed to being witches during the Salem trials is that they themselves believed in their susceptibility to temptation, and under harsh interrogation became convinced that they actually had colluded with the evil one.

It is interesting to compare the Salem witchcraft trials, which most people understand as the archetype of New England witch hunting, with the witch trials that preceded them. Their similarities and underlying differences are revealing. Between 1647 and 1692, the forty-five-year period before the Salem trials, fifty-seven people were brought to trial in New England on charges of witchcraft. Their trials produced sixteen convictions, four confessions, and as many as sixteen executions.

During 1692 and 1693, the time of the Salem witch hunt, 156 people were accused. Their trials produced thirty convictions, forty-four confessions, and nineteen executions. (One additional person died under interrogation, and four more people died in prison awaiting trial).

At first glance, comparing the early forty-five-year period of witch hunting with the Salem trials seems to indicate that they represent two distinctly different experiences. Averaging the early-period executions against the forty-five-year timespan suggests that during the early period about once every four or five years there would be a show trial resulting in a conviction and execution that served as a cautionary tale for the rest of society. At Salem, though, witch hunting went out of control for over a year, reached a crisis, and then ended permanently. While the differences between the two periods seem striking, mapping out the trials and executions by their exact dates and locations reveals a very different story.

All the people executed for witchcraft in the early period were executed, not during a forty-five-year interval, but during a sixteen-year period between 1647 and 1663. That was followed by a twenty-five-year interval without a single execution. It was succeeded by the 1688 execution of a confessed witch in Boston, which set the stage for Salem. In reality, then, there were two periods of intense witch hunting in New England separated by a whole generation without a single death. And that was not the only surprise revealed by the data.

During the early period of witch hunting Connecticut proved to be much, much harsher in its treatment of suspected witches than Massachusetts. Between 1647 and 1654 Massachusetts acquitted half of the people it brought to trial for witchcraft. In Connecticut, and the then New Haven colony, all seven of the people charged during this period were convicted and hanged. Whereas in Massachusetts a person had a fifty-fifty chance of gaining their freedom, to be indicted for witchcraft in Connecticut during these years was a death sentence.

That pattern of unyielding persecution of suspected witches by Connecticut began to change in 1655 through the efforts of one person, John Winthrop, Jr., son of the Massachusetts governor who so carefully documented the *maleficia* of Margaret Jones. Winthrop, Jr. was an equally capable but much different person than his father. He served as governor of Connecticut for nineteen years, from 1657 to 1676. (He sat out one of those years because Connecticut had term limits on the governor's office—a law they changed so he could serve continuously.) He was the founder of three towns: Ipswich, Massachusetts, and Saybrook and New London in Connecticut. Winthrop was an industrial entrepreneur who raised money in Europe to build an advanced iron foundry in New England in the 1640s, when the region was still regarded as almost wholly a wilderness. He was also New England's most sought-after physician. Winthrop's medicines and healing powers were deemed to be so effective that people wrote to him from the West Indies and Europe seeking medical advice, and the people of New England flocked to him for medical care. He was the leading scientist in colonial North America, too, and a founding member of England's Royal Society, which today is still one of the leading scientific institutions in the world. He was both a charter member of the society, and its first colonial member.

Winthrop was all these things because he was, first and foremost, an alchemist—one of those early modern scientists dedicated to employing an alchemical blend of science, religion, and magic to harness the occult forces permeating nature and do God's work in the world. Winthrop founded New London to be an alchemical research center, and he traveled through Europe recruiting other alchemists to come to America and pursue a vision of godly perfection, intended to improve the world and hasten Christ's return. The very name "New London"—which the Connecticut Assembly thought so brash in its ambitions that they rejected the use of the name on two different occasions—reflects the scope of Winthrop's vision for his new town, and his belief in alchemy's power.

As an alchemist, a practitioner of the occult, and someone who had studied natural magic, Winthrop was considered a reliable authority on the various uses of magic. And, because he was from a leading Puritan family and had impeccable political and religious credentials, he was for the most part above suspicion regarding his own magical pursuits. So as early as 1655 (1653 in New Haven colony), when there were suspicious cases involving accusations of magic and witchcraft in Connecticut, magistrates looked to Winthrop to help determine whether the suspicions of witchcraft were justified. Once Winthrop was involved, witchcraft prosecution in Connecticut changed dramatically.

From 1655 to 1661, after executing every suspected witch it had prosecuted before that time, no person accused of witchcraft in Connecticut colony faced conviction. That's because, as a consultant in these cases, Winthrop consistently found grounds for suspicion (which validated the fears of the accusers), but no confirmation that the suspect had actually used diabolical magic (which freed the accused). Connecticut's pattern of prosecution and conviction was effectively stalled by Winthrop, who, when elected governor of the colony in 1657, gained additional authority over the legal process. Unfortunately though, the brake Winthrop's influence put on witch prosecution was only temporary.

In 1661, Connecticut sent Winthrop to England on what could best be described as an emergency diplomatic mission. After an eleven-year period without a monarch on the throne (following the execution of King Charles I by his Puritan enemies in 1649), England restored the monarchy in 1660, installing Charles II, son of the beheaded king, as the country's ruler. The new monarch had ample reason to want to exact retribution on his New England colonies, which had supported the war against his father, especially as it was believed they were harboring several of the regicides, the men who had signed Charles I's death warrant. Connecticut was in a particularly vulnerable position, since the colony had been founded without royal permission and had never sought to obtain a royal charter giving sanction to its existence. Faced with the possibility of a royal takeover of the Connecticut government, Winthrop was sent on a mission to try to smooth things over with the king, and, if possible, secure Connecticut a royal charter. This was a tall order for Winthrop to fill—especially since his father-in-law had been one of the regicides, but he had little choice but to accept the assignment and sailed down the Connecticut for England in the summer of 1661.

In Winthrop's absence, witchcraft trials began anew, first with a case in October 1661 in which a divided jury found Nicholas and Margaret Jennings of Saybrook "probably" guilty of witchcraft, a qualifier that saved them from execution, though its near certainty set the stage for the witch hunt that followed. The following March in Hartford, an eight-year-old girl named Eizabeth Kelly awoke with excruciating stomach pain. She screamed for her father and told him that Goody Ayres, a woman known for spreading stories of encounters with the devil, was tormenting her. Though her father at first resisted the child's entreaties to send for the magistrates, she continued her accusations throughout her illness. When Elizabeth died, saying with her last words, "Goody Ayres chokes me," the magistrates were sent for, and all hell broke loose in Hartford.

Kelly's death unleashed a torrent of witchcraft executions. New witchcraft victims screamed their presence, as the Hartford Witch Hunt saw a year of panic that produced eight witchcraft trials in as many months. The entire colony was gripped by fear that it was under diabiolical assault as witnesses were deposed, suspects interrogated, and trials set. The trials themselves became riveting performances of social pathology, where, in the absence of an authoritative moderating presence like Winthrop, witch haters had a field day. Rejecting guidelines by English authorities that it not be used, two accused persons in the Hartford trials were subjected to the water test. In this test, suspects were bound hand to toe and dropped into water (in the Hartford cases, most likely the nearby Connecticut River) to see whether they would float or sink. If they floated, they were deemed guilty; if they sank without surfacing, they were innocent. The theory behind the test was magical, but with a spiritual foundation, and it made sense, but only in a world where religion, science, and magic were inseparably intertwined. Since a witch had, in covenanting with the devil, rejected the waters of baptism, the reasoning went, the waters would reject the witch, causing her or him to float to the surface. In Hartford, both suspects failed the test, and as a result, fled the colony before their prosecution continued.

They had good reason to flee. The ministers and magistrates leading the prosecution, this time concurring with the advice provided in the English and continental witchcraft manuals, were unstinting in the zeal with which they pressed their cases. Suspects were pressed, verbally abused, harangued, and browbeaten in the effort to wrest confessions from them. Although there are no formal trial transcripts, the surviving fragments of paper summarizing witnesses' testimony bear witness to the excruciating drama of the court proceedings. Under interrogation by Joseph Haynes, the "lewd, ignorant, and considerably aged" Rebecca Greensmith became so enraged she "could have torn him in pieces," she said, "and was as much resolved as might be to deny her guilt." But as Haynes persisted in his evidentiary assault, Greensmith crumbled. She felt "as if her flesh had been pulled from her bones . . . and so could not deny any longer." Her subsequent confession provides indication of the salacious nature of her questioning, as, in her confession she admitted that the devil had had "frequent use of her body . . . with much seeming delight to her."

By the time John Winthrop, Jr. returned to Hartford in June 1663, four people—Rebecca Greensmith, her husband Nathaniel, Mary Sanford, and Mary Barnes of Farmington had been hanged. As many as five others, certain they were heading for execution, had fled the colony, forfeiting all their possessions, before their trials were complete. One man had been acquitted, and another suspect, Elizabeth Seager, had been narrowly acquitted but had already been charged with witchcraft a second time.

Winthrop must have been disheartened at how far his more cautious approach to witchcraft prosecution had been superseded in his absence. But, as the returning governor, and the man who had succeeded in his unlikely mission of securing a royal charter from Charles II (an extremely favorable one at that, which gave Connecticut colony virtual independence from crown rule 113 years before American independence), Winthrop had a great deal of political and social capital at his disposal, and he immediately started using it to take control over the witch hunt.

Elizabeth Seager, awaiting her second trial, was the first to benefit. Winthrop appears to have engineered a compromise with her accusers that once again found her not guilty of witchcraft, but guilty of the lesser charge of adultery. A strong-willed and sharp-tongued woman, however, Seager continued to antagonize her neighbors and was indicted a third time for "continuing to practice witchcraft" in the spring of 1665. This time, her accusers seemed determined to get a conviction, so Winthrop allowed them to get one. He remained away from her trial, though as governor he could have presided over it and served as chief prosecutor. When the expected guilty verdict was returned, however, Winthrop refused to enforce it. At a special meeting of the governor and magistrates, he declared Seager's conviction "obscure and ambiguous" to him, and deferred sentencing to a later date. Then he waited nearly a year, until judicial reforms he had had written into the royal charter went into effect. These gave the governor power to "impose, alter, change, or anul any penalty" and to "release or pardon any offender." Winthrop then set Seager "free from further suffering or imprisonment." For the first time in Connecticut's history, a convicted witch did not hang.

Why was Winthrop, himself a magic practitioner, so much more reluctant than many of his contemporaries to support witchcraft convictions? Winthrop, a very astute politician, was careful never to put his reasons in writing, but from the body of his voluminous correspondence to other political leaders, alchemists, and clergy, one infers that Winthrop saw from his own magic experiments that successfully practicing magic was extremely difficult and that most people accused of doing so simply weren't up to the task. Whether or not that was the underlying reason, Winthrop never wavered in his commitment to protecting accused witches from unwarranted convictions.

Many of Connecticut's magistrates followed the governor's lead in exercising forbearance in subsequent witchcraft cases, which was not the case for many ordinary citizens still convinced that witchcraft was dangerous, and that their communities were under diabolical assault. As much as they admired their charter-winning governor and medical expert, some people quietly wondered just why the alchemical governor was so soft on witchcraft prosecution, especially after the Seager case.

Tensions over how to handle suspected witchcraft assaults came to a head in the 1669 case of Katherine Harrison of Wethersfield. This proved to be Connecticut's single most important witch trial, for it was the pivotal case in the transformation of witchcraft prosecution in Connecticut. Harrison was an outspoken Wethersfield medical practitioner, astrologer, and widow who had risen from servant status in her youth to become a person of substantial means. In May of 1668, Harrison's neighbors began collecting depositions charging her with witchcraft and a variety of *maleficia*, including inflicting illness leading to death, shape-shifting and appearing in spectral form, and astrologically divining the future. She was accused of magically causing the death of three people, two of them children. One witness reported seeing her as a black dog in the moonlight, another as a calf's head that morphed into Harrison herself on a hay cart, and yet a third saw her as a dog-like thing, but with her own head, walking to and fro in the observer's bed chamber. Several people reported that she had made numerous astrological predictions of future events, from marriages to future sicknesses and death. By the time Harrison was formally indicted in May of 1669, more than thirty witnesses from up and down the Connecticut River Valley had testified against her, but testimony offered by Winthrop and the magistrates resulted in the jury being unable to reach a verdict. Harrison was ordered imprisoned until the court met again the following October, when the jury would be reconvened to render a decision.

Someone, probably governor Winthrop, ordered Harrison released from jail and held under house arrest in Wethersfield until the trial. This provoked howls of protest from a frightened community. Thirty-eight Wethersfield residents, including two ministers and the local physician, signed a petition protesting Harrison's release and demanding her immediate incarceration. They also demanded that Harrison's prosecution be taken away from Winthrop, who, as governor, was the ex officio prosecutor, and handled by the colony's foremost lawyer, who could be trusted to press the case without favoring Harrison. Winthrop had clearly overstepped his bounds. Releasing Harrison not only called into question his impartiality but also, less directly perhaps, raised questions about his own magical practices.

When the jury reconvened on October 12, 1669, they found Harrison guilty. But once again, as in the case of Elizabeth Seager, Winthrop did not let the conviction stand, but his views on witchcraft were so suspect at this moment that he could not simply reject the verdict without provoking a fear-generated firestorm. So, he employed a different strategy.

Before passing sentence on Harrison, the Winthrop court asked for input on a number of issues central not only to Harrison's case, but to all witchcraft cases. Most importantly, they sought clarification regarding the evidentiary standards necessary for conviction. For answers, they turned to a triumvirate of ministers headed by the Reverend Gershom Bulkeley. This was not accidental. Bulkeley was a close friend of the governor and, like Winthrop, was a physician and alchemist. Bulkeley had studied alchemy under Winthrop's direction and he shared Winthrop's interest in natural magic and, most important, his skepticism toward witchcraft allegations.

Bulkeley's written response to Winthrop's and the magistrates' questions—especially the one regarding the standards of evidence necessary to convict a suspected witch—seems tailor-made to help Winthrop address the challenge he faced over Harrison's conviction. It did so through a change so subtle it went all but unnoticed by historians for many years. But for all its subtlety, it was a change that ended witchcraft executions in Connecticut forever.

Witchcraft, under English law, was a capital crime, and as such, punishable by death. The most important standard of evidence imposed in capital cases was that there had to be two eyewitnesses to the commission of the crime in order to convict. Without a second witness, it was simply one person's word against another, and that was insufficient proof to take away someone's life. Before the Harrison case, the two-witness rule had been interpreted loosely in witchcraft cases. The person who saw Harrison as a dog-like thing with her own face was one witness to her witchcraft and the person who saw Harrison appear as a calf on a hay cart was a second witness, though the two had actually observed two different events. The minsters were asked to tell the court exactly what evidentiary standards should be used in witchcraft trials to fulfill the two-witness requirement.

Bulkeley's written response to the question was simple, but profoundly important. It called for applying the exact same standards used in other capital cases to witchcraft charges. A witchcraft conviction could be valid only if there were two witnesses to the exact same act at the exact same time. Though on the surface the decision seemed to be reaffirming the traditional standard for capital case conviction, it dramatically contracted the grounds for convicting a witch. Much of the evidence against any witch suspect was automatically negated, because the spectral apparitions, familiars, and other preternatural encounters people reported with suspected witches almost always happened when the witnesses were alone. Witchcraft accusations began in people's imaginations, and they gained credibility when people told their stories to neighbors. These stories spread and the rumors spread, but the actual encounter with witchcraft was always an individual affair.

Based on the ministers' findings, Harrison was freed after agreeing to leave the colony. Moreover, as the new standards for conviction and underlying caution regarding witchcraft accusations became accepted by others, witch killing in New England ended for a generation.

Only in 1692, when an entire group of girls publicly writhed in alleged witch-inflicted agony in a Salem Massachusetts meetinghouse was the more-guarded interpretation of the two-witness rule fully met in a witchcraft case, with consequences so horrific that the ensuing tragedy in Salem has become the icon of witch hunting.

In Connecticut however, witch killing was over. Connecticut had been transformed from a state known as New England's fiercest prosecutor of witches to one that would never kill another witch, a generation before the Salem nightmare began. (During the time of the Salem trials, Connecticut would experience a brief flurry of witch trials, but, as in the case of Katherine Harrison, cooler heads prevailed and executions were forestalled.) The irony of Connecticut's great shift in attitudes toward accused witches is that it was brought about by a governor who himself knew the occult, practiced natural magic, and understood first-hand the limits of what magic could do. Together with a minister and protégé who shared his practice and understanding of the occult, he implemented a minor change in a legal interpretation that put a permanent end to a terrible state-sanctioned punishment.

FURTHER READING

Parts of this chapter are taken from Walter W. Woodward's "New England's Other Witch-hunt: The Hartford Witch-hunt of the 1660s and Changing Patterns in Witchcraft Prosecution," *Organization of American Historians Magazine of History* (July, 2003), 16–20 and "Witchcraft, Alchemy and Authority in the Connecticut Witch-Hunt of the 1660s," in *Prospero's America: John Winthrop, Jr., Alchemy, and the Creation of New England Culture, 1606–1676.* (Chapel Hill, 2010) 210–52.

For more information on Gershom Bulkeley, see Richard G. Tomlinson's *Gershom Bulkeley, Zealot for Truth* (Create Space Independent Publishing, 2018).

For more information on witch trials in general, see Richard S. Ross's *Before Salem: Witch Hunting in the Connecticut River Valley 1647-1663* (McFarlane, 2017); Cynthia Wolfe Boynton's *Connecticut Witch Trials: The First Panic in the New World* (History Press, 2014); and Richard G. Tomlinson's *Witchcraft Prosecution: Chasing the Devil in Connecticut* (Picton Press, 2012).

BENJAMIN COLLINS, ROCK STAR

A carver from Columbia was a master of the Puritans' only art form—the gravestone.

In the early 1700s cemeteries in Connecticut's Puritan towns took on a new and vital role in social and cultural life, and gravestone carvers became our earliest "rock stars." Traditionally, the houses of the first settlers, clustered around village greens, had been the source of local identity and unity, but the second and third generations' dispersal to outlying farmsteads made day-to-day, face-to-face community-wide interaction a thing of the past. To counteract the increasing isolation, town fathers and local ministers conspired to transform their local cemeteries into vibrant symbols of community connections, not just to God but also to their past and to each other. Almost every aspect of Puritan death and burial rituals were changed. Most notable were the transformations in the design of and importance placed on carved gravestones.

Seventeenth-century gravestones had been simple rough stone slabs or shaped stones carved with medieval death's-heads, crossed bones, scythes, and other symbols of death. The eighteenth-century saw those death's-heads transform into more refined (and far less threatening) images of winged faces representing the souls of the people who had died. Vines, tendrils, and other signs indicating the soul's transition from death to new life at the moment of Christian resurrection replaced symbols of death, and stones began to include life-summarizing epitaphs. In a society that normally rejected artistic expression as too worldly, the town cemetery became a gallery of vivid remembrance. One of the few places where all town members gathered frequently (thanks to comparatively high colonial mortality rates, especially among children),

RUTH SHAPLEIGH-BROWN

the "yard" became an essential site of local identity, self-expression, and community.

Stone carvers, each with a distinct approach to depicting the story of remembrance, became well known and their work widely distributed. Their particular stylistic patterns remain clearly recognizable after nearly three centuries of New England wind and weather.

One of the rock stars of Puritan gravestone carving was Benjamin Collins of Columbia, Connecticut. A patriarch of the Eastern Connecticut Ornamental Style, his signed stones date from 1726 to 1759, the year he died. Collins brought a cabinet-maker's sense of style to his work, which made it very popular. His delicate, leaf-like border panels and feathered, Indian-headdress-like-wings grace stones in Pachaug, Danielson, Ledyard, Hebron, Tolland, Scotland, Norwich, Colchester, New London, Lebanon, Plainfield, Coventry, Franklin, Windham, and Mansfield Center. In Columbia alone, there are forty-one Collins markers, many carved from the distinctively blue-hued schist he quarried at his own farm. Collins made rich use of symbolism, such as the winged hourglass ("time flies") carved into the marker of his son Zelotes, and the sun, moon, and stars (together symbolizing the promise of the Resurrection) he placed on the stone of the wealthy Zerviah Buckingham. As a parishioner of the leading New Light evangelist Eleazar Wheelock, it is not surprising that in almost every stone Collins carved there is a heart, a symbol of both the new birth in Christ (an essential component of the Great Awakening) and eternal life. Collins's graceful style made him a recognized master of the most important art form of his time and region. Two of his sons, Josiah and Zerubabel, followed in their father's footsteps. Zerubabel became a well-known gravestone carver in his own right, working until his death in 1797. He carved his father's gravestone using his own distinctive style.

Almost every Connecticut town has a cemetery where you can view the stonework of celebrated early New England artists such as Benjamin Collins while paying respects to the towns' early inhabitants. One afternoon, make a thermos of tea and go see the Puritan past in a new and artful light. For more information about gravestones in Connecticut visit the Connecticut Gravestone Network at ctgravestones.com.

ELEAZAR WHEELOCK, THE GREAT AWAKENING, SAMSON OCCOM, AND MOOR'S INDIAN CHARITY SCHOOL

Before Eleazar Wheelock was a famous Great Awakening evangelist or founder of the Indian School that became Dartmouth College, he was minister to a troubled village church.

Eleazar Wheelock (1711–1779) is remembered today as the founder of Dartmouth College, an Ivy League school in Hanover, New Hampshire, consistently ranked among the world's leading academic institutions. Most studies of Wheelock, and there have been many, focus on the immediate events surrounding that college's founding and Wheelock's role as college president during Dartmouth's early years. This limits our understanding of both Wheelock and Dartmouth, because most of the events that led Wheelock to establish the college took place not in New Hampshire, but in the small Connecticut village of Lebanon Crank, today called Columbia. That was where Wheelock lived most of his life, and where he served as local parish minister for thirty-five years. This was also where Wheelock first earned his reputation as one of the Great Awakening's greatest and most sought-after evangelists, a celebrity status that brought him both fame and notoriety. It was in Lebanon Crank that Wheelock undertook the education of the twenty-year-old Mohegan convert to Christianity Samson Occom, who also played an instrumental, perhaps the most important, role in the founding of Dartmouth. Lebanon Crank was also where, based on Occom's remarkable educational performance, Wheelock established Moor's Indian Charity School to educate indigenous missionaries and teach them the skills needed to become evangelists to their own people. This school became the proof-of-concept Wheelock used to advance the New Hampshire college project.

For all these reasons, this story about Eleazar Wheelock focuses on his years in Lebanon Crank, his life as a minister, his work as a New Light evangelist, his relationship with Samson Occom, the founding of More's Indian Charity School, and how they all affected and were received by the members of the community he served. The goal is to show how Wheelock's life in Connecticut paved the way for, and was crucial to, his later move to New Hampshire and the founding of Dartmouth. Beginnings matter, and to understand the man who founded Dartmouth, we need to know more about what happened in the place where he spent most of his life.

The only image of Eleazar Wheelock created by a contemporary is a portrait by the Connecticut painter Joseph Stewart, who was a student at Dartmouth in 1779 when Wheelock died there at the age of sixty-nine. Stewart's painting, commissioned by the college, was completed in 1796, seventeen years after Wheelock's death. Glad as we are that this presidential portrait exists, I think it limits our view of Wheelock as much as it provides one. To envision the Eleazar Wheelock of *this* story, you must imaginatively erase many years, quite a few pounds, and some signs of illness to visualize the twenty-four-year old minister who came to Lebanon Crank in 1735 and oversaw its congregation for the next three and a half decades.

That twenty-four-year-old, who accepted an invitation to "preach on probation," knew he was coming to a troubled church. Twice before the small Puritan congregation in the start-up village, established as Lebanon's second ecclesiastical society in 1716, had gone to the considerable effort and great expense of finding and hiring a minister, and both times things had gone terribly wrong.

The first minister, Samuel Smith, relinquished his office due to mental health issues. He died, probably by suicide, on the same day his successor William Gager was ordained. Gager's ministry was also troubled. He served nine years but was forced to resign after several scandalous reports of public drunkenness. Two flawed and failed ministers in succession did not reflect well on Lebanon Crank's church-founding efforts, and the young congregation was under considerable pressure to make its third choice a good one.

In a larger sense, though, Lebanon Crank's two failed ministries were emblematic of a more general trend. In the 1730s, Puritan New England was in deep spiritual and moral decline. Historians cite many causes

Joseph Steward, The Reverend Eleazar Wheelock (1711–1779). HOOD MUSEUM OF ART, DARTMOUTH: COMMISSIONED BY THE TRUSTEES OF DARTMOUTH COLLEGE.

for this: economic ambition and greater access to consumer goods, land shortages and high mobility, changing modes of child-rearing, and a rising sense of personal independence, especially among the young. The fire of religious zeal that energized New England's founding generations had, by the 1730s, been replaced by spiritual apathy among most people, and a religion of forms and rituals among the godly.

On the surface, perhaps, New England Puritanism *appeared* as strong as ever. Government was still run as a godly commonwealth. Everyone was still taxed to support their town's church and minister, and the church was still seen as the religious and moral arm of the state. Everyone still was legally required to go to church twice on Sunday. And people still drank deeply from the well of Calvinist guilt they had absorbed through childhood catechisms, family prayers, and weekly sermons. By today's standards, one suspects they would look and even seem *very* religious.

Nevertheless, the excruciating psychological and spiritual tension once generated by the Calvinist belief that only a small and select group of people were chosen by God to be saved, and that the vast majority of people were utterly and inescapably damned to spend eternity in hell, had waned. For New England's seventeenth-century Puritan *founders*, life had been a constant soul-searching battle between hope and fear, seeking on the one hand the inner spark of religious fervor that indicated God might have chosen them as one of his saints, while on the other simultaneously fighting the terrible fear that they were most likely doomed to hell. But *that* fire had gone out of Puritanism, and in its place was something much more formal and far less powerful.

By the 1730s Puritanism was a religion of forms and rituals, in which believers' faith was measured by whether they lived Christian lives and acted with scrupulous piety." Ministers called this "godly walking," and being a godly walker became the accepted standard for admission as a full communion-taking member of a Puritan congregation. Only a few people in any community fit that description. The rest came to church out of habit, or only when they had to, not feeling bound by the imperatives of godly walking nearly as much as the pursuit of more worldly goals. If they feared the damnation that might fall on them as a result of their spiritual apathy at all, it was not enough to make them alter the way they lived.

The Connecticut General Assembly had tried to check the colony's spiritual and moral decline by insisting that church attendance be officially monitored, and that laws against lying, swearing, drunkenness, and unseasonable meetings of young people were strictly enforced, but this did little to reverse the decidedly downward spiritual trend. Just as Wheelock was beginning his ministry, the Lebanon parish from which his new congregation had been hived off called a special meeting to determine what to do about "the purity of their church," which, they said, "seems dayly to be declining."

Reversing this spiritual decline would present a special challenge for any minister, but it was one the young Wheelock readily embraced. The son of a prosperous church deacon from nearby Windham and a recent prize-winning Yale graduate, Wheelock had already turned down a ministerial offer on Long Island and arrived in Columbia confident in himself and his abilities, ambitious to make his mark on the world, and filled with a sense of mission. He set out to wake the slumbering religious zeal of his twice-burned congregation and met with an almost astonishing degree of success.

Wheelock was one of two ministers whose 1735 preaching efforts helped launch a revival of religion in New England. Scholars cite Northampton minister Jonathan Edwards's success in instilling religious zeal among his town's young people that year as the earliest stirrings of the phenomenon known as the Great Awakening. Edwards reported of his congregation that summer that, "All seemed to be seized with a deep concern about their eternal salvation." But Edwards also noted that he was not alone. A similar "deep concern" had come to Connecticut, "in a part of Lebanon called the Crank, where the Rev. Mr. Wheelock, a young gentleman, is lately settled." Although Wheelock had not been ordained until early June, by year's end he had brought more than one hundred new members into the Lebanon Crank church.

What made it possible for Wheelock to succeed in converting spiritual apathy into religious zeal? Well, to begin with, he was blessed with some extraordinary abilities. Benjamin Trumbull, the early Connecticut historian who saw him preach, described Wheelock as "a gentleman of a comely figure, of a mild and winning aspect." In other words, he was good looking, and good-natured, too. "His voice," Trumbull wrote, was "smooth and harmonious, the best that ever I heard." And, "he had the entire command of it." In other words, Wheelock was an extraordinary orator, with a beautiful and powerful speaking voice.

Yet it was the way he used that voice that made him so effective. Wheelock, like Jonathan Edwards, deployed his oratorical power not to reinforce the formal pieties of the "godly walkers," but to instill, deep, soul-wrenching fear; to bring to life with terrifying effectiveness the torments and never-ending agonies that accompanied damnation. "His preaching and addresses were close and pungent," Trumbull wrote, meaning they were short, strict, piercing, and persuasive, "and yet winning, beyond almost all comparison, so that his audience would be melted even into tears, before they were aware of it."

Wheelock was relentless in his assault on spiritual apathy, and on all whose hearts were hardened to their own sin. "The audience," Trumbull said, "were pressed by all means to be Christians indeed, and not to deceive themselves. He insisted that all, without exception, who would not believe, would most certainly be damned."

Wheelock brought to the pulpit a fervent, evangelical, emotional preaching style that was the antithesis of the logical formulaic sermons of the godly walkers. And to augment the emotional impact of those sermons, he altered the music sung in his church from the old monotonous psalms of the Bay Psalm Book to the new, harmonious hymns of Isaac Watts. Wheelock won many new followers, from the ranks of both those who had been spiritually apathetic and the piously observing but spiritually weak (as far as Wheelock was concerned) godly walkers.

To protect his congregation's newfound zeal for Christian virtue, Wheelock set up church tribunals, with himself at the head, to examine, try, and judge violations of spiritual and moral authority. With the zealotry of the true believer, Wheelock called inhabitants of Lebanon Crank, high and low, to account for fighting, fornication, drinking, lying, stealing, beating slaves, or not coming to services. Even as he built a large following, there were those in Lebanon Crank and elsewhere who saw his judgmental, evangelical, and emotional preaching style as an unwelcome departure from the more staid school of godly piety. Their opposition was, however, at least in the early days of Wheelock's ministry, relatively ineffective. Wheelock's star was fast-rising, and with the 1740 appearance of an English itinerant Anglican evangelist named George Whitfield, it would soon blaze a trail all across New England.

With Whitfield, the spiritual awakening Edwards and Wheelock had launched locally five years earlier became a trans-New England phenomenon. Whitfield toured Connecticut and Massachusetts in the summer of 1740 delivering more than one hundred sermons in forty-one towns in forty-six days, many in open fields to enraptured audiences numbering in the thousands. Like Edwards and Wheelock, Whitfield deployed conscience-pricking emotional preaching to awaken his auditors to the peril of their unsaved conditions. Like Wheelock, he preached in a flamboyant, charismatic style, but with extravagant bodily gestures and tearful outbursts that took such sermonizing to new dramatic heights. Emphasizing with vivid imagery the desperately real danger of hell those before him faced, Whitfield insisted that to be saved Christians had to experience an inner spiritual conversion, be "born again," in a way that was immediate, overpowering, and spiritually transcendent. Whitfield completely rejected the idea that piety, church attendance, family prayer, or moral living—the foundation of the godly walker's assurance—were signs of salvation. Piety counted for nothing, he insisted, unless one had actually experienced a spiritually transcendent rebirth.

Whitfield's effect on audiences was astonishing. People shrieked in fear, cried in agony, fell senseless to the ground in spiritual trances. Some wept for joy as they felt the spirit within them; others praised God and sang hymns of praise.

Whitfield electrified all New England—and he drew to his side men like Wheelock and Wheelock's brothers-in-law, the Reverend Benjamin Pomeroy of Hebron, and James Davenport of Long Island, who thought Whitfield's presence heralded a moment of great Christian transformation. They emulated his style of preaching, becoming itinerant "sons of thunder" themselves—traveling emissaries of God who precipitated in full force the event known as the Great Awakening—a movement that would both renew and divide the old Puritan church.

Wheelock became one of the most important ministerial voices of this new movement. In 1741, while maintaining his duties in Lebanon Crank, he also took his ministry on the road, preaching soul-wrenching, fear-inducing sermons across the land. Invitations poured in as Wheelock became a revival rock star. Between the summer of 1741 and the fall of the next year, Wheelock preached in at least twenty towns other than his home parish, and received invitations from a dozen more. His power to awaken people to their spiritual deficiencies, to "wound them," or put them "under concern," was extraordinary, and a tremendous asset to congregations on the verge of renewal. "I can't be deny'd of you," wrote a minister from Marlborough, Massachusetts, urging him to come and preach. A Boston congregation playfully threatened to hold him captive unless he agreed to preach there one more day.

Wheelock was with Jonathan Edwards in Enfield in July 1741, when Edwards preached the now-famous sermon reminding the godly walkers before him they were just "sinners in the hands of an angry God," and he canceled his trip home after that sermon to help manage the wave of spiritual fear and anxiety Edwards's sermon had triggered.

New England that year was on spiritual fire and Wheelock was one of the matches. In congregations long characterized by staid and placid formalism, people sighed, groaned, cried out, writhed in contortions, and trembled in arm-waving, breast-beating panic as the visiting preacher Wheelock scourged them with images of God's impending wrath and the need to be born again. Despite an exhausting travel schedule, Wheelock inspired a second awakening within his own church. A visitor from Windsor wrote of the "Glorious workings of the spirit" in Lebanon Crank, which, Wheelock later noted had brought in more than three hundred converts.

By late 1741, an exhausted but spiritually vibrant Wheelock was convinced that what was happening was not just a Great Awakening, but a sign that the millennium—the long-awaited return of Christ to rule on Earth for a thousand years—was underway. "The Work of God spreads gloriously in the land," he wrote Edwards. ". . . and I do Verily believe these are the beginning of the glorious things that are spoken of Concerning the City of God in the Latter Day."

One of the surest signs that the Awakening had millennial significance was the fact that Native Americans, who for generations had actively resisted English missionaries, were suddenly taking real interest in Christianity. Puritans believed that before Christ would return, all people, including New England's original inhabitants, had to become Christians. To Wheelock, these new Indian conversions were profoundly important. He once wrote a group of Iroquois sachems, "I have had you upon my heart ever since I was a boy . . . I have prayed for you daily for more than thirty years, that a way might be opened to send the gospel among you, and you be made willing to receive it." After more than a century of false starts, it seemed in 1741 that that time was at hand. Moved by Awakening preachers such as Wheelock, and especially his brother-in-law James Davenport, more than fifty native people were attending services at Groton; thirteen Niantics worshiped at East Lyme; one hundred Narragansetts at Westerly, Rhode Island; and twenty Mohegans, including Samson Occom's mother and aunt, began attending the church at what is now Uncasville. Wheelock wrote expectantly to his fellow ministers about the "Great Work" underway among tribes where there were "many . . . converted, and the rest under concern."

What a heady thing it must have been to be Eleazar Wheelock at that moment. Though just in his thirties at the end of 1741 he was one of the best known and most sought after preachers of the Great Awakening, a leading figure in a spiritual movement that seemed about to bring on the Christian fulfillment of days. His words could shake people to the core of their beings, had brought hundreds upon hundreds into Christ's fold already, and word-wounded thousands more. Who would have thought that the confident young man who had arrived in a small, out-of-the-way parish just six years before could rise to such heights so fast? Surely, this was God's work, and Wheelock was his messenger.

But even at this moment of spiritual triumph, events were unfolding that would challenge the legitimacy of the Great Awakening, the spiritual fervor of its evangelists, and make Wheelock and his clerical relatives a focus of sharply critical scrutiny.

In part, they brought it on themselves. From the Awakening's earliest days, the evangelists held up their soul-wrenching sermons as the antithesis of and antidote to the spiritless preaching of the non-revivalist ministers who held most of New England's pulpits. Calling themselves the "New Lights"—a phrase Wheelock helped coin—and the traditional Puritan establishment the "Old Lights," the evangelists made their Awakening sermons an almost constant attack on the very ministers from whose pulpits they often preached. At first, perhaps in surprise, or forbearance, or uncertainty as to how to react, the Old Light ministers remained silent. But by the end of 1741, they, and the godly walkers in their congregations who had been horrified at the wild spiritual theatrics that had invaded their sanctuaries, had had enough.

Led by Boston minister Charles Chauncey, the Old Lights (clergy and laity together) launched a counterattack in which Wheelock and his ministerial relatives became prime targets. They stopped opening their pulpits to the traveling ministers and became openly critical of the New Lights' evangelical fervor. Early in 1742, after a member of a congregation Wheelock had visited attacked him in writing for his violent rhetoric, extreme gestures, fist-pounding outbursts, and his practice of judging the state of others souls (thus usurping the authority of God himself), the Windham association of ministers, citing the "disorder and confusion" that the itinerants had brought to formerly peaceful congregations, cautioned both Wheelock and his brother-in-law Benjamin Pomeroy to rein in their opinions. In May, the Connecticut General Assembly passed formal anti-itinerancy laws making it illegal for any minister to preach in a church that was not his own without receiving a formal invitation. They also ordered Wheelock's brothers-in-law Pomeroy and Davenport arrested and brought to Hartford to answer for causing "great disorder" at public assemblies in Stamford. Pomeroy was released with a warning; Davenport, who lived on Long Island, was found mentally unbalanced and ordered deported.

The anti-itinerancy laws triggered nearly a year and a half of theological civil war in Connecticut and reverberated throughout New England. Congregations divided. Some of the New Light preachers and their followers, notably among them Pomeroy and Davenport, were energized by the establishment's opposition and went to ever further extremes. These would ultimately lead to Pomeroy being deprived of his income, and Davenport being publicly disgraced.

For Wheelock, though, the establishment pushback forced him to reassess not the importance of the Awakening, but its unintended consequences. He began to question the extremes with which some of the awakened expressed their evangelical fervor, and he noticed with alarm the way ordinary parishioners, convinced they now had direct contact with the Holy Spirit, began to see themselves as authorities in spiritual matters, even to the point of challenging Wheelock himself on the purity of his faith.

Wheelock came to realize that without curbs on spiritual enthusiasm, the Awakening could lead to spiritual anarchy. The idea of a church where every person was his own religious authority was simply anathema to him. So, gradually, he pulled back from the forefront of the New Light movement. He curtailed his itinerant preaching and adopted more cautious interpretations of the visions his awakened converts experienced. When James Davenport set up an unlicensed evangelical academy called the Shepherd's Tent in New London, and, in a fit of evangelical fervor, stripped off his pants in public and threw them into a bonfire, Wheelock printed a public letter criticizing the "fiery, harsh, censorious driving zeal" of Davenport and his followers. Wheelock's changing attitudes to the Awakening's energetic spiritualism did not go unnoticed. "I must say you are strangely fallen from what you seemed two or three years ago." wrote a New Light convert in November 1744, "Take Heed you have not the blood of souls on your door."

As Wheelock stepped back from the itinerant movement, he put renewed emphasis on his work in Lebanon Crank. It was a good time to do so, for in his extended absences, there had been some significant backsliding. In May 1743, he wrote a fellow minister, "I . . . continue among my dear flock though the love of many seems to be waxing cold." We do not know whether Wheelock's congregation's chill came from backsliding evangelical converts or formerly quiet godly walkers empowered by recent events, but Wheelock's response to this congregational resistance was to more forcefully assert both his ministerial presence and his authority. This included a new round of church tribunals aimed at regulating moral behavior, enforcing the Biblical Ten Commandments, and thwarting public expressions of displeasure about his ministry. Among other cases, Wheelock's court tried his predecessor William Gager, now a local school teacher, for public drunkenness, and it brought charges against two church-goers for laughing and scoffing during one of Wheelock's sermons. Though it is evident that Wheelock had a large and loyal base of parish support, it is also clear there were those among the congregation less enthusiastic about his ministry, and henceforward they would pose an ongoing challenge.

One of the wedges between Wheelock and his parishioners that remained a constant throughout his thirty-five-year tenure was sharp disagreement over his compensation. To attract Wheelock to settle among them, the town, reeling from its failed first and second ministers, had offered him a substantial piece of land and given him a large, newly built house as a settlement, a kind of signing bonus. At the same time, though, they had written an annual salary agreement whose payment provisions could be interpreted ambiguously. At the end of Wheelock's extraordinarily successful but also extraordinarily expensive first year, the church's lay leaders had elected to interpret the contract in the way most favorable to the town's ratepayers, rather than to the new minister. This surprised and disappointed Wheelock, who had a very well-established sense of his own value, and he had argued for more compensation, but to no avail. In the years following, even as he grew the church; developed a large, loyal personal following; and became a New England ministerial celebrity, the congregation held its penurious line on his salary. This left Wheelock chronically lamenting, and not at all quietly, the financial burden under which he suffered. He did manage, though over time, to build up substantial personal holdings in both land and material possessions.

The son of a wealthy Windham merchant, Wheelock had married Sara Davenport Maltby, widow of a wealthy New Haven merchant and daughter of a leading Connecticut minister, just after accepting his ministerial post. He had arrived in town accompanied by two slaves, a sure sign to the town's relatively poor farmers that he was not a young man in financial need. Coupled with his hard line on local morality, the church trials that undoubtedly won him both enemies as well as friends, and his later itinerancy, which kept him absent the parish for long periods without reducing his salary, one can readily see why the ratepayers of Lebanon Crank felt justified in taking a hard line on money matters. Yale President Ezra Stiles once described Wheelock as "ambitious and haughty" with "much of the Religious politician in his make." Nowhere was Wheelock's economic ambition more transparent than in his chronic financial carping with his parish.

To supplement a ministerial income he always thought far too small, Wheelock focused on the "Latin School for Latin Scholars" he had conducted from his home since shortly after his arrival in Lebanon Crank. Running such a school was a practice not uncommon among ministers. This was a secondary school for students already proficient in reading and writing. Of the sixty-six boys known to have attended it, almost all were between the ages of twelve and eighteen and sons of prospering area farmers. The course of instruction Wheelock offered, which included lessons in the Latin required for college entrance, lasted forty-five to forty-eight weeks. The students would live in the Wheelock household and their fathers paid for tuition, use of the schoolroom, firewood, and the cost of books.

Ironically, it was this Latin school, rather than the ministry, that would sustain Wheelock's awakened sense that he was an important agent helping to fulfill God's unfolding plan for humankind. Even as the Great Awakening itself devolved into theological feuds and congregational fractures and Wheelock found himself increasingly on the spiritual defensive, his godly path forward appeared at his school in the form of a Mohegan mother seeking an education for her son.

Sarah Occom came to Lebanon Crank from the tribal land still in Mohegan possession near Norwich in the late fall of 1743. She wished to talk to Reverend Wheelock about her son Samson. Sarah had been among the first Mohegans converted by the New Light preachers, and her seventeen-year-old son Samson "fell under concern" and then "found a Hope" shortly thereafter. An eager convert, Samson yearned to read and understand the Bible, so he had gotten an English primer and with the help of nearby Anglo neighbors had taught himself to read. His motivation, Occom later wrote, was "to teach Mohegan children to read and to

Instruct them in Christianity." The young man had also recently been named to the Mohegan Tribal Council, which for many years had been in a major land dispute with Connecticut. Having a tribal council member proficient in reading English would have been an invaluable asset during negotiations, so that may also have factored in Occom's desire to master the language. Whatever his motivations, by the time Occom reached age nineteen in 1742, he had taught himself to read some of the New Testament, but he wanted more. Having heard about Wheelock's school, he asked his mother, who knew Wheelock, to see if the minister might agree to instruct him in reading. Occom envisioned spending two or three weeks with Wheelock and using that experience to inform his continuing self-education.

Talking with Sarah, Wheelock immediately realized the potential importance of helping foster the formal education of an indigenous Christian missionary, and he told her he wanted to see her son as soon as possible. Samson came to Lebanon Crank in early December 1743, expecting, he later wrote, to stay with Wheelock a few days. Instead, he was with the minister for the next four years.

Wheelock took Occom into his school and his home as a charity student, meaning he paid no tuition, and began teaching him English, Greek, Latin, and Hebrew. Simultaneously, he initiated Occom into the undoubtedly more *wrenching* process of forced assimilation into Anglo-English cultural ways and lifestyles. From the beginnings of colonization, the English believed that "civilization" (the adoption of English cultural norms) was a prerequisite to "conversion." One could not live as a true Christian without adopting the disciplined English customs they believed made Christian behavior possible—in conversation, personal relations, dress, diet, work, and religion. For Occom and all the indigenous students who would come after him, learning English with Wheelock included learning to *be English* at the same time, a transformation that struck at the very core of their identity.

In the account books recording expenditures laid out for Occom while he attended the school, the most money was spent on English clothing: multiple pairs of shoes, coats, pants, stockings shirts—all expensive because all fabric was hand loomed and all clothing tailored. This was just the most visible manifestation of the school's all-out effort to affect a total transformation of indigenous student's character, the side-effects of which were both psychological and physical. Not surprisingly, the second most common expense on Occom's behalf was for medical care.

Occom was different from the other students in Wheelock's Latin school in more ways than being a Mohegan. He was older, twenty when he arrived in Lebanon Crank in December of 1743, and he suffered a serious eye condition that limited his reading and other activities. During the four years he was under Wheelock's charge, Occom was frequently ill, requiring both a physician and nursing care. But despite chronic illness, he was also an *extraordinarily* capable student, and Wheelock lost little time in showing off his new Mohegan protégé!

During his first year as a student, Wheelock took Occom to commencement ceremonies at Yale. This was no doubt to introduce the Mohegan youth to what was intended to be the next stage of his education as a minister. It also served, in dramatic fashion, to announce to Wheelock's colleagues that the New Light minister was now engaged in the noble work—from the Anglo perspective—of helping fulfill God's "Great Design" of bringing the indigenous people to Christ. Still a third reason for introducing Occom to Wheelock's Yale acquaintances had to do with something less godly and more mundane—money. Wheelock would look to these same acquaintances to help finance Occom's education.

Wheelock sensed, and soon saw, that through teaching an indigenous student, new sources of funding opened up that could support both student, and indirectly, teacher. This is not meant to imply that Wheelock's primary motive for teaching Occom was pecuniary, though undoubtedly his view of economics was like that of the Pilgrim Father Edward Winslow, who exuberantly claimed that "In New England, religion and profit jump together." Wheelock was committed to Occom's education with or without outside financial support, but realizing other people might want to aid that goal, he sought to fully exploit that potential. Occom wrote that Wheelock "began to acquaint his Friends of my Being with Him, and of his Intentions in Educating me, and the Good people began to give some Assistance." Overall, between 1746 and 1748, Wheelock received over £350 in support for Occom. This was a figure significantly higher than an English student's tuition and boarding costs, though so was the real cost of supporting Occom. Whether or not the donations for Occom met or exceeded the expenses incurred on his behalf, the real importance of them is that they showed Wheelock that there would be widespread potential funding for an expanded indigenous education scheme.

Occom, who lost nearly a year to sickness during his matriculation, left Wheelock's Latin School after four years, having overstrained his eyes to such a degree that he could no longer pursue his studies. But long after he departed Lebanon Crank in November of 1747, Occom's and Wheelock's lives remained deeply enmeshed. For the next two decades Wheelock served as Occom's English advocate, counselor, champion, and also exploiter, as Occom became first a teacher among the Montauks, then a missionary to the Delaware and Iroquois, an ordained minister on Long Island, a missionary to the Oneida, and an overseas fundraiser for the Indian school Wheelock set out to create on the American frontier.

Occom became the inspiration, proof of concept, living brand, and most successful development officer for the Wheelock-conceived Grand Design that led to the founding of Dartmouth. Without Occom, Wheelock's project would not have succeeded, and might not have even been conceived. There would not have been a Moor's Indian Charity School in Lebanon Crank or a Dartmouth College in New Hampshire, and Eleazar Wheelock's legacy would have been as a long footnote in the story of the Great Awakening. Similarly, without Eleazar Wheelock, it is highly unlikely Occom would have become a Christian minister, or the author of the first best-selling publication by an American Indian, or a hymnist whose compositions are still sung today. Both men benefitted from, and ultimately came to feel great disappointment in, the other. But the disappointment came later. In 1747, theirs was a world brimming with positive potential.

From Wheelock's perspective, educating Samson Occom had proven to be an unqualified success. Occom, Wheelock reported, "has been useful beyond what could have been expected of an English Man and less than half of the Expense." And even as he worked to help Occom secure a position as a minister to an Indian community, Wheelock began to think of scaling up the educational approach so successfully used with Occom in an unprecedented way: through creating an Indian school to educate natives from many tribes in English ways and Christian doctrine, with the goal of preparing them to become missionaries to their own people. Such an approach would have, he reasoned, many advantages. An Indian who naturally understood the language of the people he served would be four times as effective as an English missionary who struggled with that language, plus an Indian could be maintained at half the price. They would automatically understand the customs of their tribe, too, something English missionaries often found difficult. They would have more influence with the natives than an English minister because Indians mistrusted the English, believing they only intended to steal their land. Furthermore, in a school with Indians from many tribes, the students could easily learn each other's languages and form networks of mutual assistance. As the millennial promise of the Great Awakening *revival* faded before his eyes, Wheelock's innovative concept for an Indian missionary school became a *new* millennial vision, the Grand Design that would shape the remainder of his life.

Wheelock may have envisioned locating his Indian missionary school on the Anglo-Indian frontier rather than in his Connecticut village from the start. In 1752 he joined a group of other prominent Connecticut petitioners in asking the legislature to grant them permission to establish four new towns in an area west of New York near the Delaware River. The land they sought was claimed by Pennsylvania, but the Connecticans asserted their colony had prior right of possession by virtue of their 1662 Royal Charter, which preceded Pennsylvania's charter by nineteen years. The stated goal of the Susquehannah Company, officially formed a year later in Wheelock's natal town of Windham, was "to spread Christianity as also to promote our own interest," a mission unusually well matched to Wheelock's own apparent ambitions. The Connecticut legislature, not anxious to enter into a land war with Pennsylvania over a far-from-clear-cut charter claim, stalled on the westward expansion question, but that did not inhibit the efforts of the petitioners to advance their scheme.

In 1754 Wheelock wrote John Brainard, an English missionary in New Jersey, telling him of his Indian mission school plan and asking Brainard to send two likely young Delaware boys to Connecticut to be his students. It is likely that Wheelock envisioned the boys playing a role similar to that of Samson Occom. Wheelock would educate them in Connecticut and then use them as the "proof of concept" for the Indian missionary school he would implement among the Delaware Tribes on the Susquehannah Land Company's western frontier. The outbreak of the French and Indian War that same year, however, coupled with the positive reception the new Indian school received in his hometown, deferred, but did not alter that plan.

Fourteen-year-old John Pumshire and eleven-year-old Jacob Wooley arrived at Lebanon Crank after a two-hundred-mile journey on foot on December 18, 1754, becoming Wheelock's first Indian school students. The reception of the two boys by the people of Lebanon Crank was—considering the recent outbreak of Anglo-Indian hostilities—surprisingly positive. A number of people donated clothes, fabric, shoes, food and cash to support the boys' education. And, as the boys started passing through the very difficult transition period of learning English lifeways—Pumshire became so ill he returned home, only to die shortly after—Wheelock used their presence to promote the expanded Indian school concept to potential backers. He sought to turn the French and Indian War—for which New England's colonies would provide a steady stream of men and pay a significant toll in lives—to the project's advantage. His would be a school not just to convert heathens into Christians, but also to transform potential frontier enemies into British allies. Joshua Moor, a prosperous farmer from nearby Mansfield, was one of the scheme's first major donors. He gave two acres of pastureland near the Lebanon Crank green, along with "a small House and Shop," to the school, with the promise of greater gifts to come. In anticipation and encouragement of those greater gifts, Wheelock named the new school Moor's Indian Charity School, after this promising benefactor. Other donors responded to Wheelock's steady stream of funding requests, as additional Indian students arrived, slowly at first, but in ever increasing numbers. There were four students in residence in 1757, five in 1759, and seven in 1760. That year, Wheelock expanded the school's enrollment to include English boys who felt themselves called to become Indian missionaries. In 1761, with eleven indigenous male students enrolled, Wheelock also began admitting native girls, who came to learn the English housewifery skills needed to support mission activities. By 1765, Moor's Indian Charity School enrollment reached as high as forty. Throughout its years in Lebanon Crank, as many as one hundred Mohegan, Pequot, Narragansett, Niantic, Montauk, Delaware, Mohawk, and Oneida and other native students attended the school. It was an impressive assemblage, and Wheelock viewed their presence in near-millennial terms. He told George Whitfield in 1759 that God had "opend . . . such a Door for the Grand Design that he was almost persuaded "the Time for calling in the poor Creatures into his Trinity and Kingdom is just at hand."

Despite its growth and apparent local support, the school's Lebanon location remained a matter of wartime exigency. In 1757, still plumping for the Susquehannah Land Company territory, Wheelock told a correspondent, "It would be much advantage of the school to remove it perhaps some hundred miles." A series of disastrous British military setbacks that year, including the well-known Massacre of Fort William Henry, made removal of the school little more than a pipedream, but Wheelock's preference for a frontier location for the school remained a constant, both during and after the Seven Years War, even as the school itself became a fixture in the local community.

What was the experience of being educated at Moors Indian Charity School like for the indigenous boys and girls who attended it? How did an English town sending sons to fight a war against Indians allied with a hated European rival react to the new school and the pervasive local indigenous presence it produced? How in turn did people's attitudes toward the minister's school affect the town's relations with its minister? The answers to these questions are crucial to fully understanding how Moor's Indian Charity School came to finally leave Lebanon Crank for Hanover and become Dartmouth College.

Wheelock's Latin School and Moors Indian Charity School both existed in Lebanon Crank at the same time, though it is unclear whether for practical purposes they were melded into one school, or operated independently of each other. The Latin Scholars lived in Wheelock's house, and the Charity School students lived in another house across the street, but Wheelock housed the Indian students in his own home when they were ill, so in some situations at least, housing overlapped. Most of the Latin Scholars were paying students and all of the Indian scholars were not, but the degree to which that created functional social or class divisions between the two groups is also unclear. There seems to have been frequent interaction among the two school's students, particularly seen in recreational activities, but again, there is no indication of what that suggests about the schools' organization and operations. All in all, there are more questions about the two schools' co-existence than answers, but it is significant that there were two distinct schools run simultaneously by Wheelock and not one.

Who taught the Indian school students? Wheelock hired "religious, faithful and learned" schoolmasters, usually recent college graduates, to handle regular instruction, while he served as head master and overseer of the school. Wheelock also increasingly acted as perpetual fundraiser as he planned the physical removal of the school from Connecticut. Masters usually served a couple of years before moving on, though Bezaleel Woodward, a local Yale graduate who served as a school master, remained with the school for many years, and then supervised the transfer of the school to New Hampshire, where he taught many more years at Dartmouth as Professor of Mathematics and the school's first librarian.

Indigenous boys received formal instruction in reading, writing, liberal arts and sciences and particularly religion, which included lessons in music and singing hymns. Girls, whose admission was predicated on their acquiring the English housewifery and clothes-making skills they would subsequently use as missionary wives or helpers, received classroom instruction in reading and writing in Wheelock's home, but only one day a week. The rest of the time they lived in the households of local women hired to teach them the basic arts of homemaking. For practical purposes, this meant they became unpaid indentured servants in English households, and because they were indigenous, it is likely they were saddled with the worst of their households' daily chores.

For the boys, the school day began early and continued into the evenings. Indian scholars were to be clean, dressed, and ready to be summoned by the blowing of a conch shell for morning prayers before sunrise in fall and winter, and at six in the morning in the summer. Morning devotions were followed by a short break. Then, another prayer preceded morning classes, which lasted from nine in the morning until noon. After a two-hour break, classes resumed until five in the evening. The boys gathered for evening prayer at sunset, and then did homework. On Sundays, they attended Wheelock's morning and afternoon church services at the adjacent congregational church, whose exterior was painted sky blue as a symbol of its New Light theological leanings. Between the church's two Sunday services, the school's Master evaluated their behavior, instructed them in the Westminster catechism, or led reading exercises.

At the beginning of their education, students were taught English reading, writing, and speech, and given a total immersion into English cultural norms. Later, Latin and Greek was introduced. The primary teaching method employed was memorization and recitation. Importance was also placed on good penmanship, learned by copying Latin phrase books. Samples of the boy's Latin handwriting were sometimes sent to donors, both to express appreciation for their support and to provide tangible evidence of the success of the school's educational efforts.

To supplement their academic training, the indigenous boys learned English husbandry skills by working on Wheelock's farm. This unpaid service was intended to help offset the cost of their upkeep. Many boys complained about being overworked as farm hands, and Wheelock more than once had to defend himself from charges that he was exploiting them. The father of the Narragansett Charles Daniel withdrew his son from the school because of what he saw as the imbalance between Christian education and agricultural training. "To work two years to learn to farm," he wrote Wheelock, "is what I don't consent to, when I can as well learn him that myself and have the profits of his labor." Some students at Moors school became apprentices to local tradesmen, to acquire useful skills such as carpentry, joinery, or blacksmithing.

To outside visitors among the English, the school was impressive. John Smith of Boston, who visited Lebanon Crank in May of 1764 to see for himself what others had reported, sent friends a glowing report. He arrived as the evening prayer service was beginning and was "movingly touched" to hear an Indian youth leading a hymn as he "set the Time and the others following him & singing the Tenor and Base with remarkable Gravity and Seriousness."

At five the next morning, Smith was even more impressed at the students' performance during devotions and the follow-on lessons. "It is really charming," he wrote, "to see Indian Youths of Different Tribes and Languages in pure English reading the word of God and speaking with exactness and accuracy on points (either chosen by themselves or given out to them) in the Several arts and sciences." Wheelock rode out with his visitor as he was leaving town and stopped at a farmhouse where one of the female indigenous students was living. Wheelock called to the farmer who then called the girl outside. Smith wrote that "it was exquisite to see the Savageness of an Indian molded into the Sweetness of a follower of the Lamb."

Molded seems a fairly accurate way of describing what happened to the students at Wheelock's school. But how exactly did that molding process work, and how did the students being molded feel about it? Here, the record tells a different, and not nearly as positive a story as Smith's account.

The transition from living in a Native American community to being educated under English government must have been painful, if not traumatic, for every child who went through it. Coming from the far less hierarchical and more permissive environments of indigenous cultures to the rigidly hierarchical and structured world of an eighteenth-century English colonial town would certainly have been wrenching, even to those with prior contact with English society.

Wheelock's Anglo-centric sense of cultural superiority blinded him to the deeply embedded racism of his attitudes and values. This made it impossible for him to see the difficulties incoming students faced during the transition as anything other than deficiencies to be eradicated.

"None know, nor . . . well conceive of, the difficulty of educating an Indian," Wheelock wrote George Whitfield. "They are used to set upon the ground, and it is as natural for them as a seat to our children. They are not wont to have any clothes but what they wear . . . . They are not used to any regular government, the sad consequences of which you may a little guess at. They have never been used to the furniture of an English house, and don't know but that a wine-glass is as strong as a hand-iron. . . . They are as unpolished and uncultivated within as well as without."

Wheelock insisted students be completely separated from their home communities and families—if he could manage it—throughout their education. He admitted that he believed if he kept the students isolated from their previous state of nature, he could impose strict government and discipline "as severe as shall be necessary, without opposition from, or Offence taken by any. And who does not know, that Evils so Obstinate as those we may reasonably expect to find common in children of Savages, will require that which is severe."

To be sure, the *English* boys in the Latin school *also* faced strict discipline and corporal punishment. The proverbial injunction to "spare the rod and spoil the child" was taken quite literally in this era. But Wheelock's candid comment suggests that a much harsher standard of discipline was applied to the assimilating Indian School boys than their Latin School counterparts.

How did the students react to this forced immersion into English culture? Many found it a traumatizing, even an impossible experience. Of the fifty-nine Native students for whom we have arrival and departure dates, nearly one in five (11) stayed at the school less than a year, half of them only a few months. Another one in six (10) went home between their first and second year. Sixteen of the withdrawing students were boys; five were girls.

Longer attendance at the school did not necessarily bring better adjustment to the English regime, either. Of those who stayed more than two years; three were expelled for disciplinary reasons, and others were corrected—often repeatedly—for behaviors that reflected conscious resistance to a strictly regulated English life, willful transgressions for which students were held strictly to account.

We do not know the specifics of the corporal punishment handed out to students, though we do know it was used. And, as in the church tribunals Wheelock employed with his congregation, punishment at the Indian School also included public confession, humiliation, and shaming.

Mirroring the church court practice, students were made to sign a public confession, written by Wheelock, the school master, or the student themselves, acknowledging the nature of the sins they had committed, for all transgressions of school policy were couched as breaches of God's law. Presumably, as in the church courts, this confession was read before the master and assembled students prior to the administration of whatever other punishment might take place. This public shaming was an intentional part of the reproof.

In one confession, the Delaware Jacob Wooley acknowledged "several gross breaches of the Law of God" in the summer of 1763. He had been guilty of drinking strong drink to excess; and of being "in a very sinful Passion of Anger" . . . "swinging my fists' stamping my feet . . . attempting to throw my Bed and Bed Clothes out the Chamber window while repeatedly "daring God Almighty to damn me." When Wheelock urged him to stop, Wooley had only "increased it with more violence."

Clearly, Wooley had a lot of pent-up anger. But in the confession, he "repented the way he had dishonored God, and hurt the school, and asked forgiveness of Mr. Wheelock, the master and of the Whole Family and School." Presumably his confession preceded some kind of corporal correction, which was followed by a probationary reintegration back into the school community.

Wooley's confession mirrors similar confessions among other male students, several of whom became repeat offenders. Like the male students, girls too exhibited behaviors that, from a distance, seem almost consciously targeted to resist school standards. The Narragansett Mary Secutor confessed to drunkenness and lewd conduct twice in three months during 1768. In her confession, written for her by Wheelock, she admitted that she got drunk after Sunday services, came into the school, and behaved herself in a "lude and very immodest manner among the school boys while profaning the name of God." In another, she confessed to going to the tavern, and tarrying there with much rude and vain company until "a very unseasonable time of the night while dancing and engaging in unseemly and wicked conduct, particularly drinking too much spiritous liquor."

The ease and frequency with which students gained access to liquor locally, and the welcome they received in Lebanon Crank's tavern, raise questions about how Wheelock and the Indian School were received in the local community. Clearly, though the initial reception had been positive, some locals were not hesitant to help undermine the school's intentions for the students, whether from economic self-interest, resentment at Wheelock, or an intentional effort to disprove the school's view of the Indians' potential. But other townspeople actively supported the school. Many Lebanon Crank residents, including the housewives paid to instruct the girls in housewifery, the tradesmen who took the boys on as apprentices, and a wide variety of people who provided goods and services to the school, gained economically from the students' presence there.

Passing comments outline these varied points of view. One writer noted—though only after Wheelock had moved the school to New Hampshire—that the presence of the boys playing games around the school had been a positive feature of village life. "It seems very melancholy to see the green so clear of such a number of sprightly youth as was wont to be there," they said. Others found the Indian boys' presence a way to exercise their racist prejudices. Wheelock once lamented to a school supporter the difficulty of finding suitable apprenticeships for the students who were to become blacksmiths. "The greatest difficulty" he said, "is that their fellow apprentices, English boys, will despise them and treat them as slaves." Such attitudes were by no means restricted to the young. David Crosby, a friend of Wheelock's, wrote of a conversation he had in a nearby town with two men critical of the school. They called Wheelock's attempts to Christianize the Indians "as altogether absurd and fruitless" and said that they could "never respect an Indian, Christian or no Christian so as to put him on a level with white people . . . to eat at the same table." In such an environment, it is easy to see how extraordinarily difficult it would be for Wheelock's students to successfully endure the cultural changes the school attempted to impose on them. The price of becoming Christian was to accept membership in a society where one would always be seen as inferior, and it is no wonder so many of the students ultimately recoiled at the Anglicization efforts, and why their work as missionaries or schoolteachers lasted only a short time before they rejected their English schooling and returned to an indigenous lifestyle. The complicated combination of encouragement to sin and exposure to overt racism the Indian students received in some quarters at the Crank, could not be fully offset by the support and encouragement they received in others. In fact, the mixed signals from the white community must have made adjustment to English culture even *more* complicated, confusing, and problematic. And, it may well have been a significant but unspoken factor in Wheelock's early-arrived-at but slowly realized decision to move his school farther from English settlements and closer to the indigenous frontier.

By 1761, Wheelock had concluded that in order for the mission school to be truly successful, the Indian youth had to be separated not only from their tribal homes but also from the corrupting influences they found in settled English communities. The tide of the French and Indian War had turned in favor of the British, and he now began to see a relocated mission school as a potentially major contributor to the post-war Christianization and pacification of formerly hostile native groups. With the help of British Superintendent of Indian Affairs Sir William Johnson, he recruited young Mohawk boys, among them Joseph Brant, to the Indian School in 1761, and he began sending Indian School graduates as missionaries and teachers to Iroquois country. Under Wheelock's direction, Samson Occom made three trips to the Oneida Tribe in two years. At the war's successful conclusion in 1763, Wheelock sent General Jeffrey Amherst, British Commander in Chief in North America "A Proposal for Introducing Religion, Learning, Agriculture, and Manufacture Among the Pagans of America," offering to relocate his school to an area in close proximity to frontier tribes in return for a very substantial land grant and British endorsement of the project. Amherst did not respond, but Wheelock, who was now pursuing relocation offers on several fronts, appeared to be fully committed to relocation.

Late in 1764, following repeated urging from George Whitfield and advice from another English minister that "An Indian minister in England might get a Bushel of Money for the School" Wheelock arranged for Samson Occom and Norwich pastor Nathaniel Whitaker to travel to England on a fundraising tour. Occom preached more than three hundred sermons in English and Scottish cities and towns and raised more than £12,000, a huge sum at the time, efforts for which he was barely compensated by Wheelock. This, along with what Occom came to believe was a misappropriation by Wheelock of the funds he had raised for the Indian college, later led to a permanent split between the two men.

While Occom and Whitaker raised money, Wheelock, acting much like a modern corporate executive, shopped his school relocation around to various government agencies to see which might come up with the best offer. By July 1765, in a letter seeking advice and possibly an offer from Sir William Johnson, Wheelock wrote of a large tract of land offered by New Hampshire Governor Wentworth, other large subscriptions for the Kennebec River in Maine, a £1,000 resettlement offer from the nearby Connecticut town of Hebron, and a £600 offer from Lebanon Crank if he would commit to stay. Additional offers came in from North Carolina, and late in the game, from Pennsylvania to settle in lands he had long favored. But by then it was too late. New Hampshire's Governor Wentworth had offered Wheellock a large grant of land in the coveted Cowass intervale along the Connecticut River, and perhaps most persuasive, a charter for his new college. New Hampshire was, at the time, New England's fastest growing region, witnessing the settlement of one hundred new towns between 1760 and 1774. Wheelock chose Hanover, then called Dresden, as the site of his college in 1769, and on December 13, 1769, Governor John Wentworth signed the Charter for Dartmouth College, and in August of 1770, Wheelock completed the relocation of his school and family from Lebanon Crank to the New Hampshire frontier.

Wheelock's increasing involvement in the 1760s with fundraising for and planning the relocation of his school came at a cost, though not a big one to him, perhaps—of disengagement with his church. In 1766, following the massive success of Occom's fundraising trip—Wheelock asked the Lebanon Crank congregation to release him from his ministerial duties. This triggered a four-year period of increasingly unpleasant confrontation between Wheelock and his congregation of more than thirty years. The church made one more half-hearted effort to compete with the capacious offers Wheelock had secured from other places, but it is unlikely they thought he would accept it, and he didn't. The congregation then, before releasing Wheelock from his pastoral obligations, attempted several times to find a new minister. These efforts were thwarted, at least once by Wheelock himself, who told a candidate the church sought to hire that the congregation had effectively cheated him out of his rightful salary. By the final days of his ministerial tenure, the confrontations had gotten personal. During his last year at Lebanon Crank, Wheelock told parishioner Hannah Dunham "your tongue if not your heart seem to be set on fire of hell."

In response, Dunham sent Wheelock a short poem that reached all the way back to the Great Awakening and forward to the creation of the Indian School to make a double jab at Wheelock's ministry. Calling Wheelock's church a Shepherd's Tent—a reference to the place where Wheelock's brother-in-law had stripped off his pants during the height of the Great Awakening enthusiasm, Dunham wrote

> I can't my father's house come near,
> My shepherd's tent pass by
> But hell and potash give a smoak
> And ingin arrors fly.

When Wheelock finally moved the school out of Lebanon Crank in 1770, only two of the school's Native American students, the Narragansetts Abraham and Daniel Symons, accompanied him. Several of the local families most engaged in the school when he was there also went with him. From the Lebanon Crank congregation, once the foundation of his support, there came now a chorus of recrimination. "Parish people continue in status quo," wrote Bezaleel Woodward just before he left to join Wheelock in Hanover. "Revilings don't yet cease."

Small matter, though. Eleazar Wheelock—congregational minister, celebrated New Light evangelist, and founder of Moors Indian Charity School—was now a chartered college president.

FURTHER READING

Douglas L. Winiarski's *Darkness Falls on the Land of Light: Experiencing Religious Awakenings in Eighteenth-Century New England* (Chapel Hill, 2019)

Dick Hofnagel and Virginia L. Close's, *Eleazar Wheelock and the Adventurous Founding of Dartmouth* (Hanover, 2002)

Colin G. Calloway's *The Indian History of an American Institution: Native Americans and Dartmouth* (Hanover, 2010)

Joanna Brooks's, *Collected Writings of Samson Occom, Mohegan* (Oxford, 2006).

THE HANGING OF MOSES PAUL

Throngs came to see Mohegan minister Samson Occom preach to the Wampanoag killer Moses Paul moments before his execution.

On September 2, 1772, thousands gathered in New Haven's First Congregational Church to watch a rare encounter between two Native Americans. One represented what many colonists believed most Indians in New England *had* become—dissolute, drunken, and prone to violence—while the other was what colonists hoped Indians *could* become—Christian, educated, much how the Anglo-Americans saw themselves.

The occasion was the hanging of thirty-two-year-old Wampanoag Moses Paul and the execution sermon the Mohegan Presbyterian minister Samson Occom was to deliver to the condemned man. Paul was to be hanged for murdering Moses Cook, a fifty-two-year-old white man. Paul had hit the man in the head with an iron bar while in a drunken rage at being thrown out of a tavern. His public execution would be the first in New Haven since 1749. The rarity of the event, plus the fact that Paul's execution sermon would be delivered by another Indian, drew the "very great Concourse of people," reported in the *Connecticut Journal*.

Execution sermons were a regular feature of colonial capital punishment, and, along with the executions themselves, they drew thousands of spectators. Virtually all of the 460 public executions in New England before 1800 were preceded by a sermon written for, to, and about the condemned person, delivered by a minister whose goal was to transform the spectacle into a moment of profound moral and spiritual significance. More than sixty execution sermons were published in New England before 1800; they formed America's first true crime literary genre. Samson Occom's sermon for Moses Paul, the first published writing by a Native American, became "the first Indian best seller." It ultimately appeared in nineteen editions, avidly consumed by readers eager to know what a "praying Indian" had to say to a dying one.

Paul had asked to have Occom preach his execution sermon because he believed he was being hanged for being an Indian. Paul admitted to killing Cook, but insisted on appeal that Cook had first taunted, threatened,

Mr. Occom's Addrefs

TO

HIS

INDIAN

BRETHREN.

On the Day that MOSES PAUL, an Indian, was executed at NEW-HAVEN, on the 2d of SEPTEMBER, 1772,
for the Murder of MOSES COOK.

I.

MY kindred Indians, pray attend and hear,
With great attention and with godly fear;
This day I warn you of that curfed fin,
That poor, defpifed Indians wallow in.

II.

'Tis drunkennefs, this is the fin you know,
Has been and is poor Indians overthrow;
'Twas drunkennefs that was the leading caufe,
That made poor Mofes break God's righteous Laws.

III.

When drunk he other evil courfes took,
Thus hurried on, he murdered Mofes Cook;
Poor Mofes Paul muft now be hang'd this day,
For wilful murder in a drunken fray.

IV.

A dreadful wo pronounc'd by God on high,
To all that in this fin do lie;
O devilifh beaftly luft, accurfed fin,
Has almoft ftript us all of every thing.

V.

We've nothing valuable or to our praife,
And well may other nations on us gaze;
We have no money, credit or a name,
But what this fin does turn to our great fhame.

VI.

Mean are our houfes, and we are kept low,
And almoft naked, fhivering we go;
Pinch'd for food and almoft ftarv'd we are,
And many times put up with ftinking fare.

VII.

Our little children hovering round us weep,
Moft ftarv'd to death we've nought for them to eat;
All this diftrefs is juftly on us come,
For the accurfed ufe we make of rum.

VIII.

A fhocking, dreadful fight we often fee,
Our children young and tender, drunkards be;
More fhocking yet and awful to behold,
Our women will get drunk both young and old.

IX.

Behold a drunkard in a drunken fit,
Incapable to go, ftand, fpeak, or fit;
Deform'd in foul and every other part,
Affecting fight! enough to melt one's heart.

X.

Sometimes he laughs, and then a hideous yell,
That almoft equals the poor damn'd in hell;
When drown'd in drink we know not what we do,
We are defpifed and fcorn'd and cheated too.

XI.

On level with the beafts and far below
Are we when with ftrong drink we reeling go;
Below the devils when in this fin we run,
A drunken devil I never heard of one.

XII.

My kindred Indians, I intreat you all,
In this vile fin never again to fall;
Fly to the blood of CHRIST, for that alone
Can for this fin and all your fins atone.

XIII.

Though Mofes Paul is here alive and well,
This night his foul muft be in heaven or hell;
O! do take warning by this awful fight,
And to a JESUS make a fpeedy flight!

XIV.

You have no leafe of your fhort time you know,
To hell this night you may be forc'd to go;
Oh! do embrace an offer'd CHRIST to-day,
And get a fealed pardon while you may.

XV.

Behold a loving JESUS, fee him cry,
With earneftnefs of foul, "Why will ye die"
My kindred Indians, come juft as you be,
Then Chrift and his falvation you fhall fee.

XVI.

If you go on and ftill reject Chrift's call,
'Twill be too late, his curfe will on you fall;
The Judge will doom you to that dreadful place,
In hell, where you fhall never fee his face.

1 Broadside. Mr. Occom's Address to his Indian Brethren On the Day that Moses Paul, an Indian, was executed at New-Haven, on the 2d of September, 1772, for the Murder of Moses Cook. COURTESY OF THE AMERICAN ANTIQUARIAN SOCIETY

Nathaniel Smibert, Portrait of Reverend Samson Occom, ca. 1751-1756, oil on canvas, 30⅛ in. x 24¹⁵⁄₁₆ in. (76.52 cm x 63.34 cm) BOWDOIN COLLEGE MUSEUM OF ART, BRUNSWICK, MAINE, BEQUEST OF THE HONORABLE JAMES BOWDOIN III

and then severely beaten him. Those circumstances, Paul argued, should have led to a charge of manslaughter for which the punishment should be branding, not hanging. Paul further insisted that a prejudiced jury had rushed to a faulty judgment, and that he deserved a new and more just trial. His appeals had been denied, but Occom's presence—as the then-most-celebrated native minister in America—would implicitly underscore the injustice of his conviction.

Occom, however, though he recognized and called out whites' pervasive anti-Indian prejudice, attributed Paul's fate to his sin of drunkenness. He told Paul, "Whatever partiality, injustice and error there may be among the judges of the earth . . . You have despised yourself . . . and now, poor Moses, Your sins have found you out." Occom's sermon warned all who listened of the wages of sin and explicitly cautioned Indians against alcohol, especially when foisted on them by whites eager to take advantage of

Adna Tenney, Samson Occom. Hood Museum of Art, Dartmouth. Gift of Governor Benjamin Franklin Prescott, Class of 1856, and others.

them. "You have been cheated over and over again, and you have lost your substance by drunkenness. O fools, when will ye be wise?" Occom's harsh message was tempered in the end by his insistence that, even at the moment of death, Paul's true repentance might lead to heavenly salvation. His earthly life might be ending, but a far better and eternal life with Christ, might be about to begin. And on that note, Paul was taken, with Occom at his side, to the gallows and hanged.

ROUGH JUSTICE FOR NATHAN HALE

No court-martial, no Bible, no last letters—why did revolutionary war hero Nathan Hale receive such rough justice?

Each of us has lived through some of them. Some of us have lived through many of them. They are events of such profound impact that they are seared into our memories the instant we hear about them. They change our world, and the very news of their occurrence changes us. Ever after we connect such events with the moment when, and the place where, we learned about them.

Where were you when John F. Kennedy was assassinated? Where were you when the *Challenger* exploded? Where were you when Bobby Kennedy died, when Martin Luther King was shot, when the Berlin Wall came down? Some moments hit harder because they hit so close to home. The primary school tragedy at Sandy Hook was one of those moments for Connecticans, and before that, that awful morning in New York that has permanently changed the way we think about the date September 11. Every year, for the rest of our lives, each of us will relive our experience of that 9/11 morning in 2001 when nearly three thousands of our fellow Americans died. It was a day filled with horror and with heroism. And I suspect that, on that date, you may give special thought to the 411 heroes—343 firefighters, 60 police officers, and 8 paramedics—who marched up those flights of stairs and died trying to save their fellow countrymen.

That's a crucible of heroism we should—no, we morally *must*—never forget. But this story is about another fire, and a different hero, whose heroism has a curious parallel to 9/11. I'm talking about twenty-one-year-old

1858 Depiction of Nathan Hale's Last Words. Note the clouds of smoke rising in the background. NEW YORK PUBLIC LIBRARY DIGITAL COLLECTION

Connectican and state hero Nathan Hale, who gave his life for his country almost two and a half centuries ago.

Academic historians have not generally been kind to heroes, because creating heroes and crafting histories are often at odds. Scholars practicing their learned specialties are generally more interested in approaching sources critically rather than reverentially, and having done that, let the chips fall where they may. The results have not always been pretty. Often, as historians have clarified historical recollections, they have called into question, or at least complicated, older heroic narratives. So it is with Nathan Hale.

Recent years have seen a substantial new outpouring of writing on Hale. One impetus behind this new work was the 2003 acquisition by the Library of Congress of a manuscript history of the American Revolution written by Consider Tiffany, a Connecticut storekeeper from Hartland. Tiffany's multi-chapter, pen-and-ink history of the war provides a previously unknown account of Hale's arrest as a spy in 1776 that corroborated some prior evidence and supplemented other sources, but overall, cast our state's hero in a whole new, and not very flattering, light.

Tiffany confirmed, for example, reports that the person who exposed Hale as a spy was the famed Robert Rogers, and not Hale's loyalist cousin Samuel, as some sources had suggested. Rogers was the founder of Roger's Rangers—the crack colonial militia unit whose unconventional bush-fighting tactics made them the elite fighting units of the French and Indian War and the recognized progenitor of today's Army Special Forces. One of the reasons Rogers, who himself was very much a hero to his contemporaries during the French and Indian War, is less well-known today is because during the American Revolution he sided with the British. When Nathan Hale, having volunteered to spy for George Washington, was traversing Long Island seeking intelligence in the late summer of 1776, Rogers was there recruiting men to join his unit of redcoat rangers. In Tiffany's account of Hale's capture, the astute Rogers, having sized up Hale as a possible patriot spy, began shadowing him. He dressed as a civilian, represented himself as a patriot sympathizer, and befriended Hale at a local tavern. Rogers conspicuously drank a "toast to Congress," and won the youthful Hale into his confidence by telling the young man that he, Rogers, was doing undercover surveillance for the Long Island patriots. This led Hale to disclose his own secret mission. According to Tiffany, at a second meeting, arranged by Rogers, Hale again was enticed to talk more freely about his intelligence-gathering activities. Rogers, having heard all he needed to hear, suddenly stood up, revealed his true identity, called forth a company of British troops he had arranged to have standing nearby, and arrested Hale as a spy.

At this point, Tiffany tells us, Hale acted like anything but a hero, "denying his name, and the business he came upon." And, he continued vehemently denying that he was Nathan Hale, or that he had anything to do with spying, all the way to the New York headquarters of British commander William Howe. There, Tiffany noted, "several persons recognized him and called him by name, upon which he was hanged as a spy."

Tiffany's account of Hale's panicky effort to save his skin certainly contrasts with the story given by William Hull, Hale's friend and a fellow American officer. Hull reported that upon being arrested, Hale immediately "declared his name, his rank in the American Army, and his object in coming within British lines." No panic, no denials. Hull's story also insisted that Hale continued to display the same kind of manly composure and fortitude right up to the gallows, where he supposedly said the famous last words, "I only regret, that I have but one life to lose for my country."

Now clearly, both of these stories can't be right, and in fact it is most likely that neither of these stories is completely right. Mary Beth Baker, who has written a considered analysis of both these primary Hale sources and their authors, points out that neither Consider Tiffany nor William Hull were eyewitnesses to Nathan Hale's arrest or his execution, and that their accounts are, at best, based on hearsay evidence. Moreover, she calls our attention to the fact that each of these authors had a strong personal agenda influencing their narratives.

Tiffany, who penned his account of Nathan Hale's capture more than a decade after Hale's hanging, had actually been under house arrest in Connecticut's northwest hills at the time of Hale's capture, having been accused, quite accurately, of being a loyalist. Tiffany's manuscript history of the American Revolution, in which the Hale story appears, was a diatribe *against* the American cause, and a prophetic lamentation, complete with supernatural portents predicting the impending collapse of the very dis-United States. It was that rarest of all things, a history written by the losers, and it reflected in tone and text the bitterness of the defeated.

Hull, whose stirring account of Hale's selfless valor is the bedrock document of Hale's reputation for heroism, was, unlike Tiffany, a patriot through and through. Perhaps Hale's closest friend in the military, Hull earned his own reputation for bravery in the Revolutionary War battles of White Plains, Trenton, Princeton, Stillwater, Saratoga, Fort Stanwix, Monmouth, and Stony Point, and he was honored by both Washington and Congress. In 1805 he became Governor of the Michigan territory and, at the outbreak of the War of 1812, he was made a brigadier General and commander of the Army of the Northwest. Although Hull's account of Hale's execution was, like Tiffany's, based on second-hand information, he had first heard of Hale's death the day after his execution, during a flag-of-truce conference with British Captain John Montresor, who had actually witnessed Hale's hanging. Because Hull got his information about Hale's death so near to the actual event, and from an eyewitness, one might assume that his account should be considered inherently more reliable than Tiffany's. But consider this. Hull's account of Hale's death was not mentioned by anyone until 1799, almost a quarter century after Hale's execution. Furthermore, it was not published until forty-nine years after that, as part of a posthumous biography of Hull "assembled" from manuscripts (which subsequently disappeared) by Hull's daughter and grandson. In shaping *their* biography, Hull's descendants had an agenda no less forceful than Consider Tiffany's, for they were trying to repair Hull's, by then, completely shattered reputation.

Hull had fallen into disgrace after he had surrendered Detroit to the British during the War of 1812 without so much as firing a shot. He reasoned that the Americans could not overcome the combined force of the British army and their Indian allies, and that to fight them would have led to havoc along the Michigan frontier. So Hull had chosen to take the personally dishonorable course of surrendering to the enemy without a fight in order to achieve what he believed would be the virtuous outcome of not wasting American lives. Unfortunately for Hull, his contemporaries, including the officers who served under him, did not see his behavior in that light. Hull was court-martialed for cowardice, convicted, and sentenced to be shot. Though he was given a reprieve by President James Madison, the disgrace of the surrender dogged him to his death in 1825. The biography assembled by his descendants was an all-out effort to redeem Hull's battered reputation, and the story of Nathan Hale was central to that effort. By drawing a close and personal parallel between Hale and Hull, the biographers suggested that Hull's surrender of Detroit without a fight (an act considered as dishonorable as spying had been before Hale's heroic death changed how people thought about it) could, like Hale's execution, be seen as intensely patriotic and self-sacrificing if viewed in the appropriate context. The axes being ground by the Hull family in their version of the Nathan Hale story were no less personal and no less sharp than the ones in the account rendered by Consider Tiffany. And it is naïve to read either Hull's or Tiffany's account of Hale's capture and execution without being fully mindful of the agendas that informed their production.

But that's part of what makes the Hale story so interesting and timeless. The evidence about Hale is fragmentary, contradictory, and full of gaps. And because of that, historians studying Nathan Hale have to make choices about whose evidence to believe, and how best to account for lapses in the record about which we know so very little with complete certainty. This has produced accounts of Hale the Hero, Hale the Incompetent, Hale the Naive, and even—this from an undergraduate student—Hale the Idiot.

Yet there is one thing upon which virtually all sources about Hale agree, and it is the thing about Hale that makes him truly admirable. At the same time, there is one usually overlooked factor about the Hale story that helps explain one of its ongoing mysteries: Why the young patriot was subjected by the British to such uncommonly harsh and summary justice. Surprisingly, that overlooked factor is the very thing that connects Hale to 9/11.

Whether Hale was exposed as a spy by Robert Rogers or by his cousin Samuel Hale; whether he immediately admitted his actions when he was arrested or tried to save his skin by lying; whether he said, "I only regret that I have but one life to lose for my country" or something longer and less memorable; whether he was a good spy or an incompetent spy; whether he was adequately prepared for his mission or sent as a sheep to the wolves, there is one thing about Nathan Hale that his contemporaries, both American and British, and the historians who followed them have all agreed upon: When the chips were down, and it was clear he would pay the ultimate price for his actions, Hale acted with great courage and composure. He died a good and an honorable death as an American patriot. And for that "grace under pressure"—the writer Ernest Hemingway's definition of courage—in the service of liberty, Hale is, at least in this writer's estimation, entitled to lasting honor as an American and a Connecticut hero.

This is especially true given the extraordinarily harsh circumstances surrounding his execution. Hale was not the first spy captured by the British or the Americans, but he was the first spy to be executed by either side in the War for Independence. Moreover, he was hanged within hours of his arrest, having been denied the benefit of trial by court-martial required under the English Articles of War. In his final hours, Hale was even denied access to a Bible, and his last letters, one to his commanding officer Thomas Knowlton and the other to his brother Enoch, were opened by the British and never delivered.

Observers trying to account for this rough justice in the case of Hale have often attributed it to battlefield pressures faced by British commanders and to the facts that Hale had (in at least one account) both openly confessed to being a spy and was found with incriminating evidence on his person. Both arguments are weak. The idea that British General Howe sentenced Hale to immediate death because he needed to get back to battle is without foundation. Hale was captured during a significant lull in the New York campaign. Firing had stopped almost a week before Hale's capture, after the September 16 Battle of Harlem Heights, and would not begin again in earnest until the end of October, with the Battle of White Plains. Nor should we assume that Hale's public confession abrogated the military requirement that spies be convicted by a formal court-martial. To discover what did in fact trigger the inhumane treatment of the condemned Hale, we must look elsewhere. George Dudley Seymour, perhaps the foremost Nathan Hale biographer, noted that "When Hale was brought to the Artillery Park for execution, he must have seen a drifting pall of smoke rising from the great fire then raging in the city." It is to that pall of smoke and the city's great fire that we must turn to for answers.

On the night of Friday, September 21, 1776, the same evening that Robert Rogers arrested Nathan Hale, a great reddish light appeared just after midnight on the streets of southern Manhattan. The fire that was the great light's source started at a tavern near White Hall. Brisk southerly breezes quickly spread its embers to nearby houses, whose wood frames were tinder-dry after a long, unusually rain-free summer. In minutes, the tavern fire became a conflagration.

The fire raged with inconceivable violence," a British officer later reported, "and in its destructive progress swept away all the buildings between Broad Street and the North [Hudson] River, as far as King's College, a few only excepted. Long before the main fire reached Trinity Church, that large, ancient and venerable edifice was in flames, which baffled every effort to suppress them. The steeple which was one hundred and forty feet high . . . resembled a vast pyramid of fire, exhibiting a most awful and grand spectacle. Several women and children perished in the fire. Their shrieks, joined to the roaring of the flames, the crash of falling houses and the widespread ruin which everywhere appeared formed a scene of horror great beyond description, which was still heightened by the darkness of the night.

As terrible as the fire was, it was not unexpected. The question of whether the American army, if forced to evacuate the city, would burn New York rather than turn it over to the British had been thick in the air as smoke for months. Such fears were not without substance. From the Americans' perspective, allowing the British to make their winter quarters in a major port town while they were forced to fend for themselves in the frozen countryside seemed pointless if not strategically foolish. Prior to the Continental army's evacuation, Washington's trusted advisor General Nathaniel Greene had urged firing the city as a strategic necessity.

"Two-thirds of the property . . . of New York . . . belongs to the Tories," he reminded Washington. "I would burn the city and suburbs . . . for the following reasons. If the enemy [takes] the city, we never can recover [it] without a superior naval force. . . . [We] will deprive the enemy of an opportunity of barracking their whole army together . . . [and] deprive them of a general market. All these advantages would result from destruction of the city, and not one benefit can arise to us from its preservation.

British commanders not only expected that a retreating American army might try to torch New York, they were also certain of which group of soldiers Washington would call on to light that torch. New Englanders, unlike their New York or Pennsylvania counterparts, were strongly in favor of the city's destruction. They had long viewed New York as a kind of commercial Sodom and Gomorrah and had nothing but contempt for the possibility of letting the city fall under British control. Nathan Hale's friend Gilbert Saltonstall had written to him ten months before the Great Fire saying, "I wish New York was either raz'd to the foundations, or strongly garrisoned by the American forces. I greatly fear the Virtue of the New Yorkers whose Religion is trade, and whose God is Gain."

On September 2, as the Americans were preparing their evacuation plans, a British officer had written home from Long Island, "I have just heard there has been a most dreadful fray in New York. The New Englanders insisted on setting the town on fire and retreating; this was opposed by the New Yorkers, who were joined by the Pennsylvanians, and a battle has been the consequence, in which many lost their lives." Another letter written two days later to a gentleman in London lent credence to the rumor. It reported that escapees from the city had informed the British generals that "Washington had ordered three battalions of New York provincials to leave New York, and that they should be replaced by an equal number of Connecticut troops, but the [New York troops] assured that the Connecticans would burn and destroy all the houses, peremptorily refused to give up their city."

Such reports, intriguing as they are, say more about the rumor machines that accompany armies in the field than about Washington's intentions for New York. Not that he hadn't considered burning the city. He certainly had. On September 2, the same day he was allegedly positioning troops to torch the city, Washington had written Congress asking guidance on whether the city should be destroyed. "If we should be obliged to abandon the town ought it to stand as winter quarters for the enemy?" he had asked. The alternative, he made clear, was the city's destruction. Congress, most likely reasoning that if Washington actually burned New York, the British would feel free to fight fire with fire in any American city, responded immediately and emphatically. "Congress would have special care taken," they instructed Washington, "that no damage be done to the said city by his troops, on their leaving it." And for Washington, who throughout his life embodied the concept of civilian control of the military, that was that. The city he evacuated two weeks later was left very much intact.

Fears of an American plot to torch the city, however, did not leave with him. New York loyalists and their liberating British military leaders continued to worry about Washington's intentions, and so, when the hell-on-Earth that would be called the Great Fire swept through the city the Friday night of Nathan Hale's capture, those who fought the fire and those who fled the fire automatically laid the blame on a patriot plot. That produced horrific consequences.

Newspaper accounts printed after the blaze had destroyed more than one thousand buildings—between 20 and 25 percent of New York's total building stock—describe in great detail the retribution pro-British mobs extracted from those they thought responsible for setting the flames. The *St. James Chronicle* of London, calling the fire an atrocious act, reported that one William Smith, an officer in a New England regiment, "was taken with a match in his hand and sacrificed on the spot to the fury of the soldiers" who were there fighting the fire. The *Gaines Mercury,* also of London, reported that "several persons were discovered with large bundles of matches, dipped in melted resin and brimstone, attempting to set fire to the houses. . . . One White, a carpenter, was observed to cut the leather buckets which were used to carry water to the fire. This provoked the spectators to such a degree, that they instantly hung him up." In the propaganda war to shape public opinion after the blaze, the reports published in English and Loyalist newspapers tried to establish conclusively that the Great Fire of New York was an act of arson ordered by the American command.

> *Thus the persons who called themselves our friends and protectors, were the perpetrators of this atrocious deed, which in guilt and villainy, is not inferior to the Gunpowder plot . . . Our distress was very great before, but this disaster has increased [it] ten-fold. Many hundreds of families have lost their all and are reduced from a state of affluence to*

the lowest ebb of want and wretchedness - destitute of shelter, food or clothing.

Although the debate over its cause has raged centuries longer than the fire itself, the majority of historians have concluded that New York's Great Fire of 1776 was started accidentally and was spread, not by arsonists, but by the strong south winds blowing across Manhattan that night. As to those supposed patriot arsonists whose names appeared in the Tory newspaper accounts of the fire, we are left only to speculate. Their names appear only in those accounts. But as to the burning question of whether Nathan Hale's real mission was to torch New York, as William Henry Shelton argued in 1915, the idea that Washington would send an arsonist to torch New York via the circuitous route through Connecticut and Long Island seems hardly credible. And certainly, if the British had had actual evidence that Hale was an arsonist, they would have trumpeted it loudly to the enraged and homeless loyalists of New York seeking revenge for their suffering, and in the trans-Atlantic newspaper battle for public opinion.

Yet, though Hale was not an arsonist, it is to that pall of smoke hanging over New York that one must turn in order to understand the rough justice he received from the British command. New York was still smoldering, and the rage of both the army and the populace over what they were convinced was an act of arson was still white hot. Hale, a New England officer, although captured on Long Island as a spy gathering intelligence, nevertheless matched precisely the image of the arsonist both the British generals and the loyalist citizenry had expected Washington to send to burn their town. Hale might not have been an arsonist, but in the search for a symbol of revenge for arson, he would serve just fine.

It is smoldering anger over Washington's presumed use of New England troops to burn New York, that explains Hale's being immediately sentenced to death without benefit of court-martial, the British command's refusal to give Hale the comfort of a Bible on that Sunday morning of his death, as well as the fact that they both opened and refused to deliver his last letters.

And, that smoldering anger over Washington's presumed use of New England troops to burn New York also explains one more thing. Four days after Hale's execution, a British officer wrote a letter from New York to a friend in England describing what had happened to Hale following his execution. "We hanged up a rebel spy the other day," the officer wrote, "and some soldiers got out of a rebel gentleman's garden, a painted soldier on a board, and hung it along with the Rebel: and wrote upon it, General Washington, and I saw it yesterday beyond headquarters by the roadside."

A hanging cardboard cutout soldier named General Washington and a "New England spy" named Nathan Hale hanging conspicuously side by side along a busy road provided a pure, and undoubtedly welcome, message of vengeance and revenge to New Yorkers furious at the burning of their city.

Whenever we try to visualize Nathan Hale, I suspect almost all of us imagine him young, handsome, and brave, standing defiantly on the gallows uttering his final patriotic words. If we are to fully understand the circumstances of his execution, however, we must also see the bloated, distorted body of that same young man hanging from a tree days later, and next to his grotesque form a hanged cutout of a soldier with the name Washington painted on it. War creates heroes, but it also turns people into hateful, unreasoning, vengeful creatures hell-bent on extracting revenge. And that brings us back to the fire with which this story began, and the days of fear that followed the 9/11 attack.

The cruel and inhuman treatment of Nathan Hale by the British, as a scapegoat for an enemy they thought they knew but could not see, is a reminder of how easy it is to brand a whole people as evil because of the acts of a few. It is also a call, even in times of terror, for us to judge others carefully, cautiously, and with reason.

FURTHER READING

Virginia DeJohn Anderson's *The Marty and the Traitor: Nathan Hale, Moses Dunbar and the American Revolution* (New York Oxford University Press, 2017) is the most recent book on Hale.

M. William Phelps's *Nathan Hale: The Life and Death of America's First Spy* (New York: Thomas Dunne Books, 2008) offers more information.

There are also several sources on Washington's various spy rings that include discussions of Hale, including Kenneth A. Daigler's "Nathan Hale and the British Occupation of New York City" in *Spies, Patriots, & Traitors* (Georgetown University Press, 2014), 93–110.

The most important set of sources on Hale's life was compiled by George Dudley Seymour. It is called *Documentary Life of Nathan Hale* (New Haven, 1941).

The entire issue of *Connecticut History* (now *Connecticut History Review*) vol. 45 no. 1 (Spring, 2006) was dedicated to Nathan Hale; it is very useful, especially Mary Beth Baker's, "Nathan Hale: Icon of Innocence."

On Hale and the New York fire, see William Henry Shelton's, "What Was the Mission of Nathan Hale?" *Journal of American History* 9 no. 2 (April–June, 1915): 269–89.

More recently written is Benjamin Carp's, "The Night the Yankees Burned Broadway: The New York Fire of 1776," *Early American Studies* 4.2 (Fall, 2006): 471–511.

For the narrative of Consider Tiffany, see James Hutson, "Nathan Hale Revisited," *Library of Congress Informational Bulletin* (July/August, 2003) https://www.loc.gov/loc/lcib/0307-8/hale.html.

THE MAP THAT WASN'T A MAP

There was a time when Connecticut stretched from Rhode Island to the Oregon coast.

Connecticut's most important map wasn't really a map. It was, instead, a royal charter. The Charter of 1662—arguably the most important document in all of Connecticut's history—contains among its other provisions a written description of the colony's boundaries that served the same function as a drawn map.

> *We, of Our abundant Grace . . . have given, granted, and confirmed . . . unto the said Governor and Company . . . all that Part of Our Dominions in New-England . . . bounded on the East by . . . Narraganset-Bay . . . on the North by the Line of the Massachusetts-Plantation; and on the South by the Sea; and in Longitude . . . From the said Narraganset-Bay on the East, to the South Sea on the West Part*

The South Sea is the Pacific Ocean, an entity well known to early navigators, but whose exact location in relation to Connecticut colony was unclear. What Charles II effectively granted Connecticut through that grandiose wording was a swath of land some 70 miles wide stretching from the Narragansett Bay on the east to the northern California/Oregon coast just west of Mount Shasta. If that landmass was still part of the Nutmeg State, the modern cities of Albany, Scranton, Erie, Cleveland, Detroit, Chicago, Des Moines, Omaha, Cheyenne, and Salt Lake City would all have Connecticut addresses.

Historians have long marveled at the generous provisions of Connecticut's 1662 charter. In addition to the transcontinental footprint, the king also granted Connecticut virtually complete governmental autonomy over a century before the Declaration of Independence. The charter's provisions in this regard were so complete that when other states scrambled to create new constitutions at the start of the American Revolution, Connecticut simply replaced the name of the king with "the people of

Connecticut Royal Charter of 1662. Framed in wood from original Charter Oak.

Connecticut" and continued using the charter as its constitution until 1818.

Charles II's generosity to Connecticut is made even more surprising by the fact that he had every reason to be furious with his New England subjects. Connecticut was a Puritan colony, and the Puritans had been instrumental in the execution of his father, Charles I. In fact, at the time the charter was issued, rumors (which subsequently proved true) were flying around London that several of the regicides who had signed the king's death warrant were being sheltered from prosecution in New England.

So why did the king give so much to a colony he had many reasons to punish rather than reward? In part, because of the persuasive powers of Connecticut's Governor John Winthrop, Jr. Winthrop, who in addition to serving as Connecticut's governor for nineteen years was also America's leading scientist, used his London scientific connections to gain access to the king's patronage network, and ultimately the monarch himself. Charles II appears to have warmed to Winthrop—with whom he shared a surprising physical resemblance—seeing him as an ideal person to help institute a royally conceived plan to combine all the colonies of New England into a single entity under crown rule. The generous charter provisions to Connecticut were part of an effort to win Winthrop over to this plan. When Winthrop, after receiving the charter, refused to comply with Charles's consolidation scheme, the king issued new competing charters that quickly reduced Connecticut's transcontinental holdings to a small area of land east of the Connecticut River.

Connecticut's officials, however, steadfastly maintained that the Charter of 1662 was the only valid Connecticut charter, a position that helped them lay claim to large areas of Ohio (the Connecticut Western Reserve and the Firelands) in the early days of the new United States. Connecticut's imprint still looms large in those parts of the Midwest, a direct result of the provisions found in the 1662 map that wasn't a map at all.

LEAVING CONNECTICUT, SHAPING AMERICA

In the face of a troubled economy and few job opportunities, thousands of young people left Connecticut to shape their futures elsewhere. The year was 1817.

For some years now, Connecticut has faced a serious out-migration crisis. In response to an array of seemingly intractable economic problems centered around jobs, income, and taxes, people of all ages have been voting with their feet to seek their futures elsewhere. Connecticut's population has been declining in real numbers since 2013, and in 2018 a national study by United Van Lines showed Connecticut had the third highest net rate of out-migration of all states. Perhaps the most disturbing aspect of this population loss is to be found in the number of young people who have grown up in Connecticut, only to move away as young adults.

As far back as 2009, the state's first-ever Economic Strategic Plan noted soberly that, "Since 2000, Connecticut has lost a higher percentage of its twenty-five- to thirty-four-year-old population than any other state in the nation." The plan left no doubt as to how serious a problem this loss is. "Connecticut is at a crossroads," it said. "The workforce is aging, as talented, young workers are leaving the state and population and job growth are stagnating." One of the state's first priorities moving forward, it said, needed to be creating an economic climate in which our children can not only afford to live in Connecticut, but will be able to prosper. To date, such efforts have not reversed the tide.

As sobering as such statistics are, we can perhaps draw some solace from the fact that this is not the first time in which Connecticut has faced a crisis over the loss of its people, especially young people, to other, more hopeful, places. Two centuries ago, in May 1817, Connecticut Governor Oliver Wolcott issued a remarkably similar note of concern in his gubernatorial report to the state's General Assembly. "An investigation of the causes which produce the numerous emigrations of our industrious and enterprising young men," he said, "is by far the most important subject which can engage our attention."

Connecticut in the early nineteenth century, as in the twenty-first century, was hemorrhaging its young people, the lifeblood of its future, to other, more economically attractive, locations. And it had been doing so for a long time. On January 1, 1801, the first day of the nineteenth century, the newly chartered Connecticut Academy of Arts and Sciences, in its first project as an organization, sent a circular letter to each of Connecticut's 107 towns, asking them to provide detailed answers to 113 questions. One of the items of interest to the academy was, "Emigrations from the town or society." In their responses, most towns left no doubt that outmigration had been a real problem of significant duration.

The towns of Haddam and Killingworth, for example, both reported that "Emigrations from this town have been very numerous." Coventry said, "There have been many emigrations from this town to the new countries, so that of late the number of inhabitants has not greatly increased." Farmington, with a population of 2,809 people in the 1800 census, reported that 147 families and forty or more young unmarried persons of both sexes had left the town, for a total loss of 775 people, almost a quarter of the town's population. Durham explained that, "The reason that there has been no more increase of population for many years is, that individuals and families have removed almost perpetually to other places." Lebanon suggested that but for out-migration, its population might be triple its current count. "Emigration for more than 30 years has been so constant, that it is judged that if all who left the town who are still living and their descendants and the descendants of those who are dead were to return, they would treble the number of inhabitants." Clearly, Governor Wolcott's 1817 message calling outmigration "the most important subject which can engage our attention" was addressing a real and serious problem. But where were all those people going? Where did the grass look that much greener?

Although they dispersed to sites both far and near, one area in particular proved the most powerful magnet for Connecticut expatriates. This was the part of Northeast Ohio stretching 120 miles west from the Pennsylvania border, and from the forty-first degree of latitude to forty-second degrees and two minutes, a place many people called "New Connecticut" but which was also known, and is today still called, Connecticut's Western Reserve. This was a part of its original charter territory that Connecticut reserved ownership of when it ceded the remainder of its charter lands to the newly formed United States in 1786.

Now anyone who visits the Western Reserve today cannot help but be struck by the way in which that region seems to be a mirror image of Connecticut in town layout, naming patterns, and architecture. From Claridon to Hudson, Stowe to Strongsville, the area roughly between Youngstown and Cleveland appears to be nothing less than Connecticut West.

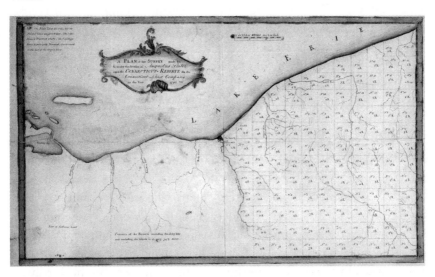

The importance of the grid system used to lay out the Western Reserve lands cannot be overstated. Augustus Porter upon the Connecticut-Reserve for the Connecticut Land Company in the Year 1796. WILLIAM L CLEMENTS LIBRARY UNIVERSITY OF MICHIGAN

Why, I wonder, did so many people decide to leave Connecticut in the late 1700s and early 1800s? What were the push factors driving them out, and the pull factors drawing them to the Western Reserve instead of other places? What was the experience of removal like? Who went? How did they travel? How long and how hard was their journey? And how did the people who stayed in Connecticut feel about the emigration of so many of their children?

Generally the motives driving so many people from the Nutmeg state to uproot themselves and their families and head west were the same two factors that have propelled much of human mobility in all times and places: the rhyming twins of need and greed. By 1750, much of Connecticut's arable land east of the Great River had been farmed out. Fields that had once been astonishingly productive were now only as good as fallow periods and limited manure could make them. In addition, everywhere one looked there was confirmation that New England's lifestyle had had remarkably beneficial effects on Old English bodies. Not only had the descendants of the Puritan first comers lived long and healthful lives, they had obeyed the Biblical injunction to be fruitful and multiply with relish. English emigrants who settled in Connecticut lived twice as long as those who went to Virginia. They lived a decade longer than those they left behind in England. Infant mortality rates were low, marriages early, and child-bearing years long. The result was a colonial population explosion that had left Connecticut fathers scrambling to find sufficient agricultural land to pass on to their many children.

Between 1730 and 1760, Connecticut's population more than tripled, from 38,000 in 1730 to 70,000 in 1749, increasing to over 130,000 by 1760. On the eve of the American Revolution in 1774, it was close to 200,000. Town populations began to outstrip the local agricultural capacity. The abundant 150 acres of land granted to the average first comer, was soon whittled down by inheritance divisions to just enough land to get by, and then not even that. In the 1730s, the voracious demand for more land was satisfied by the sale of three hundred thousand acres in the northwest Connecticut hills, but by 1750 the last of the colony's public lands were gone. Meanwhile, in the Land of Steady Habits, no habit was steadier than regularly producing children, so the need for additional farm land for rising generations became a Connecticut constant.

For a time, this need was partially met—or at least was intended to be met—by sale of the lands claimed by the newly formed Susquehannah Land Company along the fertile valleys of the Susquehanna River near present-day Wilkes Barre and Scranton, within the bounds of Connecticut's 1662 charter, a huge area the developers not-so-creatively called Westmoreland. The problem was, the land Connecticut claimed was also claimed by Pennsylvania. This led to a generation of inter-colonial conflict—often violent—that was ultimately decided in favor of the Keystone State.

Land-hungry Connecticans, especially those who had served in the expeditions against Canada during the French and Indian War and the American Revolution, were also attracted to the northern Connecticut River Valley. Up the valley these land hungry migrants came, bringing their families, possessions, and Connecticut town names with them. They settled in Windham, Windsor, Orange, and Essex Counties (among others) and created Guilford, Pomfret, Hartford, Wallingford, Brookfield, Norwich, Middlebury, Salisbury, Goshen, Bethel, and the list goes on. This desire to carry old Connecticut to new lands was so strong that twenty-five of the 211 Vermont town names appearing in America's first census, about one out of every eight towns, was named after a Connecticut town of origin. So many Connecticans moved north into this previously unsettled region in the years after the French and Indian War that when the inhabitants assembled to declare themselves "a free and independent jurisdiction, or state," on January 15, 1777, they declared that they were forever hereafter to be "called known and distinguished by the name of New Connecticut, alias Vermont."

For most migrants, Vermont soon proved to be too hilly, rocky, and cold, and in the years after the American Revolution, many looked to lands in Western New York state, promoted by speculators such as Oliver Phelps, who in 1787 contracted to buy over six million acres in Genessee County for resale to New England outmigrants from his land office in Suffield. These lands were indeed attractive, but the biggest plum in the west for land speculators, would-be settlers, and the people of Connecticut collectively, were the five thousand square miles of territory included in the Western Reserve.

"Adventuring in lands and procuring inhabitants to settle them," was in the late eighteenth century, as the Connecticut diplomat and profiteer Silas Deane noted, "the best branch of business in America." So it is not surprising that the agreement Connecticut made with the United States carving out the Western Reserve from the rest of the Northwest Territory prompted a decade-long debate over how the reserve land should be sold, who should sell it, and what should be done with the proceeds. For a long time, the debate proceeded in a desultory fashion, no doubt in part because at the time the Ohio country was the scene of many of the deadliest battles between Indians and whites in American history. Mad Anthony Wayne's decisive victory at The Battle of Fallen Timbers near present-day Toledo in 1794, followed by the 1795 Treaty of Greenville in which the indigenous tribes were forced to cede most of Ohio to the Americans, effectively cleared the Western Reserve for white settlement. Simultaneously, the Jay Treaty with England meant the British would also vacate their frontier forts in the northwest. Not surprisingly, once the land could be settled without undue concern about Indian conflicts, agreement on how to dispose of the Western Reserve lands was reached the same year.

The reserve land was sold in the fall of 1795 for $1,200,000 in notes to the Connecticut Land Company, a syndicate of venture capitalists whose names read like a Who's Who of Connecticut's venerable Standing Order. Names such as Edwards, Bull, Griswold, Root, Stoddard, Holbrook, Lyman, Morgan—families whose members had been part of the ruling oligarchy of Connecticut for generations—were interspersed with the names of the newly wealthy. The biggest investor was Oliver Phelps of Suffield. Phelps was already heavily invested in the Genessee country of New York when he signed on for $168,000 of the debt. The smallest investor, Sylvanus Griswold, put himself on the hook for a hundredth of that amount.

A fifty-person surveying team led by Moses Cleveland of Canterbury was sent out the following spring, and in 1796 and 1797, the Western Reserve was mapped, staked, and made ready for sale. The surveying method Cleveland's party used both copied and departed from that used by the surveyors of the United States Northwest Territory, from which the Western Reserve had originally been carved. The grid system employed in the Northwest Territory was used, but in modified form. It had divided up the landscape into uniform rectangular townships that were six miles square, subdivided into sections that were one square mile each. The Connecticut Land Company laid out townships that were only five miles square, also subdivided into sections of one square mile. The Connecticut land speculators, unlike the US government, did not specifically reserve one section of each township for support of public schools. The irony of this, of course, is that when the state of Connecticut originally sold the land, it dedicated all proceeds from the sale to support public education— but only for schools in Connecticut.

One cannot overestimate the importance of the uniform grid system used in the Northwest Territory and the Western Reserve in the history of westward expansion. Laying out distant and unknown lands into packages of the same size and shape turned an irregular and unknown landscape into a standardized commodity that could be bought and sold at standardized prices, located with specificity on a map, and easily exchanged for other parcels of land of the same size and shape by people who had never actually laid eyes on it. The Western Reserve surveyors began in the southeast corner of the reserve and numbered the townships south to north in sequence until they came to Lake Erie. Each vertical strip of townships was called a range. Ranges were numbered from east to west. Thus, a prospective purchaser sitting in Lyme or Bloomfield, Connecticut, could look at a map and see that the land he was being offered in Range Three, Section Thirteen was adjacent to both Lake Erie and the Ashtabula River, while the land in Range Twelve, Section Six was along the Cuyahoga River just south of the proposed town of Cleveland. The language of range and township became the *lingua franca* of westward expansion, and letters to and from the reserve are loaded with discussions of the qualities of various places to settle, all described in reference to the grid system.

To ensure that each investor got a proportionate share of the reserve's better and lesser quality lands, the Connecticut Land Company distributed the surveyed land through a cumbersome lottery system that resulted in all proprietors gaining landholdings scattered throughout the region.

An unintended consequence of this mode of distribution was that the subsequent sale of these randomly drawn parcels of land to settlers produced a settlement pattern in northern Ohio significantly different than the one through which Connecticut itself had been settled. Whereas the most common form of settlement in old Connecticut had been clustered settlement by congregations in new towns that later grew and spread out by hiving off daughter towns, settlement in the Western Reserve was, from the beginning, much more individualized and broadly dispersed. Land was usually purchased not by congregations, but by individuals who chose their location based on what they could find out about specific parcels being offered, and what they could afford. For many years, the cabin in the clearing—not the inviting village—was the most common sight in the region many settlers called New Connecticut.

In any event, at the same time as the Connecticut Reserve was being made ready for sale, a kind of westward fever had gripped the East. People were on the move, and their direction was toward the setting sun. In early March of 1795, the *Connecticut Journal* ran a story from Albany, New York, indicating that "upwards of 1200 sleighs, loaded with women, children, and furniture, coming from the east, have passed through this city within three days. . . . The current of emigration," it noted, "flows incessantly through this city." Two months later, the *Norwich Packet* ran a story from Whitestown, New York, that reported "Land speculators are everywhere to be found, and the number of honest husbandmen who are moving westward exceed all calculation." The story estimated that fifteen or twenty boats a day, filled with families moving westward, passed by Old Fort Schuyler, near Lake Oneida. "The west," it asserted confidently, "will shortly become as populous as the Connecticut hive."

What was it that drove so many people to leave Connecticut in the early national period? Certainly, the opportunity to trade a limited parcel of worn out Connecticut land for a much larger tract of fertile and virgin soil elsewhere was primary. One astute observer in 1717 noted the similarities between the western migrants and the semi-sedentary Indian groups who had once roamed the land.

Americans, he noted, partake, in no small degree, of the habits of their predecessors, the Aborigines, who, when they have exhausted one hunting-ground, pull up stakes, and incontinently march off to another, four or five hundred miles off, where game is plenty. So with honest Brother Jonathan. When he has eaten up everything around him, and worked his land to skin and bone, and when his house is just on the point of tumbling about his ears; instead of taking the trouble of restoring the one, or rebuilding the other, he abandons both; and packing up his movables, consisting of his wife and chubby boys in a wagon, whistles himself to the banks of the Ohio.

Desire for land is only part of the story. One who reads the many accounts of this epic diaspora carefully soon finds a host of other reasons pushing migrants out of Connecticut, even as land promoters' enthusiastic accounts drew them westward. These additional factors, which built in intensity throughout the early decades of the nineteenth century, help explain why the stream of emigrants to the Western Reserve became a literal torrent after 1815.

To begin with, in the early nineteenth century, Connecticut faced an environmental crisis on several fronts. Today, concerned with global warming, we have almost forgotten that early America was held in the grip of a period of intense cold known as the Little Ice Age. This severe cooling of the earth's temperature, which lasted roughly from 1450 to 1850, had internal cycles of warmer and colder weather, and the decade from 1810 to 1820 proved to be the coldest period ever recorded in North America. Growing seasons were shortened by several weeks, and Connecticans were required to heat their homes eight months out of twelve. To make matters worse, the biggest volcanic eruption ever recorded took place in 1815 on Mount Tambora in the Indonesian archipelago. The four hundred million tons of gas released by the volcano shrouded the earth in vapor, producing in 1816 what became known as "the year without a summer." In New England, snow fell during every month of that year. Crops failed and firewood, the victim of a major tree-felling hurricane that blasted through New England in 1815, was in critically short supply.

117

The climatic crisis created an economic crisis for marginal farmers, many of whom simply threw in the towel and joined the hopeful heading west.

Some people had political reasons for leaving New England. Although the country's founders had not envisioned the creation of political parties, hoping to establish a nation where every leader was a part-time, selfless public servant, the mere act of ratifying the US Constitution had produced two sharply divided political parties, the Federalists and the Jeffersonian Republicans. Nowhere were those divisions felt more strongly than in New England (and especially Connecticut), where a deeply entrenched, venerable Federalist elite—the Standing Order—was being challenged by a fast-growing coalition of Republicans and their allies, deeply resentful of the ways in which the Federalists had clung to the reins of power. A writer in the *Worcester Spy* noted that in addition to "the sterility of our soil, and the coldness of our climate," some people were emigrating because of the "overbearing oppression of the predominant party; a party who would "not employ, or buy of a Republican, if they could possibly obtain the same of a Federalist . . . . Has a Republican an equal chance with a Federalist in this region in commerce, at the bar, in physic, in divinity, or in any other profession whatever? We know they have not." Others echoed the criticism, pointing out that Connecticut's Federalist elites had even used the bankruptcy and imprisonment laws to enrich themselves at the expense of the state's less well-to-do Republicans. Calling the laws allowing for seizure of debtors' property "weapons in the hands of your party to assist them in perpetuating their own power and to . . . oppress political opponents," a Republican writer for the *Hartford Times* claimed that for many Republicans, "Emigration or imprisonment seems to be the only alternative. Federal[ist] policy has driven [Republicans] . . . to this dreadful situation; they must leave that party or leave this state."

Such criticism of Connecticut as a state whose government was so hostile to political opponents that it sent them into exile raises the interesting possibility that Ohio's Western Reserve, rather than being a place to which Connecticut's political culture was transplanted, became more like its antithesis, a stronghold of political exiles espousing anti-Federalist party principles. Telling, perhaps, is the fact that in every presidential election up until 1836, Ohio voters chose the Federalist's opponent.

Other motivations discussed as causes of out-migration from Connecticut include religious intolerance, as Connecticut forced its citizens to support the established Congregational church until 1818, and inequitable taxation. Connecticut laws taxed farm families as much as 70 percent more than those who worked in manufacturing or other employments, so for hard-pressed farmers the state's tax burden was another factor driving removal.

To summarize: A shortage of land, a multi-stranded environmental crisis, political repression that spilled over into economic and social life, religious intolerance, and inequitable taxation were all factors behind the thousands of individual decisions made by Connecticans in the early 1800s to pick up stakes and head west.

But who went? And how, having made the decision to go to the Western Reserve, did they get there? Existing sources provide two images of Connecticut's outmigrants, one that's a bit too close-up, and another that's a bit too distant. The too-close image comes from the numerous diaries, journals, and travel narratives recorded by various individuals who made the trek west and lived to write about it. These indispensable accounts by people such as the surveyor Seth Pease; missionaries Joseph Badger and Thomas Robbins; the physician Zerah Hawley; the English traveler who published as D. Griffith; and the young woman in search of a husband Margaret Van Horn Dwight give us indispensable detail about the journeys to and conditions in the early Western Reserve. But as good as these accounts are, they are also idiosyncratic records of a single person's observations, one sojourner's interpretation of their own unique experience. The too-far image of the migration, on the other hand, is the collective view of the effects of migration as revealed by the historical census data records. Their focus is hazy, a snapshot taken at ten-year intervals, but they give us a sense of some characteristics common to the migrants as a group.

The census data tells us that the population of New Connecticut was different in significant and important ways from old Connecticut. Not surprisingly, given the effort it took to literally begin the world anew in the wilderness, people there were much younger than the folks back home. Old Connecticut was then, as today, a graying population. More than one

119

of every six people in Connecticut was forty-five years old or older at a time when only one out of three people could expect to reach their sixtieth birthday. On the Western Reserve, the number of adults over forty-five was fewer than one in ten. Also, unlike old Connecticut, where women slightly outnumbered men throughout the period of westward migration, the Western Reserve population was skewed toward males by a ratio of 54 percent to 46 percent. Underscoring the gender disparity, travel writer John Melish urged emigrating New Englanders "to take a greater portion of the blooming Yankee girls along with them, and not suffer nearly seventeen thousands of them to pine away as old maids in their own country, when it is seen they are so much wanted in this."

Another important but predictable finding from the census data is that while Connecticut's population was relatively stable, the population of the Western Reserve was booming. Ohio experienced a 236 percent population increase between 1810 and 1820. It would be nice of course to be able to chart that growth year by year, but such data is simply unavailable.

If the census data gives us an insight into how Connecticut's Western Reserve was taking shape demographically, the journals and diaries left by travelers and emigrants give us a view of what the experience of removal and resettlement was like. While each account is a personal one, some observations seem appropriate to all of them.

To begin with, the journey west was both long and hard, between five hundred and six hundred and fifty miles, depending on the route selected and destination. Road conditions ranged from very bad to deplorable for most of the journey. In heavy rains, roads became mud pits and streams impassable. In some low-lying or wetland areas, efforts were made to ameliorate the muddy conditions by building "corduroy roads" of logs placed perpendicular to the direction of travel, which provided their own unique kind of jarring discomfort. The generally awful state of the heavily traveled routes may help explain why many people preferred to pull their goods westward on sleds during the winter snowpack, a fact that also underscores the different climatic conditions of the Little Ice Age.

The would-be emigrant had choice of two possible routes to the Western Reserve. A northern route went up the Mohawk Valley and crossed New York to Buffalo. There a choice had to be made between taking a boat along Lake Erie's southern shore and risking the Lake's unpredictable conditions or staying land-bound and following the rugged trail along Lake Erie's shoreline. The second, southern route to the Western Reserve crossed Pennsylvania along the old Forbes Road cut during the French and Indian War, crossed the mountains into Pittsburgh, and then followed a number of different trails into the reserve at Youngstown. Neither route was a cakewalk, and neither offered significant advantages over the other in terms of time or distance. Which route an emigrant family chose came down largely to personal preference.

Although there was significant variation in the duration of the journeys westward, travelers averaged twelve to fifteen miles a day depending on the terrain and weather. Six weeks was the average duration, though as transportation improvements such as canals and better roads came into play in the late 1820s and 1830s, travel time decreased. A determined Zerah Hawley made the journey to Ohio from Connecticut in only twenty-three days in 1820. Reverend Joseph Badger, who did a lot of preaching along the way west, took over four months.

No matter how long the journey took, it was an experience no traveler would ever forget. In addition to the considerable physical dangers of traveling bad roads, fording swelled streams and rivers, and climbing and descending high mountain passes, migrants commonly experienced inhospitable treatment at over-crowded and often squalid inns and taverns. They slept fitfully among strangers; ate bad food with rowdy, drunken, and sometimes dangerous fellow migrants; and fought off both homesickness and fear of the unknown. Henry Leavitt Ellsworth sought to procure for himself some "instruments of death"—that is, handguns—prior to leaving Connecticut, to protect himself from the rare, but not unknown incidence of highway robbery.

For many Connecticut émigrés who had lived their entire lives among the remarkably homogenous and un-diverse population of the Nutmeg State, the journey west brought their first exposure to groups of people who spoke a different language, embraced a different culture, and held different values than they. Many found such contact disconcerting, some found it offensive and frightening. Consider, for example, the prim and proper Margaret Van Horn Dwight's description of the Germans she encountered violating Connecticut's time-honored blue law conventions for Sunday deportment at an inn in Hanover, Pennsylvania, in 1810:

> *I should not have thought it possible to pass a Sabbath in our country among such a dissolute vicious set of wretches as we are now among— I believe at least 50 dutchmen [Germans] have been here today to smoke, drink, swear, pitch cents, almost dance, laugh and talk dutch and stare at us. They come in, in droves, young and old—black and white—women and children. It is dreadful to see so many people that you cannot speak to or understand.*

Though the road west brought migrants significant exposure to people, cultures, and conditions previously unknown, it is also clear that these Connecticut ex-patriots were never far removed from some connection to the state they had left. All along the way, in town after little town (many of which are now all but forgotten), migrants reported running into people they had known in Connecticut who now resided in this or that way station along the route west. The roads to the Western Reserve, particularly the northern routes, were studded with Connecticans who had chosen to seek their fortunes in the west, just not as far west as the Ohio country. Perhaps they were people who had started out for the Western Reserve and found other possibilities along the way, or maybe they found the road west a road too far, or simply realized there were better opportunities closer to their original home. For now, all we can say is that the tens of thousands of Connecticut natives who started out for New Connecticut in the early 1800s found thousands of fellow former Connecticans along the way, with whom they shared a surprisingly precious bond of common origins.

How did all these migrants feel about pulling up roots and leaving their natal state? Some undoubtedly felt a pioneer's excitement at facing a world that was all possibility. Others, perhaps the younger sons not in line to inherit the family farm, seethed with resentment about being forced into exile. Some, it is clear, saw having to leave Connecticut for the west as a sign of shame, a visible symbol that they were the expendable ones.

How else can we explain Margaret Van Horn Dwight's comment on day two of her journey?

The country we pass thro till we are beyond New York, I need not describe to you, nor indeed could I, for I am attended by a very unpleasant tho not uncommon companion—one to whom I have bow'd in subjection ever since I left you—Pride. It has entirely prevented me seeing the country lest I should be known . . . and so I suppose it will attend me to the mountains, then I am sure it will bid me adieu.

Hiding in the wagon so she would not be recognized. This is an aspect of out-migration that we rarely encounter, or even think about. Once we do, though, it complicates long-standing views of Anglos hot in the pursuit of manifest destiny. Surely, Connecticans left their state with mixed emotions.

But how did those who stayed behind view their leaving? In most cases, Connecticans, at least those not involved in promoting the sale of the western lands, viewed the state's out-migration crisis with grave concern. One observer lamented that Connecticut's population had long been "kept down," and attributed it to the fact that "migration from Connecticut must have ratably exceeded the migration from any of the other states." The effect of the "fifty thousand New Englanders who have, for a number of years, passed annually over the Alleghenies" led another writer to bemoan the increasing decline of New England's political clout in favor of the new states. Other Connecticans saw the out-migration as producing not just a youth drain, but a serious capital outflow as well. "The property that is carried out by this constant stream of migration," wrote one, "cannot be much, if any, less than a million dollars yearly; which waste is not repaired."

Worse than the loss of capital for some observers was the outmigrants' potential loss of human civility. These critics harkened back to the old Puritan fears of creolean degeneracy, the not unlikely possibility that settlers living in a wilderness environment would lose their civilized qualities and return to a savage state of nature. "The transition from civilization to savageness is much easier than from the latter to the former," cautioned a *Hartford Courant* commentator. He warned of a population of "millions of our own color, flesh, and blood," who, having migrated westward, now lived "without schools, without a ministry, without religious institutes, without the Sabbath, without bibles, sunk and still sinking into the depths of moral debasement."

Another writer, who styled himself only "A Connecticut farmer," urged those thinking of leaving to reconsider before it was too late. "Few—very few I believe—of those who have sold the inheritance of their fathers to improve their fortunes in the western wilds, have fully "counted the cost" of their undertaking. For myself," he said, "I love my native state—I reverence her laws—her religion—her morals—and her habits and would not exchange them for the mines of Peru."

I love my state, too. And like the man who called himself "A Connecticut Farmer" in 1818, I lament the loss of our state's young people today, just as he lamented those thousands on the road in the early 1800s. History, however, gives us hope. For just as those thousands were pulling up stakes and heading west in the nineteenth century, a group of those who stayed behind—people with names such as Whitney, Colt, Collins, Cheney, and Root—were finding innovative ways to harness Connecticut's abundant water resources to drive new machines of their own invention, machines that would within a single generation transform Connecticut into one of the world's great industrial powerhouses. No one expected that to happen in 1820, but it did. What surprises might Connecticut have in store for us this century?

FURTHER READING

Studies of out-migration to the Western Reserve from Connecticut are few, and many tend to be dated. Particularly useful are Richard Buel, Jr.'s *The Peopling of New Connecticut: From the Land of Steady Habits to the Western Reserve* (Hartford, The Acorn Club, 2011); Chaim M. Rosenberg's, *Yankee Colonies Across America: Cities Upon the Hills* (Lanham, Md: Lexington Books, 2015); Robert A. Wheeler's, "The Literature of the Western Reserve," *Ohio History Journal* vol. 100 (Summer-Autumn 1991), pp. 101–28, http://resources.ohiohistory.org/ohj/browse/displaypages.php ?display[]=0100&display[]=101&display[]=128; Harlan Hatcher's, *The*

Western Reserve: The Story of New Connecticut in Ohio (1991); Alfred Matthews, Ohio and Her Western Reserve, with a Story of Three States Leading to the Latter, from Connecticut, by Way of Wyoming, Its Indian Wars and Massacre (Heritage Books, 2013).

The travel narrative of Margaret Van Horn Dwight, *A Journey to Ohio in 1810*, edited by Max Farrand (New Haven, 1912), is available in several reprinted versions.

FROM AFAR . . . THEY STILL LOVED CONNECTICUT

In 1858 in Galesburg, Illinois, William Ransom got homesick for Connecticut, so he decided to throw a party.

In the fall of 1858, William Ransom was really homesick. Like tens of thousands of his contemporary Connecticans who had faced such issues as tapped-out farmland, economic downturns, high taxation, climate change, and political repression, he had left Connecticut years before in search of a better life. He'd made his way to the start-up town of Galesburg in southern Illinois, becoming so successful there that people called him Squire Ransom. But that fall, instead of reveling in his Midwestern achievements, Ransom found himself longing for the place that had given him birth, the homeland that had shaped his most fundamental values. He missed Connecticut, and he wondered if there were others in Illinois who felt the same.

A man of action, Ransom decided to find out. He and a group of friends formed a committee to invite "all persons of Connecticut birth, and all heads of families of which either the husband or wife may be of Connecticut origin" to come to a "Connecticut Festival." The event would begin with a "Social Interview" at three o'clock, followed by a "Pic Nic Supper" at six, a pot-luck dinner whose offerings were to be brought by the participants. In keeping with the theme, but perhaps otherwise not such a good choice, Ransom scheduled the Connecticut party for the mid-winter date of January 7, the birthday of Connecticut Revolutionary War hero Israel Putnam. (Putnam was the leader who supposedly said, "Don't fire till you see the whites of their eyes!" at the battle of Bunker Hill.) People coming to the event were asked to bring Connecticut memorabilia with them—"paintings, relics, or other articles calculated to revive associations connected with the parent State." Hopeful that his idea would strike a chord with other expats from the Land of Steady Habits, Ransom rented a hall and even put together an ad hoc band of all Connecticut-born musicians just for the event. But as January came nearer and the Illinois winter grew sharper, an unspoken question loomed large—would anybody really come?

January 7, 1859, dawned inauspiciously. The day proved to be "one of the coldest and severest of the season." Only the hardiest dared venture out. But venture out they did. To nearly everyone's astonishment, more than three hundred former Connecticans showed up in Galesburg that snowbound day, ranging from "the old, sedate and wrinkled" to the "young, beautiful, and accomplished." Their potluck contributions created a massive New England feast that included, among a cornucopia of other dishes, oysters, baked beans, turkey, pumpkin and apple pies, fried cakes, and cranberry sauce. One cake, nearly two and a half feet high, was emblazoned with the words "Nutmeg State," and around its base were wooden nutmegs and wooden cucumber seeds (humorous nods to the Connecticut peddler's legendary reputation for engaging in good-natured trickery) "sufficient to deceive a practiced eye."

Toasts were given in profusion, among them one to "Connecticut, our common mother, home of our brightest hours;" one to "The Charter Oak, may it ever live in the memory of all;" one to "The Connecticut River—the Mississippi of New England;" one to "the Daughters of Connecticut," the "Sons of Connecticut," and "their Yankee genius." Even the town of Vernon was toasted by a man named Sage, who praised his original hometown for furnishing the "Sages of the West."

Each of the toasts was followed by a short disquisition by the person making the toast, elaborating on its significance and meaning. After everyone was sufficiently toasted, there followed a musical interlude during which the all-Connecticut band played songs with Connecticut themes such as "The Connecticut Peddler," and a hymn still heard in many Congregational churches called "Old 100" ("Praise God from Whom all blessings flow. . .).

Before the party ended and the hardy ex-Connecticans set out to brave the Illinois winter darkness sometime after midnight, participants all agreed they had enjoyed a "feast of reason and a flow of the soul," and they had formed a new organization called the Sons and Daughters of Connecticut, whose mission was to repeat the Connecticut Festival the following year. And, a year later, on January 7, 1860, they indeed met again. Despite a severe ice storm that made it impossible for many would-be attendees to get there, another three hundred people made it to the event and held an even more elaborate celebration of Connecticut ties that remained unbroken across space and through time.

The next January, however, they may or may not have held the third Connecticut Festival, for it was 1861, and there is no record extant. Abraham Lincoln—from the state of Illinois—was the new President of the United States, and South Carolina had already seceded from the Union. The sons and daughters of Connecticut, in Illinois and elsewhere, were about to become Americans at war.

One thing, however, is clear. Then and now, though many people left this state through necessity, or for opportunity, they took, and they take, their love for Connecticut with them.

ROOTED IN PLACE:
THE STORY OF LYMAN ORCHARDS

Connecticut history is family history, and few families tell that story better than the generations behind one of the state's most beloved family farms.

Every year, thousands upon thousands of Connecticut families make their way to Lyman Orchards in Middlefield. Once there, they engage in myriad family activities: picking the freshest of more than one hundred different varieties of fruits and berries, finding their way into or out of a corn or sunflower maze, shopping or dining at the farm's Apple Barrel store and restaurant, golfing on one of the farm's three championship courses, and even forming new families at the Lyman Homestead, the nineteenth-century National Register of Historic Places manse that is now a popular wedding venue. For many of those who visit, the annual trip (or trips) to Lyman Orchards is something of a family tradition. That is most fitting, because if this family-farming operation, stewarded continuously by the last ten generations of the Lyman family, speaks to anything, it is to both the importance of family and the very special ways in which families such as the Lymans have shaped Connecticut's history.

The history of Lyman Orchards is at its core that of a single extended family and those who have worked along, beside, and for them for nearly three centuries; people who, in the course of living out lives whose epicenter was a farm in Middlefield, witnessed, shaped, and literally made history. In their family's story we can see vividly the arc of Connecticut's history and America's history, from before we were even America right up to the present.

William Lyman and his son David publicly called for abolition of slavery in 1851, a time when Connecticut was deeply racist. COURTESY LYMAN ORCHARDS

The Lyman story begins, for purposes of this tale, in the year 1741, when a young man named John Lyman and his wife Hope decided to buck a historical trend. A farming son of a farmer's son, young John was one of the thousands of Connecticans trying to cope with one of history's unintended consequences. For over a century, ever since the early 1630s, the Puritan farmers of Connecticut had been working the land, bending human toil and animal power to the task of raising their families' livelihoods from ever less, and ever-less-fertile soil. The average Connecticut family had eight children, John and Hope would have nine, and all of those children, once grown, needed land of their own to raise families of their own. Over time, the pace of population growth meant that each new generation had to try to raise more food on ever smaller farms whose lands were increasingly tapped out by overproduction. Colony leaders tried to address this problem by releasing the colony's remaining land holdings to the public, and in the early 1730s the colony's last large tract of undeeded land, located in the stony northwest hills of Litchfield County, was offered for sale. John Lyman's father was one of thousands of Connecticans who jumped at the opportunity to acquire new fertile land, and he and his oldest son moved his family to Torrington. But young John and Hope did not join them. His beloved new wife was from the area near what would become Middlefield, and so there they placed *their* new family's hopes, acquiring thirty-seven acres, and then another twenty-five acres in 1741. For the rest of their lives, John, Hope and their children followed the New England way of subsistence farming, meeting as many of their needs as possible from the fruits of their own soil, and using any surpluses to purchase more land for the next generation. By 1761, two years before John Lyman died of lung disease at age forty-seven, he and Hope had acquired 187 acres. This was nearly three times what they had started out with, but still, it was barely enough to meet their family's needs.

Following his death, while one son, David, worked to build up the farm, two of their other sons fought for America's independence. One of them, Phineas Lyman, died of wounds suffered in the battles for New York and Long Island. The other, Elihu Lyman, survived the Revolution, only to die twenty years later fighting the Indian wars in the Ohio Country. For his part, David, the second-generation patriarch, followed a lifetime of farming and community leadership, and by the time his mother died in 1797, he had grown the Lyman farm to over five hundred acres.

Five hundred acres is a lot land, but in the early 1800s in the new state of Connecticut in the new United States of America, it still was not enough land to assure the future of all the Lyman family. Connecticut land was still over farmed, its fertility waning, and there was no more surplus land to sell. This had produced a massive out-migration of young Connecticans, first to Vermont, then New York, and later the Ohio country. David Lyman's son and namesake had joined that migration, buying land in Vermont, but his father was absolutely determined to root the family's future in Middlefield, and to entrust the farm's fate to his non-emigrating son William. So he took what, even for a successful man like him, was a major gamble. He literally bet the Lyman farm on an agricultural innovation closely tied to a major change just beginning to transform both Connecticut and America: the rise of the American textile industry, as evidenced by the new factory villages appearing along New England's fast-running streams and rivers. The agricultural innovation David Lyman gambled on came in the form of a small flock of Merino sheep—each ram worth a thousand dollars—recently imported to America from Spain by David Humphreys of Derby, who had been George Washington's hand-picked ambassador to Spain. Merino sheep produced finer wool than any other sheep in the world, and that wool, David Lyman reasoned, would be just the thing to fuel the growth of this fledgling industrial transformation. Lyman's gamble was a striking example of one of the guiding principles John Lyman III—Executive Vice President of today's farming operations—still uses to direct the course of Lyman Orchards. "The ability to keep a family business going into the next generation is contingent on economic viability," Lyman notes. "Adaptation to changing market conditions is essential."

David Lyman saw that agriculture in Connecticut was changing—had to change—and he took a gamble on leading that change. And it worked. At least for a while. We now know that the arrival of Merino sheep in America was the stimulus that launched an industry that became New England's largest in the nineteenth century and fueled the machine-tool revolution that made Connecticut America's industrial powerhouse.

David Lyman was in on that transformation at the beginning. By the time he made his will in 1811, he was the wealthiest man in Middlefield, with large land holdings in Connecticut, and investment lands in Vermont, New York, and Pennsylvania. The success of the Merino sheep investment spurred other speculations too, a great number of them—in fact, too many, none as good as the first. By the time of his death in 1815, David Lyman's estate was insolvent, and it was left to his eldest son William and youngest son Elihu to sort out the issues and save the farm.

They accomplished this, though it took several years. With the help of supportive neighbors, the brothers were able to maintain the Lyman farm in Middlefield and slowly unravel the tangle of affairs in Vermont and New York. In the process, Elihu died a young man after a short illness, and William became a firm temperance advocate, turning away from alcohol himself and denying even the traditional hard cider to his farm laborers. He became a man of strong religious faith, too. In the early 1830s, far, far ahead of most of his contemporaries, William and his son David were among the first Americans to recognize the injustice of slavery and join the call for its abolition.

Today, Lyman Orchards has a coveted spot of remembrance on Connecticut's Freedom Trail, the state-designated trail that documents sites embodying the struggle of African-Americans to achieve freedom and equality in the state once called by William Lloyd Garrison "the Georgia of the North." Much as we would like to believe otherwise, Connecticut was a fundamentally racist state before, during, and even after the Civil War. Twice at the end of the Civil War, Connecticans overwhelmingly voted down amendments to the state Constitution that would let African-Americans vote. For William and David Lyman to embrace the abolition of slavery as a matter of morality and conscience in the 1830s was not only extraordinary, it was risky. And for them to go on to publicly proclaim their fierce opposition to slavery in an 1851 open letter printed in the newspapers was frankly courageous. Why did they do so? As part of the Compromise of 1850, designed to close the ever-widening gulf between free and slave states, Congress had passed the Fugitive Slave Act declaring it mandatory for anyone in the country to aid bounty hunters searching for runaway slaves. For William and David Lyman, father and son, refusal to abide by the act's provisions was quite simply a matter of conscience, one more important than their own safety. "Good citizens cannot be slave catchers," they wrote, "any more than light can be darkness." Theirs is a powerful and poetic statement, but our state honors them and it today, not for the elegance of its wording, but for the moral torch it shined and still shines in a darkening world.

So, what has the Lyman family shown us during its first one hundred years in Middlefield? First and foremost, perhaps, a commitment to family cooperation that is broad and long: it extends across the generations and all along the family tree. Second, a commitment to place, this place, Connecticut, Middlefield, and most important, the family land itself. But that bond to place and family never blinded them to a third necessity: the need to adapt to an ever-changing environment, to roll the dice when necessary, and then to celebrate the victory, if victory followed, or do whatever it took to recover from the loss if it did not. And fourth, the Lyman family farm at one hundred was grounded in faith and moral courage. These characteristics, commitment to family and land, the willingness to adapt, the courage to take risks, and a foundation in faith and moral fortitude were the armor the family wore into its second century.

And they would need all of it. The Merino sheep craze in Connecticut proved short lived, and the opening of the Erie Canal in 1825 brought cheap grain and other foodstuffs from the Midwest all the way east, making much of Connecticut's agricultural production uncompetitive. Area farms adapted to practice market gardening, selling fresh produce, milk, and eggs for the new nearby cities created by the early consumer and industrial revolutions. It was a hard slog, and by the mid 1840s, William's son David concluded that to keep the family farm, the family would need more than farming to get by, and he had an idea that he thought would help the family clean up.

Since the 1820s, America's new manufacturing centers had brought an explosion in inexpensive clothes, fabrics, housewares, and other goods within reach of a new emerging American middle class. It was a new world of goods, creating a standard of living for many people that their grandparents would not have imagined. Along with new fashions, tastes, and consumer products, came new standards of personal and domestic cleanliness. Commercially produced soaps, toothpaste powders, and cleaning products filled the shelves of Main Street stores, and beautiful packages and catchy advertisements reminded people that Cleanliness was indeed next to Godliness. To capitalize on this new trend, in 1857 David Lyman II bought the rights to a new invention called the Metropolitan washing machine and started a factory to produce it in the Baileyville section of Middlefield. It was the right product at the right time, and within just a few years it made David Lyman an immensely wealthy man and guaranteed the viability of the Lyman farm during his lifetime.

Proud of his new success, while deeply mindful of his heritage, David began in 1863 to construct the Lyman Homestead on the site of the original 1741 home of John and Hope Lyman. Rather than tear down the original family home, he had oxen roll it on logs a half mile to a new location across the street from today's Apple Barrel store, where it remains today. The new homestead, every bit the showplace he intended, served as the family home to six generations of Lymans before being repurposed in the mid-1980s as a site for weddings and private functions. Once again, sensitivity to changes in the market and culture and the willingness to adapt to them propelled the family and the family farm into the future.

David Lyman II was nothing if not a man with vision. Having developed a product whose demand was so great he was sure he could sell it anywhere, he set out to bring everywhere within reach of Middlefield, whose status as an incorporated town he had helped secure in 1866. Reasoning that if he could easily get his washing machines to New York or Boston, he could distribute them worldwide, he became president of a company to build what would be known as the Air Line Railroad, and in 1867 began construction of a rail line linking fifty Connecticut towns from New Haven to Willimantic, and from there to everywhere. The greatest challenge was building a rail bridge across the Connecticut River, not because it was a difficult engineering feat, but because a generation of business interests that had made their fortunes in the steamboat and canal trades opposed him. Their opposition was so fierce that although he succeeded in getting the needed legislation and saw the rail line reach Middlefield from New Haven, David Lyman never saw it completed. He died in January 1871 at the age of fifty, two years before the railroad reached Willimantic.

After his death, David's son Charles Elihu Lyman took over management of the farm, and once again the Lyman lands experienced rapid change. While David had envisioned that the transportation revolution he brought to middle Connecticut would transform his washing machine company, Charles saw its transformative potential applying equally to the family farm. The availability of rapid transportation meant that it was now possible to get high value meat and produce products to major metropolitan cities still fresh, where they would command the best prices. So, Charles ushered in an era of crop specialization the farm had never known. Lambs were fattened for eastern markets, six to nine hundred tons of hay annually were transported to urban areas where horses were still the primary means of transportation, and the farm grew from 500 to 1,500 acres.

The most significant change of all came when J. H. Hale of Glastonbury convinced Charles Lyman and other farmers that they could profitably grow peaches in Connecticut. Peaches have a short shelf life and couldn't survive the weeks of travel it took to get them from orchards

David Lyman was instrumental in building the Air Line Railroad that connected Lyman family enterprises to the wider world. COURTESY CONNECTICUT EXPLORED

in Georgia to tables in New England. But by growing peaches in Connecticut, it was possible to meet Yankees' nearly insatiable demand for this source of preserves, jams, pies, and hand-held goodness. By the early 1900s, Lyman Orchards had over five hundred acres of peach trees, and because of the handy access to the Air Line Railroad, Lyman peaches made it fresh to every point in New England. That is, they did so until 1917, when disaster struck.

That winter a hard, bitter frost hit New England. Temperatures stayed below zero for four straight weeks. The ground froze to a depth of four feet and the peach crop that year was a total loss. Spring revealed that a substantial portion of the peach trees had actually been killed, and over the next two years still more and more trees died. By 1920 it was clear that every peach tree in New England had been destroyed by that 1917 freeze. The loss was enough to take down many farms, and Lyman Orchards, with five hundred acres of dead trees, was nearly one of them. Once again, though, the family's willingness to do whatever it takes to survive, and then take yet another risk, helped Lyman Orchards pull through. Farms the family owned in New York and Pennsylvania were sold off to raise money for the Connecticut recovery, and a new orchard crop, hardy enough to withstand cold northern winters, was planted. Lyman peach orchards, like many former Connecticut peach farms, became Lyman apple orchards.

Lyman Orchards' survival was also aided by revenue from another manufacturing company, founded by Charles Lyman's brother William. The Lyman Gunsight Company had perfected a rifle sight that became immensely popular, especially during World War I, and the diversified revenue stream it generated was extremely welcome after the peach disaster. Standard apple trees take about ten years to grow to maturity, and even with the sale of the out-of-state farms, money from the gunsight company helped see the family through the decade-long crisis. This was especially important, because just as the Lyman apple trees finally came into full production, the family faced yet another major problem.

All over New England, thousands of acres of newly mature apple trees planted by farmers trying to come back from the peach tree die-off were about to come into production, glutting the market with apples all

THIRD NEW ENGLAND FRUIT SHOW, BOSTON, NOVEMBER, 1913.
THIS UNIQUE DISPLAY WAS THE CONTRIBUTION OF THE CONNECTICUT POMOLOGICAL SOCIETY.

For Lyman Orchards, the transition from peaches to apples as a matter of survival. COURTESY LYMAN ORCHARDS

at once. The result, it was clear, would be financially disastrous. Prices of newly ripe apples would fall to nearly nothing, and much of the crop could be expected to rot unsold. What was needed was a way to extend the time the apples would stay fresh.

Charles Lyman had died in 1923, but John Lyman, Sr., his successor in managing the farm, introduced a way of sustaining freshness to Middlefield. Once again, faced with major problems in the present, the family invested in the future, building a cold-storage facility with a capacity of forty thousand bushels of apples. The new cold technology kept the apples fresh much longer, enabling the farm to both extend the growing season and begin marketing to the wholesale side of the apple business.

Apple orchards now became the core of Lyman Orchards diversified farming operation, aiming to meet the needs of a society that was rapidly urbanizing and suburbanizing. Within a generation, general stores became supermarkets, and fruit carts became produce sections. The Lyman farm, now in its seventh generation of continuous family management, changed with them. By 1949, it was clear that food marketing and farm operations had both changed so dramatically that a corporate structure for the farm was now in the best interests of both the farm and the family. Lyman Farm, Incorporated, was formed with John Lyman, Sr., its first president, and the heirs of Charles Elihu Lyman as directors.

As Connecticut and American society changed in the 1960s and '70s, the farm, as it had done so many times in the past, tried to anticipate where the parade was going and get there slightly ahead of the movement. Just as the average American was beginning to learn about things like cholesterol and saturated fats, a decision was made in 1960 to phase out the farm's high-fat milk-producing Guernsey dairy herd. In 1963, long before farm-fresh goodness became a mantra of the food advertising industry, Lyman Orchards was investing in controlled-atmosphere storage that preserved apples in a nitrogen-rich environment with only 5 percent oxygen. This extended the period an apple retained its farm fresh goodness from fall all the way through the following spring and into summer.

In the 1970s and 1980s, before any of us had even heard of America becoming a "leisure society" and when a phrase like "locavore food movement" would have provoked laughter, Lyman orchards anticipated both. And what they did, they did well.

In 1972 the Apple Barrel Farm Market opened, which placed Lyman Orchards squarely in the forefront of an emerging locavore foods movement. In addition to a fruit sales area, the uniquely designed circular store included both a deli and a bakery, where the farms' popular apple pies were made by hand. The pies became so popular that in 1996 the farm formed a wholesale pie operation that today sells pies, based on generations old recipes, to family-owned grocery chains in a dozen different states.

Earlier, in 1969, in fields where cows and sheep once grazed, Lyman Orchards opened a new eighteen-hole golf course designed by the legendary golf architect Robert Trent Jones, Sr. It is the only public Robert Trent Jones, Sr. course in the world. Buoyed by the enthusiastic and sustained public response to this course, the family opened the first nine holes of a second eighteen-hole championship golf course in 1994, this one designed by Hall of Fame golfer Gary Player. That course was supplemented in 2012 with the opening of The Golf Center and Apple Nine course, intended to help train a new generation of golfers while meeting the needs of a changing and more time-pressured golfing community.

Even as Lyman Orchards adapted to meet the needs of Connecticans increasingly devoted to outdoor leisure activities, they were helping set standards for an emerging agritainment movement. The pick-your-own-fruits market, which had begun here in the early twentieth century with home canners looking for bargains, was modified to meet the expectations of new consumers interested in quality, freshness, and a fun family activity. Lyman Orchards became a five-month pick-your-own must-go-to destination, whose reputation as a family outing destination was further augmented with the 2000 introduction of the four-acre Lyman Orchards corn maze, an attraction that has helped raise more than half a million dollars to fight cancer. This was augmented with the three-acre sunflower maze, supporting Connecticut's Children's Medical Center in 2007. And that was only another aspect of Lyman Orchard's late-twentieth-century adaptation to an ever-changing market.

How is Lyman Orchards today different than when John and Hope Lyman founded it in 1741? Well, like Connecticut itself during the last three centuries it has changed again and again. What began as thirty-seven acres is now eleven hundred acres. What was a subsistence farm is now a major commercial farm operation, golf center, food purveyor, agritainment and agritourism destination, and the twelfth-oldest family business in America. Ten generations of the same family have invested their lives and fortunes in this same piece of Connecticut land and earned their destinies here. Lyman Orchards's story is their story, and it is Connecticut's story, and your and my story, too.

Today the Lyman family faces the same challenge with which it began so long ago: How do they adapt to remain economically viable as a family farm not just for the present but for all the generations to come? The answers to that question have changed continuously, and they will keep changing—maybe even faster—for the foreseeable future. Yet, armed with the principles that have sustained their family from the beginning: commitment to family and land, the willingness to adapt, the courage to take risks, and a foundation in faith and moral fortitude, it is not unlikely that the Lyman family farm will still be going and growing strong in Middlefield, centuries after this writer has gone to memory.

FURTHER READING

Historian Diana McCain has written and published a novel about the first five generations of Lyman farm owners, *Thy Children's Children* (Create Space Independent Publishing Platform, 2016), available on Amazon.

A well-presented history of the farm and its record of change and adaptation is on the Lyman Orchards website (lymanorchards.com).

Much of the information used in this chapter came from interviews with John Lyman III in preparation for a 2016 talk I gave celebrating the family farm's 275th anniversary. You can hear interviews with John Lyman III on the *Grating the Nutmeg* podcast "Lyman Orchards Turns 275" at http://gratingthenutmeg.libsyn.com/9-lyman-orchards-turns-275-and-whats-it-all-about-summer-edition, as well as on the podcast with novelist/historian Diana McCain called "Staying on the Land: Five Generations of Pioneers" at http://gratingthenutmeg.libsyn .com/46-staying-on-the-land-five-generations-of-connecticut-pioneers.

CONNECTICUT'S SLOW WALK TOWARD EMANCIPATION

When it came to ending slavery, Connecticut wasn't exactly in a rush.

Many people believe that as a northern state Connecticut would have been in the forefront of states supporting the emancipation of enslaved African-Americans. A review of the history of emancipation in Connecticut, however, reveals a record that is both mixed and sobering.

After American independence, Connecticut, like many of the northern states, examined whether slavery was compatible with American ideals. It decided, in a half-hearted way, that it wasn't. Connecticut chose to emancipate its enslaved people, but, concerned about the property rights of owners, did so very gradually. In 1784 the state passed legislation freeing any child born to an enslaved woman after March 1 of that year. However, that child was not to be freed until they reached the age of twenty-five. That would delay the earliest emancipation until 1809, a year after the Constitution outlawed the importation of slaves to the United States. Notably, the 1784 Connecticut Emancipation Statute did nothing to free the child's father or mother. Later, the state passed laws lowering the age of emancipation and forbidding the sale of any slaves out of state (where emancipation laws could be circumvented), but slavery continued in Connecticut well into the nineteenth century.

Encouraged by vocal abolitionists such as Jonathan Edwards, Jr. and Theodore Dwight, many Connecticut masters freed their slaves well before the emancipation laws required them to do so. By 1800 there were more than 5,000 free blacks in Connecticut. Some leading Connecticans, including such prominent people as Noah Webster and the jurist Zephaniah Swift, felt such early emancipation was ill-advised. They believed slow emancipation was important for both public safety and the welfare of the enslaved.

Connecticut's blacks, on the other hand (both free and enslaved) not surprisingly thought otherwise, and they were a steady voice urging and acting for faster emancipation. In the end, slavery remained legal in the

Land of Steady Habits until 1848, though the number of enslaved people reported in census figures dropped to ninety-seven by 1820 and seventeen by 1840.

Opposing slavery was never the same as advocating equality, and here in the state William Lloyd Garrison called "the Georgia of the North," racism remained deeply entrenched long after slavery ended. Views on Civil War emancipation were mixed. While Connecticut Republican Governor William Buckingham personally traveled to Washington to urge President Lincoln to emancipate enslaved people months before the Emancipation Proclamation was issued, other political leaders protested vigorously that the war was only being fought to save the Union, not to end slavery. After the Emancipation Proclamation, which freed slaves only in the states then in rebellion against the United States, took effect on January 1, 1863, Connecticut's State Democratic Convention adopted a resolution saying the proclamation "would disgrace our country in the eyes of the civilized world, and carry lust, rapine, and murder into every household of the slaveholding states."

A similar popular racist response met the 1865 passage of the Thirteenth Amendment, which ended slavery nationally. When the Republican-dominated Connecticut General Assembly sent voters an amendment to the state constitution removing the word white from the description of who could vote in state elections, a provision that would have given the vote to free black Connecticut men, the electorate soundly rejected it, preferring to maintain political inequality as the policy of the state. The Fifteenth Amendment to the US Constitution guaranteeing blacks the right to vote in every state, that was subsequently passed by Congress and ratified in 1870, was intended to address the ongoing racism of states like Connecticut as much as racism in the South.

While the Civil War that ended slavery did indeed pit the North against the South, it is sobering to recall that our nation, including the majority of people in Connecticut, remained united by deeply embedded racism for at least another century.

THE IRISH IN CONNECTICUT

From hated newcomers to people in charge, the Irish have been shaping Connecticut for nearly four centuries.

Since the early 1600s, more than seven million Irish men and women parted with home, family, friends, and history, and left Erin for the American hope of a better life. Many found it; many did not. But in their coming, they transformed America and America transformed them. Today, nearly forty million Americans claim an Irish heritage, and American culture has been profoundly and indelibly influenced by its Irish inheritance. Hundreds of thousands of Erin's children made their way to Connecticut, at different times and for many different reasons. When and why a particular Irish person, family, or migrant group came to the Land of Steady Habits had a marked influence on their reception here, on the people among whom they settled, and the places in which they settled. This is a brief account of how the Irish helped create Connecticut, even as they made Connecticut their home.

Americans commonly think about Irish immigration only in terms of the Great Hunger of the mid-nineteenth century. This is unfortunate, for it ignores the long history of Irish emigration before and after that desperate time. Between Connecticut's founding in 1636 and American independence almost a century and a half later, nearly 400,000 Irish immigrants came to the New World, some voluntarily, others against their will. Most of them came to North America, but decidedly *not* to New England. Early Irish migrants intentionally avoided the northern colonies if they could, settling instead in the Mid-Atlantic and the South. They had good reasons for doing so. Long-standing victims of English persecution, they knew New England was populated almost entirely by

Puritans who shared the same anti-Catholic and anti-Irish prejudices as their English counterparts. To make matters worse, New Englanders' anti-Catholic hostility had been amplified by a long series of conflicts with French Catholic Canada, which regularly sent converted Catholic-Indian allies to devastate New England's frontier settlements. On top of religious hostility and ethnic racism, colonial New England also offered newcomers precious little in the way of economic opportunity. Unlike the tobacco-rich Chesapeake, it was a region of small family farms and subsistence agriculture, with long winters, stony soil, and no cash crop.

Despite the dismal prospects, some Irish did find their way to colonial Connecticut, though often not by choice. At least 1,400 Irish Catholic men, women, and children were forcibly transported to New England as servants in the aftermath of the Puritan Oliver Cromwell's suppression of the Irish Rising in the early 1650s. We know little about the fate of most of these people, but we do know that Edmund Fanning and his family, who had led resistance to Cromwell's army during the horrific siege of Limerick in 1651, was transplanted to New London and sold as indentured servants to future Connecticut governor John Winthrop Jr. in 1654. Fanning served out his five-year term as a servant, then went on to become a successful merchant and a founder of the town of Stonington. Other Irishmen fought their way into Puritan acceptance by providing military service in Anglo-Indian conflicts. At least five Irish men—James Murphy, Daniel Tracy, Edward Larkin, James Welch, and John Roach—distinguished themselves fighting for Connecticut in King Philip's War in 1675 and 1676, for which they received both recognition and bonuses of land.

Forced transportation of Irish servants to Connecticut continued, intermittently, throughout the colonial period. A 1764 *Connecticut Gazette* advertisement, for example, offered "a Parcel of Irish servants, both men and women, to be sold cheap, by Israel Boardman, Stamford." In 1783, ship captain Robert Winthrop sold some of his cargo of 231 formerly imprisoned Dubliners at New London. This influx of involuntary Irish migrants may have buttressed the thriving eighteenth-century trade in flaxseed that developed among Connecticut farmers (who grew the seed), New York merchant go-betweens and Ulster and Leinster farmers who supplied flax for Irish linen producers. Of all colonies, Connecticut was America's biggest exporter of this specialized seed crop.

Estimating how many people of Irish origin were in Connecticut during the colonial period is problematic. Evidence is fragmentary and numbers vary. One historian found 205 men and 5 women with Irish surnames in Connecticut records before 1800. Many of these were presumably married, and, given New England's average family size of eight children, the total number of colonial Irish Connecticans may have been in the low thousands. This (and the multi-national—Irish, Scottish, Welsh and Breton—possibilities inherent in the term Celtic) may explain why another investigation found more than eight hundred Celtic names on the military rolls of Connecticut men who fought for American independence. Even in the low thousands, though, the Irish represented a very small percentage of Connecticut's total population of 208,870 in 1782, in all likelihood less than the state's estimated 2.8 percent black population of 5,885.

However large or small their numbers, there is little evidence of Catholic religious practice among these early Irish colonial migrants. That's not surprising, since celebrating mass was outlawed in Connecticut until 1818, and no priests lived within its borders until a decade after that. Rather than trying to cling to their roots and faith, New England's first Irish migrants appear to have consciously downplayed their ethnicity and set aside their Catholicism (at least publicly) to better fit into Puritan society. This conscious rejection of Irish identity and religious practices as a strategic response to Puritan ethnic and religious hostility is found only during this early period. It produced in Connecticut a founding group of Irish immigrants who, to all appearances, worked hard to blend in with the Yankees around them.

That approach changed dramatically between American independence in 1776 and Ireland's Great Hunger of the mid-1840s. By then, even as the flood of famine refugees began to board the coffin ships, any hopes they had of blending peacefully into Connecticut Yankee society were as blighted as the potato plants they left behind.

Both Ireland and Connecticut changed dramatically in the early 1800s. Ireland experienced a short-term economic boom along with a population explosion from four million to seven million people between 1800 and 1821. Then, an economic collapse at the end of the Napoleanic Wars triggered a sudden and severe crisis that generated a dramatic increase in out-migration to the United States. The trickle of incoming Irish during the first 150 years of American settlement became first a steady flow, then a rushing stream. Over 100,000 people left Erin for America between 1780 and 1810, but that number increased to one million by 1840. And whereas the majority of pre-revolutionary emigrants had been northern county Protestants headed for the American South, the new Irish emigrants were Catholics from Muenster and Connaught, who clustered in the cities of the American North.

Old-line Connecticut Yankees viewed this gathering swarm with fear and loathing. Government in the Land of Steady Habits was still run, for the most part, by actual descendants of the first Puritan leaders two hundred years earlier. The citizens who voted for them were also descendants of those same Puritans. Connecticans were Protestants in faith and law, Anglophiles in disposition, and Federalists in politics, and they were facing some harsh realities. Two centuries of over-farming rocky soil and Connecticut's large average family sizes had created a situation in which families no longer had enough land to pass on to adult children, and what land they did have was essentially infertile. As a result, Connecticut, like Ireland, was, in the early 1800s, experiencing a vast out-migration of its youth to the new states of the American Midwest. The last thing Connecticans needed—or wanted—was an influx of what they considered wild, work-seeking "Papists"(a time-honored slur used to denigrate Catholics by underscoring their loyalty to a foreign Pope). Fortunately, most Irish immigrants felt the same way about Connecticut. The last thing they wanted was a place with no work and bad soil, and so, for a time, at least, they stayed away from the Nutmeg State, clustering in New York, and later Boston.

Connecticut soon found the key to its economic future through an abundance of waterpower that could drive the machines of industry and mass-produce the fabrics, guns, clocks, tools, utensils, and tin-ware needed by a modernizing society. Just at the moment when the flow of Irish emigrants became a rushing stream, the streams of New England began the transformation that would make Connecticut an industrial colossus. Yankees in the Land of Steady Habits might not want to live among Irish Papists, but they would soon find it first useful, and then necessary, to do so.

The trigger event for this transformation was the 1825 opening of the Erie Canal that linked New York City to the Midwest. Its astonishing success almost instantly made Gotham the nation's premier financial and trade center. Canal fever swept the country. In Connecticut, that fever centered on New Haven, which looked at the Connecticut River and dreamed of opening a water passage to Montreal. On July 4, 1825, city elites broke ground on the eighty-six-mile Farmington Canal, which was intended to connect to the Connecticut River via a second new waterway, the Hampshire and Hampden Canal, in Massachusetts. Hartford, New Haven's rival for commercial supremacy, immediately answered with their own Enfield Canal, intended to circumvent the traffic-stopping rapids on the Connecticut River at Enfield. Overnight, the state had launched two major construction projects of unprecedented scope and scale, which generated a massive demand for unskilled workers.

Enter the Irish. To meet the need for laborers, contractors for the Farmington Canal brought in twenty-eight gangs of Irish canal workers called *navvies* from Galway and Cork. Hartford brought in four hundred Irishmen for the Enfield Canal project. Life for the navvies was hellish. Like the Irish railroad track workers who soon followed them, they dug furiously sunup to sunset, goaded by overseer/contractors whose profits depended on how much labor they could extract every day. Eyewitnesses marveled at the physical prowess of the Irishmen as they ran full wheelbarrows up narrow planks from ditches twenty feet deep. They lived in temporary shanty camps, where overcrowding, poor sanitation, and stagnant water made disease a constant. Alcohol was woven into a workday marked by short bursts of furious digging followed by a trip to the whiskey barrel and a dram from the "jigger boss." Irish workers were paid only for the days weather and their health let them work, and they earned just seventy-five cents a day, one-third less than native-born laborers.

The navvies represented Connecticut's first major influx of practicing Irish Catholics, and the descendants of Connecticut's Puritan founders did not like it one bit. Connecticut had no resident priests and the Yankees made it clear they would like to keep it that way. When Reverend John Powers of New York requested permission to celebrate Mass for canal workers at New Haven's Protestant Seaman's Chapel on Long Wharf, he was told, "We have no Popery in New Haven, and we don't want any." Despite the overt intolerance, Popery did come to Connecticut, at first through the services of an itinerant priest from Rhode Island, who, in 1828, conducted house Masses on the east bank of the river in Hartford. The following year Hartford became home to Most Holy Trinity, Connecticut's first Catholic church and the state's resident priest, Father Bernard O'Cavanaugh. The *Connecticut Observer* was aghast. "How will it read in history, that in 1829, Hartford, in the state of Connecticut, was made the center of a Roman Catholic mission?"

Even as their numbers increased, the incoming Irish, whose speech, dress, and religion seemed an affront to Connecticut norms, faced unrelenting prejudice reflecting centuries of anti-Catholic hatred and Anglocentric racism. Newspapers demeaned Irish dress, language, character, intelligence, pugnacity, and intemperance. The Reverend Horace Bushnell, an old-line Yankee whose name is still honored at Bushnell Park surrounding Connecticut's state capitol, was a leading spokesman for this anti-Irish contempt. "If you will glance over the catalogues of our colleges and universities, the advertisements of merchants and mechanics," he wrote, "you will almost never find an Irish name among them, which shows that they do not rise among us. At the same time, If you will search the catalogue of almshouses and prisons, and potter's fields, there you will find their names in thick order." The inference was clear; as far as the Connecticut Yankees were concerned, the Irish were as inferior as the blacks with whom they competed for the worst jobs.

Despite such unstinting ethnic hostility, many of the Irish navvies made Connecticut their home. There were 720 Catholics in Connecticut in 1835, the majority former canal workers. Why did they stay? Conditions in Ireland were so stressed that going home wasn't an option. Even if it had been, grinding poverty made leaving for anywhere impossible for many. But there was also work to be had in Connecticut; not good work, perhaps, but work, and lots of it. And, in the urban ghettos coalescing

Rev. Horace Bushnell, a leading moral authority, led the charge against the Irish immigrant threat. COURTESY CONNECTICUTHISTORY.ORG

around Most Holy Trinity in Hartford and Christ Church, the parish founded in New Haven in 1832, Irish communities within communities were forming—with grocers, saloons, church societies, and political leaders all attuned to Irish needs and Irish interests in a new and not very friendly place. These became the seedbed for a new kind of Irish person, the Connecticut Irish-American, with roots in the old country, and connections—very useful ones—in the new. This new class of culture-crossing power broker appeared none too soon, too, for the 1840s brought a tsunami of Irish immigrants who would shake the Land of Steady Habits to the core.

The stream of Irish emigrants had become a torrent even before the 1845 potato famine. As early as 1839, Connecticut author Samuel Griswold Goodrich, who wrote under the name Peter Parley, wisely warned Americans that they were coming, and to pay attention. "Ireland is an unhappy country," he wrote. "Not one person in a hundred there is the proprietor of the land from which his substance is drawn . . . thousands . . . lie down every night, not knowing how they may obtain the bread of tomorrow. Our happier country is the asylum to which multitudes . . . are flying. . . . They are found by thousands in our larger cities. They penetrate the interior . . . and whether we look to their own happiness, or their influence upon our institutions, they may fairly claim the attention of every intelligent American citizen."

Claim Americans' attention they did, especially after the famine struck in 1845.

During the seven-year-long potato blight almost a million Irish people died. The British response to the disaster was totally ineffective and morally bankrupt. Elihu Burritt, the "learned blacksmith" of New Britain who had risen to become an internationally known publisher, lecturer, essayist, and radical pacifist, visited Ireland in 1847, saw the desperation there, and sent impassioned pleas to the people of New England to send aid to the starving country. This generated large public responses in New Haven, Hartford, New London, Norwalk, and Bridgeport. Lydia Sigourney, the "sweet singer of Hartford," then one of America's best-known female poets, added her voice to the call, penning "Irelands Appeal," a sentimental poem urging her readers to support the relief effort. Connecticut's

Yankees—both individuals and civic and church groups—sent aid to the distressed. And though hard-pressed themselves, many immigrants sent remits of cash to family members back home, while New Haven's Irish community collectively canceled their 1847 Saint Patrick's Day parade to send a $200 contribution to aid those they'd left behind.

Connecticans' compassion for starving people thousands of miles across an ocean did not translate into compassion for those same people once they arrived in America. And arrive they did, in numbers that had no precedent. In the face of unthinkable desperation, many of the Irish who could got out of Eire did so, even after the worst of the famine had passed. The United States counted 924,000 migrants by 1850; two million more between 1851 and 1855. Most came into the country through New York City via Liverpool. Though only 18 percent of these Gotham migrants settled in the city permanently, by 1860 one of every four New Yorkers was Irish.

Twenty-five percent of the famine's Irish immigrants came to New England. Despite Yankee prejudice, the industrial revolution in the Yankee states was now in full swing and had created an immense demand for labor. Father John O'Hanlon's 1851 *Irish Immigrant's Guide for the United States* praised Connecticut as a destination for both agricultural and manufacturing work. Elsewhere, though, he realistically described most of the awaiting opportunities: "[T]he work consists in a great part, so far as laborers are concerned, in the making and opening of sewers and trenches for waters and gas pipes, in grading, leveling, and paving streets or levees, in digging cellars and foundations for houses—all of which are mostly carried on by the use of the spade or mattock, at which the Irish excel."

An 1848 visitor to Connecticut summed up the often dangerous manufacturing opportunities available to the Irish in the Nutmeg state this way. "Irishmen were called in to dig the deep foundations of huge factories, to blast the rocks, to build the dams; and when the great structures arose, the children of Irishmen were called to tend the spindles or the furnaces."

Factories needed both skilled and unskilled laborers, but the economics of prejudice meant the Irish got the unskilled jobs. In 1850, Irish workers held two-thirds of Hartford's poorly paid, dirty, dangerous, and often only part-time unskilled positions. A Connecticut axe manufacturer wrote that he employed Irish grinders only because the death rate from accidents was so high native Connecticans wouldn't take the work. If work for men was low-paid, dirty, and dangerous, ninety percent of the Irish female immigrants became domestic servants for Yankee families who profited from their labor even as they openly mocked their Irish maids' supposedly low intelligence, lack of polish, rude manners, and heretical religion.

Poor, suffering, and generally unwanted—though needed as workhorses—the Irish spread across the state, picking up jobs as farm workers in the country or laborers in the rural factory villages. Mostly, though, they huddled together in urban ethnic enclaves characterized by poverty, squalor, disease, alcoholism, and pugnacity: "The Hill" in New Haven; "Dublin" in Danbury, Dublin and Kerrytown in Stamford, and, in a name that speaks volumes about the local reaction to the Irish presence, "Pigsville" in Hartford. The Yankees watched these Irish Catholic ghettoes grow with angry anxiety. This was the antithesis of the controlled order for which The Land of Steady Habits had always stood. Horace Bushnell warned his Puritan flock, "Catholic emigrants are pouring into our country. . . . Every one of them and their descendants is meant to be our enemies, and most of them probably will be." The *Hartford Observer* noted that allowing Catholics into Connecticut was like allowing "an invasion of savages on our western borders." A letter writer to the *Courant*, who signed his name simply "American," underscored why such concerns were warranted. "The Roman Hierarchy . . . has poured into our country her ignorant, superstitious and Priest-ridden Minions to do her work in overturning our free Government and erecting her bloody throne upon the ruins." Spurred on by such fear-mongering, it was widely believed, though never proved, that nativist arsonists set the fire that burned down New Haven's Catholic church in 1848.

The defiant Elm City Irish held services in a tent for six months, then bought a former Congregational church and renamed it St. Mary's. Shortly after that, they started a group intended to make a statement that would help thwart any future attacks. In July 1849, a group of New

Haven men formed an all-Irish militia group, the Washington-Erina Guards. The organizers were the Irish shop and saloonkeepers, skilled workers, professionals, and ward leaders who served as the ghetto community's informal leaders, providing information, credit, and links to political patronage. The Irish had learned quickly that their fastest avenue to power in America would be through politics—specifically through alignment with the Democratic party opposed to Connecticut's traditional Yankee elites who comprised the state's venerable Standing Order. The fact that the Irish were concentrated in ghettoes gave them immediate voting clout, first in local ward elections, then, as their numbers grew, in city and state elections. They used that political clout to support those who stood up for them.

Expressing fervent American patriotism along with Irish nationalism, the Washington-Erina Guards drilled for three years without weapons until the state elected a Democrat, Thomas Seymour, as governor in 1852. By then, Irish militia units had formed in four Connecticut towns. The politically savvy Governor Seymour rewarded his Irish supporters by incorporating the Irish units into the state's Second Regiment. This, to say the least, did not sit well with the old-line anti-Irish Yankees. The presence of armed Irish troops in the Connecticut militia further intensified their anti-Irish paranoia and led to the ascendance of the Know Nothings—an anti-Irish-Catholic political movement whose number-one goal was to stop immigration and end Irish voting rights. In the election of 1855, the Know Nothings took over Connecticut government, and one of Governor William Minor's first acts was to fulfill his campaign promise to disband all the Irish militia companies.

Mid-nineteenth-century, native-born Connecticans had some justification for their concerns that the Irish were taking over their state and commandeering their culture. Certainly, the newcomers were rapidly changing the Land of Steady Habits in ways the Puritan founders would never have believed possible. Between 1851 and 1855, twenty-two new Catholic churches were built in the state, and the Sisters of Mercy had also begun to establish parochial schools and asylums for Irish-Catholic orphans. Connecticut's Irish population had increased seventy-seven fold in twenty years, and already one out of every eight people in the state was foreign-born Irish.

Yet the Know Nothing's grip on Connecticut politics was short-lived, not because of an upwelling in pro-Irish sentiment, but because of a different and all-consuming challenge. With the attack on Fort Sumter on April 12, 1861, the country became embroiled in its most divisive and costly conflict in terms of human lives—the American Civil War. Suddenly, the Know Nothing governor's decision to disband the Irish militia seemed short-sighted at best. An apologetic new governor from the pro-Union Republican party, William Buckingham, requested the Irish units reactivate in defense of the Union, which they did enthusiastically. Twelve hundred Irish volunteers joined the gallant Ninth Connecticut Regiment, and marched south under an emerald-green battle flag. During the war, they saw combat in Louisiana and Virginia, but as with most Civil War units, most of the 250 fatalities inflicted on the Ninth came from disease, specifically, the malaria caught while digging a canal during the summer 1863 siege of Vicksburg, Mississippi. Altogether, more than six thousand Irish Connecticans fought for the Union in the Civil War and they won a grudging respect for their patriotism, even among their fiercest opponents. To many veterans who had fought by their side, "the Irish [now] became Americans in peace or war." But to the most resistant of the traditionalists, in uniform and out, they remained a highly suspect and inferior group of outsiders.

The Civil War ended in 1865, but the anti-Irish prejudice continued. Irish men were commonly stereotyped as slow-thinking and devious, prone to drunkenness and fighting, their wives and daughters ridiculed as lazy and incompetent. For the famine immigrants, life remained a constant struggle. Compared to the situation for those who stayed in Ireland, America might indeed have provided new opportunities, but for most that only meant the ability to rise from the pauper class into poverty. Such conditions would change, though not without struggle, for the famine generation's children, as the Irish in America began to assume their rights as Irish-Americans.

Two million Irish people came to the United States between 1870 and 1920, no longer famine migrants, but people, often with relatives already in America, seeking not just to stay alive, but to live a better life.

Connecticut was leading America's explosive industrial expansion. The third smallest of the fifty states, Connecticut ranked eleventh in manufacturing in 1900. It produced 79 percent of America's brass and copper goods, 76 percent of its ammunition, 64 percent of all clocks, and 46 percent of all hardware. It was a major producer of bicycles, automobiles, typewriters, fabrics, rifles, and rubber goods of all kind. The demand for new consumer products was insatiable, as was the demand for new factories and workers. Ireland alone could not provide nearly enough workers, so migrants from Italy, Russia, Germany, Canada, Poland, and Sweden had helped create a Connecticut in which, by 1900, immigrants and their children outnumbered the original Yankee stock.

What made this a watershed period for the Irish was that now second-generation Irish Connecticans (persons born in Connecticut to Irish parents) began to outnumber actual Irish immigrants. That changed both Irish culture in Connecticut, and Connecticut itself. Second generation Irish-Americans enjoyed significant social mobility. Retaining their sense of Irish distinctiveness, they had also thoroughly embraced being Connecticans and Americans and were rewarded with opportunities denied their parents. Unlike their fathers, by 1900, two-thirds of second-generation Irish men worked in skilled trades or higher, with economic security mirroring that of the Connecticut Yankees. Irish-American men dominated police and fire departments and monopolized the building trades. And, while 90 percent of their mothers remained domestic servants, second-generation Irish-American daughters rose to become clerks, skilled factory workers, teachers, and union organizers, too.

Better jobs came in part because of high Irish involvement in Connecticut's labor movement. Irish-Americans made up most of many unions' membership and leadership. Union involvement and political involvement intermingled. In the 1880s, the Irish-led Knights of Labor elected thirty pro-labor members to the Connecticut house. In 1901, a new labor group, tellingly organized on Saint Patrick's Day, elected Connecticut Federation of Labor president Ignatius Sullivan mayor of

Hartford. By World War I, the Irish were often the controlling factor in Connecticut's urban and state politics. In 1916, the *Hartford Courant*, noting that the mayor and the chiefs of the police and fire departments were of Irish descent claimed, "The Irish people are born politicians. They fit naturally into politics." But then, they went on to say the Irish "are apt to do well at anything they undertake." This glowing recognition of Irish ability was a complete reversal from the *Courant*'s racist anti-Irish stance during the famine years, and a sign of just how far acceptance of Irish Connecticans had advanced. Second-generation Irish-Americans were now held up as a model for the newly arrived waves of Italian, Russian, and Polish emigrants to emulate. "While they are Irish, they are more essentially American," the *Courant* wrote, even as "they are maintaining the traditions of their ancestors."

Though they found a measure of acceptance, the Irish remained different to most, and suspect to some. A few found Irish Connecticans' large rallies in support of the 1916–1919 Irish War for Independence and the Free State formed in its wake disturbing. They were a minority; most of the continuing anti-Irish feeling in Connecticut was related to Catholicism, that ancient and still-feared enemy of the Puritan founders.

Connecticans' feelings about the state's Catholic institutions were ambivalent. On the one hand, church leaders promoted old line Yankee's cherished values of temperance, education, and virtuous behavior. But on the other hand, the church hierarchy, led by Irish-American priests and bishops, still answered to a foreign pope, whose ability to command obedience from a potential fifth column of religious zealots seemed un-American, perhaps even a threat to national security. And the Catholic Church in Connecticut was both large and powerful. By the state's three hundredth anniversary in 1935, Connecticut had well over a half-million Catholics served by 292 churches, 39 religious communities, 4 hospitals, 100 parochial schools, 3 colleges, and 4 seminaries. This was a force to be reckoned with, and for some, to be feared.

So, even as second- and third-generation Irish-Americans moved up and out to the new streetcar-suburban enclaves of Connecticut's cities, they became targets of a virulent minority anti-Catholic movement that flourished in the 1920s and remained significant right up to the election of John F. Kennedy in 1960. The Ku Klux Klan, which admitted roughly 75,000 members—almost 15 percent of the native-born whites in the state—between 1921 and 1925, held anti-Catholic rallies with white robes and burning crosses throughout the state. One such rally in Manchester, Connecticut, attracted nearly ten thousand people, another in Branford nearly fifteen thousand.

Irish Catholics countered this surge of anti-Catholic hostility through increased membership in groups such as the Knights of Columbus. Founded in New Haven, Connecticut, in 1882 by Civil War veteran James Terrance Mullen and Father Michael McGivney, the Knights espoused a fervent American patriotism and pan-ethnic Catholicism that helped the organization grow to 782,000 members by the early 1920s. Resisting Catholic persecution while demonstrating American nationalism, Irish-Americans began to define themselves in a new way: as both Irish-Americans and militant American Catholics. By the 1930s, it was not uncommon for Connecticut's Irish-Americans to self-identify explicitly as Irish Catholics.

A major factor that helped the American Irish Catholic community weather the early twentieth century's undercurrent of anti-Catholic sentiment was the omnipresent and immensely appealing presence of Irish influence in American popular culture. The Irish put an indelible stamp on American entertainment, one that was decidedly Irish-American in character. It was made up of Tin Pan Alley songs such as "When Irish Eyes are Smiling" and "Mother MaCree," films like *The Fighting Sullivans* and *Yankee Doodle Dandy* and movie priests such as Spencer Tracy and Pat O'Brien, not to mention heartthrobs like Bing Crosby. Knute Rockne's Fighting Irish of Notre Dame became a legend in American football, while from his home in New London, Eugene O'Neill, the second-generation son of Irish actors, worked on the plays that won him the Nobel prize. Taken together, these cultural productions helped convey the idea that Irish-Americans were Americans through and through, but they were different Americans. And much of that difference was connected to their Catholicism.

American Catholicism in the twentieth century required rigorous and disciplined morality of its followers. Through the 1960s, perhaps, family Rosaries (a ritual using set repetitions of specific prayers counted off on a string of rosary beads) were common. Religious paintings, statuary, and other Catholic icons were a visible presence in many Catholic homes. The Latin mass, women wearing veils in church, secret confessions between priest and parishioner, and a host of ritual obligations set American Catholics off markedly from their Protestant peers.

Such differences did not, however, keep Connecticut's Irish Catholics from continuing up the socioeconomic ladder. Proof of Irish political power was everywhere. Though the Irish remained clustered in Connecticut's cities, they controlled politics statewide. In 1934, Francis Maloney of Meriden defeated a prominent old-line Yankee to become Connecticut's first Irish senator. Robert Hurley, a second-generation Irish-American from Bridgeport who gained prominence exposing corruption, became Connecticut's first Irish Catholic governor in 1941. James C. Shannon, became the second, following the death of the incumbent, James MacConaughy, in 1948. Cahir's John Dempsey became the first Irish-born governor of Connecticut in 1961, and the legacy of his remarkable decade in office is what one might describe as a tendency to award the office to people of Irish descent. Since Dempsey, half of Connecticut's governors have claimed Irish heritage, including Thomas Meskill, William O'Neill, John Rowland, and Dannel P. Malloy.

Brien McMahon, an immensely popular US Senator from Norwalk, Connecticut, set his sights on the US Presidency itself. In 1952, in the midst of the Korean Conflict, he announced his candidacy with the slogan "The Man is McMahon, and his main platform is to insure world peace through fear of atomic weapons." McMahon's diagnosis and death from cancer shortly after his announcement put an end to what many said was a high-potential candidacy. Since Senator McMahon's death, a series of Irish-American politicians have established a tradition of Irish-Connectican representation in the US Senate, including William Purtell (1952–1959), Thomas J. Dodd (1959–1971) and his son Christopher Dodd (1981–2011), and, most recently Chris Murphy (2013–present).

McMahon's belief that an Irish Catholic could become the US President despite many Americans' mistrust of Catholicism's link to a foreign pope was shared by John Bailey, the political power broker

160

who stage-managed Connecticut Democratic politics throughout the twentieth-century's middle decades. Bailey went to the 1956 Democratic National Convention intent on securing the vice-presidential nomination for then Massachusetts Senator John Fitzgerald Kennedy. He issued a document now known as the "Bailey Memorandum," which argued that, given the high Catholic population of key states, having a Catholic on the ticket would bring more votes than it cost. Four years later, in 1960, Kennedy, with Bailey as a key adviser, became the first Irish and Catholic President of the United States, a watershed moment in Irish-American history. Bailey was rewarded with the chairmanship of the National Democratic Party. Irish Catholics were rewarded with the crumbling of the final barrier to full American political acceptance. Combined with their dominance of the American Catholic Church hierarchy, and their leadership of America's most important labor unions, the Irish had indeed fully arrived. To those of us who lived through it, it seemed that with Kennedy's election—and if not then, certainly with his assassination—anti-Catholicism in America largely evaporated.

With anti-Irish discrimination largely a thing of the past, many Irish Connecticans were arriving in the new exurban suburbs. There, acceptance into the mainstream of American culture meant the Irish were now far more likely to marry outside their own group. The irony was that at their moment of greatest achievement, many Irish-Americans' identification with their Irish roots began to wane. Fewer than 50 percent of the country's Irish Catholics married other Irish-Americans in the 1960s. Interest in traditional Irish organizations such as the Ancient Order of Hibernians declined. Even Saint Patrick's Day parades, celebrated in Connecticut since the first parade in New Haven in 1842, became a challenge to fund. In 1961, television host and Irish tenor Dennis Day lamented, "I don't think Irish records sell very well now. . . . Record companies won't put them out because there's not enough demand. . . . The second-generation Irishman in this country doesn't want to sing except on Saint Patrick's Day, when they do 'My Wild Irish Rose.'"

Little surprise then, that as America faced the new challenges of the Civil Rights Movement and the Vietnam War, for some Irish-Americans the Irish green in Irish-American culture was fading to a torn and tattered red, white, and blue.

The Civil Rights Movement; the war in Vietnam; the assassinations of two Kennedys, Malcolm X, and Martin Luther King; not to mention the impeachment and resignation of a US President, shook American society to the core in the 1960s and 1970s. Primary values were called into question, as was the legitimacy of fundamental institutions. In the 1950s, to be Irish in America had meant to be a devout Catholic, a vote-the-ticket Democrat, and a fierce American patriot. The 1960s changed all that for many.

The Second Vatican Council, which met from 1962 to 1965, initiated a continuing series of profound changes in American Catholic observances that included dropping the Latin mass for one spoken in English, ending the practice of women wearing veils in church, introducing face-to-face confessions, and increasing the involvement of the laity in church affairs. Taken together, these changes transformed militant Catholicism into a kind of vernacular ecumenism, and in the wake of changing American values toward sexual freedom, birth control, and divorce, and the subsequent revelation of internal sexual scandals that shook many people's faith in the priesthood itself, the church's authority was weakened, and its institutional structure began to crumble. Regular mass attendance dropped from 74 percent in 1958 to around 30 percent today. A quarter of all American Catholic marriages now end in divorce. In small and then growing numbers, Connecticut's Catholics also left the church altogether. Vocations declined precipitously, and parochial schools closed at an alarming rate: in Bridgeport, Meriden, New Britain, Waterbury, and Putnam.

As ties to the faith weakened, so did ethnic distinctions. Whereas once an ethnically diverse white population had been clearly demarcated by racial/ethnic terms such as "the Irish race" or "the German race," the quest for social justice unleashed by the Civil Rights Movement put a focus on the nation's white/non-white racial divides that made white ethnic racial distinctions seem superfluous. In consequence, identifying as Irish-American now became a choice one consciously made, not a choice made for you at birth.

Even the century and a half long loyalty of Irish-Americans to the Democratic party loosened, as many disaffected Irish Democrats swung decisively over to the Republicans. No longer dependent on the party of Jackson and Jefferson for social protection or patronage, a significant number of Irish-American men became conservative Republicans, even in blue-state Connecticut.

Every Irish-American was now free to choose what it meant to be both an Irish-American and an Irish Connectican. Many—often the older generations—clung to the traditional Irish-Connectican trilogy: attend Mass, vote Democratic, and fly the American flag. But others, many in the rising generation of Irish-Americans, embraced an Irishness based on pride in ancestry, and immersion in the history, culture, and traditions of the old country that proved energizing. Irish traditional music and dance was at the core of this new interest. This was not Tin Pan Alley Irish identity, it was a direct connection to the homeland through the songs of The Clancy Brothers and Tommy Makem, The Chieftains and The Wolfe Tones, played with bodhrans, tin whistles, guitars, fiddles, and pipes. All around Connecticut, Irish bars spruced up and expanded. Traditional Irish organizations such as the Ancient Order of Hibernians saw their chapters grow, while relatively newer organizations such as the Irish-American Home Society, chartered in 1947, relocated from Hartford to newer suburban facilities in Glastonbury to accommodate an expanding membership. All this was before the Chicago-born, first generation Irish-American Michael Flatley developed the celebrated stage show *Riverdance* in 1994, and the 1997 film *Titanic* made almost everyone want to climb onto a ship and step dance with Kate Winslet. Such programs stimulated even greater interest in Irish culture. Around Connecticut, Caeli classes sprouted like mushrooms, along with Irish feises and Gaelic cultural festivals. The Connecticut Irish-American Historical Society was founded in Hamden in 1998. Its 350 members are the memory keepers of three and a half centuries of Irish-Connecticut history, which they share through lectures, publications, and exhibits. At both Yale and the University of Connecticut, the early twenty-first century has witnessed the development of new courses offering Gaelic and Irish literature, including an online website, leamh.org, to teach the early modern Irish language. Perhaps the single greatest indicator of the extent of interest in Irish culture in Connecticut today has been the 2012 opening at Quinnipiac University of the Great Hunger Museum, which houses the world's largest collection of material relating to the Irish famine. The annual Saint Patrick's Day Parade in New Haven, which began in 1842, is today Connecticut's largest single-day spectator event.

Coupled with Irish Connecticans' interest in connecting with traditional Irish culture, came a hunger for real connection to Ireland and its people among those whose Irish ancestry now stretched back a century or more from their ancestor's emigration. Tapping into this desire, an Irish tourism campaign to welcome all people of Irish descent back to the old country for an event called The Gathering in 2013 produced double digit increases in visitation from North America that year, and significant enough increases in ensuing years that the Irish airline Aer Lingus began non-stop flights from Hartford to Dublin in 2016.

To be Irish in Connecticut today is, for those lucky enough to claim Irish-American ancestry, a source of both identity and pride, underscored by an extraordinary long-term record of Irish Connecticans' achievements in politics, law, public safety, commerce, industry, and, culture. The fact that such achievements were made by a people once reviled as incapable, discriminated against as inferior, and treated as unwelcome interlopers in a society that took offense at their presence, is an important reminder, especially in times like these, that the very people we fear at one moment, can sometimes turn out to be the source of some of our society's greatest strengths.

FURTHER READING

For those wishing to learn more about the Irish experience in America and Connecticut, here are some useful starting points:

Timothy J. Meagher's *The Columbia Guide to Irish-American History* (New York: Columbia University Press, 2005) provides a comprehensive overview of the Irish-American experience.

Neil Hogan is the dean of historians of the Irish in Connecticut and publishes through the Connecticut Irish-American Historical Society in Hamden. His *Cry of the Famishing: Ireland, Connecticut and the*

Potato Famine (East Haven, CT: Connecticut Irish-American Historical Society, 1998) is an excellent treatment of the generation of Irish men, women, and children who came to Connecticut before, during, and in the wake of the Great Hunger. His other works include *Connecticut's Irish in the Civil War* (2015), *Wearin' O the Green: St. Patrick's Day in New Haven, Connecticut 1842-1992* (1992); *Neil Hogan and Patrick Mahoney, From a Land Beyond the Wave: Connecticut's Irish Rebels 1798-1916* (2016).

Janet Maher has produced two informative and visually rich books on the history of the Irish in the Naugatuck Valley. *From the Old Sod to the Naugatuck Valley: Early Irish Catholics in New Haven County, Connecticut* (Baltimore, MD: Apprentice House Books, 2012); and, with John Wiehn, *Waterbury Irish: From the Emerald Isle to the Brass City* (Charleston, S.C.: History Press, 2015).

"An Ethnic History of New Haven," created by the New Haven Heritage Center, highlights the Irish experience in New Haven and presents it in the context of other immigrant groups to The Elm City (http://connecticuthistory.org/wp-content/uploads/2013/04/AnEthnicHistory ofNewHaven2.pdf).

IMMIGRANTS ALL

No matter how long your people have been in Connecticut, they first came from someplace else.

All Connecticans, from the first indigenous settler to the state's most recent arrival, are immigrants or the descendants of immigrants. The Laurentide ice sheets that covered our state with a mile-high wall of ice 22,000 years ago made sure of that. Immigration has, for most of our history, steadily replenished the Land of Steady Habits with vibrant influxes of new ideas, cultural influences, and social values. Yet a curious anomaly in our immigration pattern—a break in the norm that occurred four hundred years ago—created an environment that made subsequent immigration a particularly contentious and contested process.

From 1620 to 1640, colonial Connecticut participated in what historians call "The Great Migration," the rapid immigration of some twenty thousand religiously and culturally homogeneous English Puritan refugees to the land they would conquer and remake as New England. In 1640, with the outbreak of the English Civil War, that migration stopped on a dime (or perhaps a shilling). For the next century, New England's population increased dramatically, but almost exclusively from the offspring of those original English immigrants. On the eve of the American Revolution, this extended New England cousinage numbered more than 183,000 people in Connecticut alone, an extraordinarily self-possessed, white, Anglo-Saxon, Puritan seed-stock whose issue shaped the government, economy, society, and even the land to reflect their own culture and values.

Such a homogeneous and powerful group was not likely to embrace diversity, and when the Irish arrived in the early nineteenth century, first to dig canals and build railroads, later to flee the Great Hunger, the scions of the Puritans ridiculed the newcomers' culture and condemned their religion. Anti-immigrant, anti-Catholic hostility was so strong in Connecticut in the 1850s that the nativist American Party won control of Connecticut's government on a platform to resist foreign or Roman

Catholic political or cultural incursion. The state's six Irish militia units were disbanded in 1855, a policy the state regretted when the Civil War began six years later.

For all their desire to protect their cultural patrimony by keeping out the "other," the Yankee descendants of the Puritans faced a problem of their own making. Throughout the nineteenth century they were mounting the machine-tool revolution that transformed New England into the industrial powerhouse that was the envy of the world. The new water- and steam-powered factories—the armories, textile and paper mills, clockworks, munitions plants, and brass and silver works—all depended on a labor force far beyond local capacity. And so, for all their fears, the Yankees came to rely on outsiders to literally make their fortunes, and the floodgates of immigration opened to Italians, Poles, Swedes, Germans, Russians, Finns, and Lithuanians, who worked the factories, and even the farms the Yankees had depleted and abandoned. American migrants joined the throng, too: African-Americans from the South; French Canadians from the North; and Cubans, Puerto Ricans, and Jamaicans from the West Indies. By 1940, the homogenous world of the Puritan fathers was no more. And the transformation continues. Recent decades have seen the arrival of Asians and Spanish-speaking people of many different cultures and nationalities. Each group brings new ideas, presents new opportunities, and poses new challenges. Like the Puritans of old, some Connecticans resist immigrants' challenges to the status quo as a threat to our state's—and our nation's—future. But which Connectican among us can say he or she is not also descended from immigrants who once posed the same challenge to the status quo, the same "threat" to the future?

MARK TWAIN AND THE HISTORIC HOUSE PROBLEM

Why don't we smell cigar smoke when we tour the Mark Twain house?

Since the fieldstone farmhouse of Jonathan and Tryntje Hasbrouck in Newburgh, New York, was acquired by that state back in 1850, thus becoming America's first historic house museum, our nation has been blessed with an ever-expanding supply of homes-turned-historic sites intentionally preserved so they can teach the future about the past. Like the Hasbrouck House, which had been George Washington's headquarters during a long and critical phase of the American Revolution, most early house museums had direct connections to some famous figure. America's second and third historic house museums—The Hermitage, Andrew Jackson's plantation home (Nashville, Tennessee, 1856) and Mount Vernon, Washington's home (Vernon, Virginia, 1858)—solidified a trend of famous-person house preservation that continued right into the mid-1930s. By that time there were more than five hundred historic house museums in America, each associated with someone more or less renowned.

Since then, the rise of American automobile culture, expanded federal and state support for museums, and a much greater focus on history from the bottom up has led to a vast expansion in the sheer number of house museums, as well as the types of people they represent, which are now socially, economically, and racially far more diverse and much more ordinary.

Mark Twain was an inveterate chain smoker known to smoke fifteen to twenty cigars every day. 1906 Photograph. NEW YORK PUBLIC LIBRARY DIGITAL COLLECTION

Connecticut has long been a leader in historic house preservation. As one of this country's earliest settled colonies, we have an amazing inventory of historic house stock representing virtually every style, type, and period of house design. The State Historic Preservation Office lists more than 75,000 structures on the State Register of Historic Places, and the State Historic Preservation Council, on which I sit as State Historian, annually considers dozens more to be added to the list. Although only a very small minority of these places are officially set aside as historic house museums, nearly all of Connecticut's 169 towns have one or more historic homesites (Hartford has six) dedicated to showing us how life really was back then.

But do they? This historian's answer to that question is both yes and no, and to explain why I think that, this story will bore in on what is in all likelihood our state's most famous single historic house site, The Mark Twain House and Museum in Hartford. There you can see, in high relief, what is best about historic house museums, as well as why most of them suffer from what I call "The Historic House Problem."

In my career, I have promoted the Mark Twain House as one of the country's best examples of employing the home of a famous person to teach important lessons, not just about that person, but about the times and the world in which they lived. The way educators at the museum use this classic property and its residents, both the Clemens family and those who served them, to tell stories about Gilded Age values and class distinctions is exemplary. Best of all, it is done in the clear-eyed, tell-it-like-it-is (or was) spirit with which Twain himself reported on the world around him.

Still, much like almost every historic house I have ever visited, and I've been to many, the Twain House exhibits one characteristic that is anachronistic, unrealistic, and which, for me at least, detracts from an otherwise extraordinary experience. That flaw is that it's just too damned perfect. At the Mark Twain House—or almost any other famous person's historic showcase house—you always get the feeling that the supposed residents must be expecting the President for dinner. It's just so spic 'n' span, so carefully coiffed, so T-I-D-Y. I always find myself wondering, *What was it really like here? Where did Mark Twain drop his socks? Where are the marks Suzy colored on the wallpaper?*

One thing, for example, that we definitely never encounter on the Twain House tour that had to be one of the home's most noticeable characteristics to every visitor when Twain actually lived there, is the stench of cigar smoke that must have permeated every room, every curtain, and every piece of fabric.

Twain was no ordinary smoker. He was a deeply committed, unregenerate, professional pipe and cigar smoker who mastered his craft at an early age and continued to improve upon it for the next sixty-eight years. An 1885 description of Twain at age fifty in *The Critic, A Literary Weekly*, details his dedication to continuous process improvement in tobacco consumption.

He is an inveterate smoker, and smokes constantly while at his work, and indeed, all the time, from half-past eight in the morning to half-past ten at night, stopping only when at his meals. A cigar lasts him about forty minutes, now that he has reduced to an exact science the art of reducing the weed to ashes. So, he smokes from fifteen to twenty cigars every day. Some time ago he was persuaded to stop the practice and actually went a year and more; but he found himself unable to carry on important work . . . and it was not until he resumed smoking that he could do it. Since then, his faith in the cigar has not wavered.

In the great age of industrial production, Twain turned himself into a literary factory, belching cigar smoke as the words poured forth.

Wherever Twain went, tobacco smoke followed, and one of his greatest fears was to be where tobacco wasn't. In 1867, one day before sailing to Honolulu from British Columbia, Twain found a local wholesale tobacconist and bought three thousand cheroots and fifteen pounds of tobacco. That was about one cigar per nautical mile of the impending voyage. Later that afternoon he went back and bought three thousand more cheroots. That night, shortly after beginning a farewell public lecture, Twain stopped his talk in mid-stream, called his manager up to the stage, and said, "Pond, I fear that cigar place may close before I get through here. Go there now and get fifteen hundred more of those cheroots." In the morning, Twain, and his 7,500 cheroots plus his tobacco, happily embarked for the Sandwich Isles.

Another indication of his singular estimation of tobacco's value can be found in his Hartford-penned *A Connecticut Yankee in King Arthur's Court*. In that book, a young mechanic from East Hartford is knocked unconscious in an accident and wakes up in King Arthur's medieval English court, which the mechanic found fared pretty poorly in comparison with industrial Hartford. "There was no gas, there were no candles . . . there were no books pens, paper, or ink, and no glass in the openings they believed to be windows. But perhaps the worst of all was that there wasn't any sugar, coffee, tea . . . or tobacco."

Twain knew smoking was generally unhealthy, but he saw the habit as a kind of life vest that provided a wellness safety margin. He told the story of the doctor who visited an eighty-year-old woman who was in rapidly failing health. "You must stop drinking," he told her.

"I never touched a drop of alcohol in my life," she answered.

"Then you must immediately give up smoking," the doctor said.

"I have never, ever smoked," she said indignantly.

"Well, then," the doctor replied, "there's no way I can help you. You are a sinking ship, with no freight to throw overboard."

Twain saw some of his most insightful perceptions about the period in which he lived through a thick, blue, tobacco-smoke haze. He used cigars, for example, to underscore the hypocrisy of the new, branded consumerism that accompanied Gilded Age mass marketing. In writing about cigars, he once said:

People who claim to know say that I smoke the worst cigars in the world. They bring their own cigars when they come to my house. They betray an unmanly terror when I offer them a cigar; they tell lies and hurry away to meet engagements which they have not made when they are threatened with the hospitalities of my (cigar) box. Now then, observe what superstition, assisted by a man's reputation, can do. I was to have twelve personal friends to supper one night. One of them was as notorious for costly and elegant cigars as I was for cheap and devilish ones. I called at his house and when no one was looking borrowed a double handful of his very choicest; cigars which cost him forty cents apiece and bore red-and-gold labels in sign of their nobility. I removed the labels and put the cigars into a box with my favorite brand on it—a brand which those people all knew, and which cowed them as men are cowed by an epidemic. They took these cigars when offered at the end of the supper, and lit them and sternly struggled with them—in dreary silence, for hilarity died when the fell brand came into view and started around—but their fortitude held for a short time only; then they made excuses and filed out, treading on one another's heels with indecent eagerness; and in the morning when I went out to observe results the cigars lay all between the front door and the gate.

All except one—that one lay in the plate of the man from whom I had cabbaged the lot. One or two whiffs was all he could stand. He told me afterward that some day I would get shot for giving people that kind of cigar to smoke.

Twain's smoking habit also led him to decry the new statistical approaches to public health that emerged in the early progressive era. In an 1893 essay titled "The Moral Statistician," he berated those who "are always ciphering out how much a man's health is injured, and how much his intellect is impaired, and how many pitiful dollars and cents he wastes in course of ninety-two years indulgence in the fatal practice of smoking."

"Now I don't approve of dissipation," Twain added, "and I don't indulge in it either, but I haven't a particle of confidence in a man who has no redeeming petty vices."

"The problem with agenda-driven statisticians, Twain noted, "was that they never see more than one side of the story." As a result, he emphasized, "I don't want any of your statistics; I took your whole batch and lit my pipe with it."

To be sure, Twain's smoking habit ultimately cost him much. Yale professor William Lyon Phelps, a friend and frequent visitor of Twain, reported of a 1904 visit to the author, six years before Twain's death in his seventy-fifth year, that this was the first occasion Twain looked like an old man .... "The muscles in his right cheek were beyond his control, twitching constantly during the hour I spent with him, and there was something wrong with his right eye. He had not, however, cut short his allowance of tobacco, for he smoked three cigars while I was there."

To the end, Twain claimed he was the master of his smoking habit. "As an example to others," he proclaimed, "it has always been my rule never to smoke when asleep, and never to refrain when awake." Which brings me back to my critique of the perfectionist tendencies of historic house museums.

Those who tour the Mark Twain House today never get even a whiff of the house in the way German historians once called *wie es eigentlich gewesen ist*—that is, "as it really was." Perhaps, all things considered, that's for the best, a concession to the sensibilities of a different time. But for a purist like myself, this cleaned-up version of the Twain House is a bit of a sham, a "smoke and mirrors" presentation, without, of course, the smoke. If historic house museums really want us to know how it was way back then, they might start dropping a sock or two on the floor, leaving a faded stain on a tablecloth, and setting out a (preferably dirty) ashtray here and there.

FURTHER READING

For a lengthy but readable and informative biography of Twain, see Ron Powers's, *Mark Twain: A Life* (New York: Simon & Schuster, 2007).

The annotated *Autobiography of Mark Twain*, released in three volumes between 2010 and 2015 by the University of California Press, is an extraordinary self-examination by the author himself and a must-have reference for the serious inquirer.

Recent works on Twain's family life include: *Mark Twain, Livy Clemens, and Suzy Clemens, A Family Sketch and Other Private Writings*, ed. Benjamin Griffin (Berkeley: University of California Press, 2014); and Gary Scharnhorst's, *Twain in His Own Time: A Biographical Chronicle of His Life, Drawn from Recollections, Interviews and Memoirs by Family Friends and Associates* (Iowa City, University of Iowa Press, 2010).

On how the Twain house is used by educators, see "Historic House Museums," in *Teaching History with Museums: Strategies for K-12 Social Studies, 2nd Edition* by Alan S. Marcus, Jeremy D. Stoddard, and Walter W. Woodwards (New York: Routledge, 2017), 114–36.

On historic houses as a category see *Historic House Museums in the United States and the United Kingdom: A History* by Linda Young (Lanham, MD: Rowman & Littlefield, 2017).

For a recent reassessment of the role of house museums in American historical memory, see "Open House; Reimagining the Historic House Museum," a themed issue of the journal *The Public Historian* vol. 37 no. 2 (May 2015).

HENRY GREENE AND THE
FINAL UNDERGROUND

Gideon Welles's coachman was the first African-American to break the color line in Hartford's Cedar Hill Cemetery.

Almost all of us have at least one significant encounter with the underground. It comes at the end our lives, when the earth itself becomes our final resting place. When Henry Green was buried on June 17, 1911, in Hartford's Cedar Hill Cemetery, he became the first African-American deliberately interred there as opposed to having slipped by the authorities unnoticed, which was said to have happened a time or two in the undocumented past.

Born near Richmond, Virginia, in 1844, Henry (sometimes Henderson) was enslaved on the plantation of a man named Greene, from whom his last name was derived. The early days of the Civil War found Green (as he spelled it) no longer enslaved near Richmond but living in Washington, D.C, apparently as a free man. There he met Glastonbury native Gideon Welles, Abraham Lincoln's Secretary of the Navy and a pivotal figure in the president's cabinet.

Green was retained by Welles and worked for the Welles family for the next fifty years. During the Civil War he went into battle as body servant to Gideon's teenage son Thomas, charged personally by the boy's mother with looking out for her son's welfare. According to author Jean Mitchell Boyd, who knew the elderly Green when she was a child, in one heated wartime encounter, a panic-stricken Green fled the battlefield, but then he had a vision of Mrs. Welles motioning him to return, saying, "Go back, Henry, Go back!" Reportedly fearing her censure even more than the roar of the battlefield, Green returned to his duty and her son.

When Gideon Welles retired from service in Washington in 1869, he invited Green to Hartford as a servant to the Welles family. Henry accepted, and became one of three servants, (the only male and only African-American) along with two Irish sisters, Ann and Catherine Coghlin, at the Welles home in Hartford's fashionable Charter Oak Place

Henry Green and Thomas Glastonbury Welles. COURTESY JOHN BRAINARD.

neighborhood. Welles's occupation at the time was listed as "Gentleman" and his assets were valued at a very handsome $250,000.

In his half century with the Welles family, Green, who was himself, according to those who knew him, "aristocratic," "very intelligent though uneducated," as well as thrifty, jovial, and superstitious, served both as head servant and the family's coachman. Coachman was a high-status, and high-profile, position. This was an age when the bearing of coachmen strongly reflected on the reputations of the families who hired them.

Following the senior Welles's death in 1878, Green continued to work for Welles's son Thomas, now a colonel, and later for Thomas's son in New Jersey. In his will, Gideon Welles had left explicit instructions that Henry should be buried in the family plot in the prestigious and, at the time, all-white Cedar Hill Cemetery. Green died thirty-three years later in New Jersey. In accordance with the will, and presumably Henry Green's wishes as well, his body was returned to Hartford. The cemetery honored Welles's burial request, though he was buried in the family plot without a marker. The *Hartford Times* noted Henry's burial as "a somewhat unusual distinction."

Edward Valentine Mitchell, who wrote about Green a quarter century after his passing, said Green's interment provoked "a storm of protest, the Southern press being very emphatic in its view that the color line should be drawn after death as well as before." A search of Southern newspapers for 1911, however, did not show this to be the case. Southerners, it seemed, knew exactly what category to place Henry Green in, a category that had long been part of their "lost cause" mythology. Rather than seeing Henry Green as a man whose death had broken a color barrier, the *Richmond Times* saw him as just another "faithful servant," a black man who had taken such good care of the family that they wanted him near them in death.

In 2010, descendants of Gideon Welles had Henry Green's name inscribed on the front of the family's memorial obelisk.

CONNECTICUT'S THREE HUNDREDTH– A BIRTHDAY TO REMEMBER

Connecticut has had some great birthday parties, but none as big as the three hundredth.

As one of the United States's thirteen original colonies, Connecticut has a lot of past of which to be proud and celebrate. Down through the years, as major anniversaries of our state's founding have occurred, we've found a surprising variety of engaging and frequently spectacular ways to celebrate our state's birthday. None of them, though, can top the pull-out-all-the-stops, six-month-long commemoration that marked our state's 300th anniversary in 1935. This one set a high-water mark for us to aspire to as we move toward Connecticut's quadricentennial.

On a cold afternoon in February 2010, Governor M. Jodi Rell stepped out of the State Capitol accompanied by the Governor's Foot Guard, legislative leaders Don Williams, Chris Donovan, and Connecticut Secretary of State Denise Merrill, some fifty school children, invited state officials, and a military honor guard. To the rat-a-tat beat of the foot guard's drummer, Rell led this entourage down the snow-lined sidewalk, across the street, and up the granite stairs of the Connecticut State Library and Supreme Court. Greeted there by Connecticut Chief Justice Chase Rogers, Rell and company were led into Memorial Hall, where they joined dignitaries and historians representing Connecticut's 169 towns. After songs performed by state troubadour Lara Herscovitch and speeches by Rell and others, students eagerly consumed a large Connecticut-shaped cake, and the state's 375th anniversary celebration was officially underway.

Pulled together swiftly by a group of volunteers, the year-long commemoration of Connecticut's 375th birthday was, perhaps as it should have been in a time of economic challenge, a relatively circumscribed affair. The commemorative activities built around the theme "Connecticut. Industrious. Inventive. Enduring" (the brainchild of state librarian Kendall Wiggin) included the creation of a painting of the Charter Oak by landscape artist Mark Patnode, a student art contest featuring Connecticut landmarks, a governor's summer reading program featuring Connecticut authors, admission-free weekends at Connecticut's state parks and forests and at many Connecticut museums and historic sites, and a reprise of documentaries about Connecticut history on Connecticut Public Television. A special 375th anniversary stamp was placed in twenty-eight of the state forests' letter-boxing locations. Many local historical sites, service organizations, and schools also coordinated programming with the 375th celebration. The last, and perhaps most lasting, of these events was the opening in December of a new permanent exhibit about the state's history at the Connecticut Historical Society.

Funded completely by private donations, the 375th was more limited than previous commemorations, but the enthusiastic response it generated showed Connecticans' continuing appreciation for their state's history. That appreciation was even more evident during the larger, if somewhat controversial, celebration of the state's 350th anniversary.

Celebrated from May 1, 1985, through April 25, 1986, Connecticut's 350th anniversary began with a pre-event that was, at best, politically inexpedient. In late January 1985, three months before Governor William J. O'Neill officially declared the start of the state's 350th anniversary, he, along with state politicos, held what amounted to a de facto private kickoff at the Connecticut State Library. A select guest list of about three hundred officials, including seven living governors, members of the general assembly, persons of influence, and members of the media were invited to a gathering featuring a Connecticut cake, hors d'oeuvres, wine, the First Company of the Governor's Foot Guard, and the 175-member East Lyme High School Viking Band. The evening ended with a lavish fireworks display over the state capitol. Members of the public, unaware of the event, reacted to the sudden explosions by calling in a number of alarms, which in turn produced a brief, but sharp, reaction from some newspaper columnists, who bristled at the public's exclusion from the event.

Despite this false pre-start, the 350th celebration was launched again on May 1 with O'Neill's formal proclamation. At noon, officials in Connecticut's 169 towns released more than 50,000 balloons—350 per town—special 350th anniversary flags flew, bells rang, and cannons were fired. During the ensuing year, commemorations of all shapes and sizes took place. Vernon, for example, celebrated by holding a cow-chip (dried cattle poop) tossing contest. Beard-growing contests were held in Bristol, East Haven, and Bloomfield. Middlebury held an event showcasing Connecticut wines. Connecticut Celebration 350th, established by the State Department of Economic Development (DEC) to plan the commemorative events, awarded plaques to the oldest house in each town. The exhibition "The Great River: Art and Society of the Connecticut Valley, 1635–1920" enjoyed a four-month run at the Wadsworth Atheneum.

The penultimate event was a gala parade in New Haven, held April 19, 1986, that involved approximately seventeen-thousand marchers and featured a five-hundred-piece birthday cake, "The World's Biggest Milkshake," marchers from 130 Connecticut towns, and an array of clowns and mimes. Concluding the nearly year-long celebration was "History Day at the Old State House," an eighteenth-century military encampment held 350 years to the day after the first meeting of Connecticut's General Court. Governor O'Neill, standing among actors dressed as famous historic Connecticans, including Noah Webster and Prudence Crandall, officiated at the lowering of the 350th anniversary commemorative flag to the accompaniment of several gunpowder salutes.

Reaction to Connecticut's 350th celebration was decidedly mixed. While DEC chairman Peter Burns expressed pride that more than a million people had participated in one or more of the state's events, historians were not nearly so cheerful. Then State Historian Christopher Collier lamented the celebrations' circus-like atmosphere. "The people who ran it had no sense of history whatsoever," Collier said. "They missed a great opportunity to interest people in Connecticut's history and to inform them. These people don't even know what they're celebrating." Ellsworth Grant, president of the Connecticut Historical Society, seconded Collier's critique. "From a historical standpoint," he said, "the celebration was totally inadequate. I like to recall the quotation of Carl Sandburg that whenever a society or a nation perishes, one condition can always be found: They forgot where they came from."

One of Collier's criticisms of the 350th commemoration was that O'Neill chose an arbitrary and historically questionable year to celebrate the state's birthday. Collier's argument had substance, but O'Neill's choice also had good grounds.

The question of when to celebrate Connecticut's birth is a tricky one, first raised in 1928, when state historical organizations met to begin planning what was, most certainly, the greatest commemorative event in the state's history, the 300th anniversary. There were many options from which to choose, but no clear standout. Windsor was first settled by Anglo-traders in 1633, Wethersfield in 1634. The Fundamental Orders creating Connecticut's governmental institutions were passed in 1639. Other dates also presented themselves. "The question is a curiously complicated one," noted Yale professor Charles M. Andrews. "The dates of Connecticut's founding run through at least six years, from 1633 through to 1639, and just which point in that period of six years is to become the object of our veneration has not yet become known."

The question wasn't decided officially until 1934, when Tercentenary Commission member George Matthew Dutcher announced that 1935 had been selected for the celebration because in 1635 "the beginning of settlement had been made" at all three original Connecticut River towns and a fort had been established at Saybrook. He noted that although civil government for Connecticut wasn't created until 1636, a 1936 Connecticut celebration would conflict with Rhode Island's tercentenary events. Therefore, 1935 would mark Connecticut's 300th. This set a precedent. Governor O'Neill, following the lead of the Tercentenary Commission, chose 1985 as the date of our state's 350th, and Governor Rell chose 2010 as the 375th.

There was no official celebration of the state's 325th, as it fell during the election year 1960 and also possibly because the magnitude of the 300th still rang with intimidating force in people's memories. Despite the Great Depression, Connecticut's six-month tercentenary celebration caught the imagination of an entire citizenry. At its conclusion, the *Hartford Courant* editors wrote, "It would be hard to find anyone in this state, free, sane, well, and over five, who has not participated in the festivities." Coming at the end of an era of great historical pageantry, in the midst of the colonial revival period, and at a time when the eugenics movement had increased people's interest in their historical and genealogical roots, Connecticut's tercentenary channeled all these strands of contemporary culture into a great outpouring of historical celebration. Seven years in the planning and funded by the Connecticut General Assembly to the tune of $125,000, the tercentenary generated hundreds of local events across the state, significant cultural and educational programs, and several star productions that may remain unique in our history.

While Windsor and Wethersfield had whetted the state's appetite for commemoration with major local tercentenary celebrations in 1933 and 1934, the statewide celebration of Connecticut's founding was officially bracketed between two historically significant dates in 1935: April 26, the 199th anniversary of the first meeting of the General Court, and October 12, Columbus Day.

Governor Wilbur Cross's opening of the celebration set the precedent for future commemorative inaugurals in form, but on a much grander scale than they would achieve. At noon on the 26th, while bells throughout the state pealed and car horns honked, Cross, accompanied by the foot guard, the lieutenant governor, the supreme court justices, members of the general assembly, the governor's staff, and the color bearers and band of Putnam's Phalanx marched smartly from the capitol to the Bushnell auditorium, where 3,300 representatives of fraternal, civic, military, and historical societies and the general public waited to greet them. All sang "America" and, after a poetic invocation, greetings were received from the governors of Vermont and New Hampshire, a keynote address reviewing the state's constitutional history was given by Chief Justice William Maltbie, and the self-deprecating Governor Cross officially opened the tercentenary celebration. He praised the state's history, while noting his own less-than-perfect ties to Connecticut's Puritan past: One Cross ancestor was fined for selling wine without a license, while another obtained Connecticut's first divorce, from a wife "who preferred to live in England."

In a pattern reflected throughout the tercentenary period, the official kickoff was only one of many commemorative events held on April 26. Earlier, the governor had received the first official tercentenary postage, a three-cent stamp engraved with an image of the Charter Oak. At the same time, officials at Aetna Casualty unveiled a commemorative map showing all the state's highways and featuring historical sites. At the White House, First Lady Eleanor Roosevelt attended the planting of a scion of Connecticut's Charter Oak on the White House lawn by two Connecticut Girl Scouts, and in Simsbury, the tercentenary celebration announced the forthcoming publication of a short history of Simsbury.

For the next six months Connecticut was abuzz with events celebrating its Puritan and industrial history. Almost every town sponsored some kind of ceremony. Historical societies hosted exhibits, and patriotic organizations published pamphlets. Monuments were unveiled and plaques installed. The state was awash in historical reflection.

Highlights among the hundreds of tercentenary activities included a June 1 choral concert of more than three thousand singers from seventy-three state glee clubs (accompanied by a one-hundred-piece orchestra) before an audience of more than fifteen thousand at the Yale Bowl. In September, more than four hundred thousand Connecticut school children participated in Connecticut Education Day, which focused attention on the study of Connecticut history. The tercentenary commission issued an expansive series of short monographs on colonial Connecticut history; these are still considered vital references. The *Hartford Times* published in hardback a three-volume comic-book-style history of Connecticut.

Three early-October events brought the half-year of festivities to a climax. The first was the Tercentenary Industrial Exhibition, held at the state armory in Hartford. Dedicated "to the genius of the Connecticut Yankee," the thirty-one groups of exhibits highlighted the state's history of industrial invention and manufacturing leadership. Connecticut manufacturers displayed more than ten thousand product lines with more than seven hundred thousand Connecticut-produced items. The "pageant of progress" drew more than two hundred thousand adult visitors and attracted as many as seventy-five thousand Connecticut students.

The second of the final weeks' culminating events combined early history with recognition of immigration's transformative effect. "The Making of America in Connecticut," a three-and-a-half-hour pageant incorporating historical reenactment, tableaux, dance numbers, and singing, played on The Bushnell stage for three nights to packed houses of more than three thousand viewers each night. Subtitled "A Pageant of the Races," the extravaganza blended the Puritan past with the immigration-transformed future, offering Connecticut's newcomers inclusion through assimilation.

"The Making of America in Connecticut," with six hundred cast members, was the largest performance ever staged at The Bushnell. The production was too large for the theater's facilities; actors had to wait at the state office building across the street until just before their performances, then hurry over to the theater. The pageant, which played to continuous applause from delighted audiences, presented the "story of the state's

The pageant "The Making of America in Connecticut" with a cast of over 600 people, was the largest performance ever staged at Hartford's Bushnell Performing Arts Center. FINAL BULLETIN STATE OF CONNECTICUT TERCENTENARY COMMISSION HARTFORD CT PUBLIC DOMAIN DECEMBER 17, 1935

cultural development under the influence of many nations" and recounted the state's history in four segments. The first three ("A New Colony in the Making," "A New Nation in the Making," and "The Union is Preserved") depicted significant moments in Connecticut history acted largely by costumed civic leaders and descendants of early Connecticans. These were followed by a transitional dance number titled "Connecticut Rivers and Industry," in which one hundred women in blue costumes waved their arms, imitating Connecticut's powerful rivers, while men moving in stylized mechanical fashion among them symbolized the development of industry along those rivers. This was followed by the play's longest section, "A New State in the Making," intended to show "all the foreign influences that have been blended into ours." The eight numerically largest groups of late-nineteenth- and early-twentieth-century industrial revolution immigrants to Connecticut—French Canadian, Czechoslovakian, Italian, Lithuanian, German, Swedish, Polish, and Russian—each presented a performance showing ways in which their culture had enriched Connecticut. The Germans offered a 150-voice Saengerbund Chorus, while the Italians had 50 young women performing "O Sole Mio." Czechs performed folk dances, and the Polish contingent recreated Thaddeus Kosciusko presenting credentials to George Washington.

The play's finale featured nineteen families of four representing each of the "races" in Connecticut (including the original Puritan stock) marching from the back of the theater to the stage to sign the Pact of Connecticut, a document promising the state a glowing future based on unity, good will, and understanding. While Albanians, Armenians, Danes, French, Hungarians, Irish, Norwegian, Portuguese, Russian, Scottish, Swedish, and Ukrainian families were invited to join the eight largest "races," neither the indigenous people of Connecticut nor African-Americans were included. They were not completely left out of the tercentenary celebration, however. The Mohegan Tribe celebrated during its August wigwam festival, and African-Americans held a well-attended musical performance in honor of the tercentenary at Hartford's State Theater. Still, Connecticut's Pageant of the Races excluded both groups.

The culminating activity of the tercentenary was the largest parade the state had ever seen. Twenty thousand marchers, more than one hundred

Tercentenary Parade Draws Greatest Crowd
to Hartford

The Tercentenary Parade drew nearly one-third of the state's population to Hartford. FINAL BULLETIN STATE OF CONNECTICUT TERCENTENARY COMMISSION HARTFORD CT PUBLIC DOMAIN DECEMBER 17, 1935

floats and thirty bands, and nearly five hundred schoolchildren passed before a reviewing stand of dignitaries and celebrities from a dozen states, including the heavyweight boxing champion Gene Tunney. The patriotically themed parade focusing on Connecticut history lasted nearly three hours. More than four hundred thousand people—almost a third of the state's population—watched, and in downtown Hartford telephone directories became scarce overnight as observers in office buildings shredded them into confetti to shower on marchers. The themes of the top three prize-winning floats—first place went to The First Thanksgiving Dinner, second place to The Viking Ship, and third place to The Pioneer—underscored the celebration's historical focus. One columnist noted it was "a parade worth waiting 300 years for."

A costume ball was held in New Haven later that night, and with the observance of Connecticut Sabbath the next morning (in which many churches conducted services using historical liturgies), the tercentenary celebration officially ended. In the afterglow of the celebration, Tercentenary Commission Chair Colonel Samuel Herbert Fisher received encomiums both for the scale of the events and his genius for local initiative. The *Hartford Courant* noted that the tercentenary had increased tourism, produced remarkable memorials, and stimulated important research. But the greatest benefit the *Courant* found was that "knowledge and respect for the founders and builders of Connecticut have been deepened," and respect for the "culture, skills and qualities… brought into Connecticut by the successive waves of migrations of immigrants" had greatly increased. This in turn had produced a "determination to work together for the future prosperity and progress of the state."

Connecticut's tercentenary celebration was indeed one for the record books. Today, as we are just beginning to anticipate the milestone quadricentennial anniversary of our state coming up in 2035, we might do well to study carefully what they did, adapt it for a world and a state that is very different today than a century ago, and resolve now to make our 400th anniversary just as spectacular and memorable as—and a bit more inclusive than—our 300th.

FURTHER READING

The records of the Connecticut Tercentenary Commission are at the Connecticut State Library in Hartford. Notable products of the Commission are the 30 June 1936, *Report to the Governor,* summarizing the statewide events, Connecticut Tercentenary Commission, *Report to the Governor,* 30 June 1936 (Hartford: The Commission, 1936).

Many individual towns also documented their participation in the tercentenary. Check with town libraries and historical societies.

SWEET DEMOCRACY—
THE HISTORY OF THE CONNECTICUT
ELECTION CAKE

With elections leaving people with a bitter taste in their mouths, perhaps it's time to revive a classic Connecticut tradition.

I suspect most people would agree that elections in recent years, at least some of them, have left people on both sides of the political aisle with a bad taste in their mouths. That's why it might be time to revive one of our state's oldest, and for centuries most-time-honored traditions—the Connecticut Election Cake.

What's an election cake, and why is it a Connecticut tradition? An election cake was a big, rich, fruit, spice, and sugar yeast cake baked up in huge quantities and served to all comers during the festivities surrounding first our colony's, and later our state's, annual elections. How big was a Connecticut Election Cake? This ingredient list from the election cake recipe in Amelia Simmons's *American Cookery*—the first American cookbook, published in Hartford in 1796, should give you some idea.

> *Thirty quarts of flour, 10 pounds butter, 14 pounds sugar, 12 pounds raisins, 3 dozen eggs, one pint of wine, one-quart brandy, 4 ounces cinnamon, 4 ounces fine coriander seed, 3 ounces ground allspice; milk, yeast . . . [and a very strong arm.]*

Obviously, put all those ingredients together into one cake and you've got something bigger than any oven, especially those beehive hearth ovens from the colonial era, could possibly handle. The ingredients, once made into batter, were formed into loaves—twelve to a batch—and baked into more manageable portions. But the amount of ingredients Simmons called for gives an idea of how much Election Cake was needed by the average preparer, and how important the cake figured into both official and unofficial election festivities.

The story of how Election Cake became a Connecticut tradition goes all the way back to the days of the Puritans. One of the things that made the Puritans so pure was that they didn't believe in the annual round of Catholic and Anglican holidays. They didn't celebrate Christmas or Easter or any of the numerous Saints' and Festival days, and for them, New Year's Day came on March 26—so no midnight kisses or dropping ball, either.

While they rejected all of these supposedly invented occasions for mirth, they did believe that in the year 1662 Connecticut, for reasons still not exactly clear, got something that very much was worth celebrating: a royal charter from King Charles II that gave the Connecticut colony virtual independence more than a century before the American Revolution. Unlike Massachusetts and Virginia and the other royally governed American colonies, Connecticut could make its own laws, and more important, elect its own leaders, without royal oversight. This right to choose their own leaders was seen from the start as fundamentally important and distinctive, worth celebrating and worth protecting. Our state's most iconic legend—the story of the Charter Oak—where colony officials supposedly hid the 1662 charter in the hollow of an ancient oak tree rather than give it up to a crown official demanding its surrender, was all about keeping and protecting the right to choose those who were in authority.

So, it's not surprising that on those days when Connecticans gathered to choose their leaders—back then Election Day took place in early May—these otherwise celebration-starved Puritans found reason to celebrate, and what better way to do so than with cake—and lots of it.

We know Connecticans were feasting on Election Day cakes well before the American Revolution, because the colonial records tell us so. In May 1771, for example, just after the election festivities had been concluded, the general assembly approved a bill for £2 7s 9d (two pounds, seven shillings, and nine pence) for "raisins, cloves, mace, sugar, &c. for the cake," and a second bill for £2 0s 5d (two pounds and five pence) paid to Mrs. Leslie for "baking." It is difficult to meaningfully convert colonial pounds, shillings, and pence to today's dollars and cents, but to give you an idea of how much purchasing power this involved, a pound of cheese mentioned in the same bill cost 4 pence. Using that for comparison, the ingredients for the election cake cost roughly 95 pounds of cheese and Mrs. Leslie's labor to bake it another 73 pounds of cheese. One Election Cake equaled 168 pounds of cheese.

If incorporating Election Cake into the ceremonies was an important Connecticut tradition before the American Revolution, it became even more important after. In the aftermath of gaining independence, when the newly somewhat-United States were trying to figure out how to make a government of independent states work, Connecticut, which already had 116 years of independent government under its belt by the time of the Constitutional Convention, proudly held itself up as the model for the United States to follow. The Connecticut Compromise—that decision to make representation in congress proportional in the House and equal in the Senate—was one example of this. So was Amelia Simmons *American Cookery*, that first American cookbook, published in 1796, which food historians have recently argued was part of a coordinated post-revolutionary print campaign to sell Connecticut's political order to both men and women throughout America.

As Simmons's cookbook and Connecticans themselves spread across the country to the new lands in the American West, the Election Cake tradition went with them. Election Cake recipes appear in early cookbooks in states across the nation; and they are abundantly found in the manuscript cookbooks left by individuals in our historical societies and archives. Catherine Beecher, renowned educator and the sister of Harriet Beecher Stowe, author of *Uncle Tom's Cabin*, included a recipe for Old Hartford Election Cake in her best-selling books on household economy. An election cake recipe is even featured in an issue of *Godey's Ladies Book*, one of the most popular magazines of its day, in 1863.

Reading these works, a few things become crystal clear. Election Cakes were central to the election rituals in many places, but especially here in Connecticut. And, they were not just baked for the big events in places like Hartford but in homes all around the state. Making an extraordinary Election Cake, perhaps with one's own special ingredient or unique mixing process, became a point of honor with many home keepers. Having a reputation for making delicious Election Cakes became a competitive source of status.

Election Cake from an updated recipe. COURTESY MARIE WOODWARD

The long excerpt below, from an article printed in the *Hartford Courant* at the end of April in 1867, titled "A Hartford Lady's Reminiscences," shows just how large Election Day and its dedicated cake loomed in early Connecticut's political and social circles. The unnamed reminiscing lady takes her readers on a journey back from the post–Civil War days in which she was writing to Connecticut of a half century before, where she talks about the prominence and pervasiveness of election cakes, even as she gives us a remarkably vivid sense of all the pomp and circumstance that was Election Day.

> *Will somebody who remembers it all tell about Election in old times in Hartford? Tell how gay it was, and how everybody looked forward to it; how the country people poured in, 'going down to Hartford to see 'lection'; how every house was in apple pie order, summer arrangements all completed. . . . There was a grand ball in the evening then;*

and in those times too there was an 'Election Sermon' preached at the meeting house, before the Governor and the Legislature, and grand singing by the choir, who in costumes something like those now worn at the Old Folks concerts, gave Old Hundred and various national anthems. . . . 'Election time. Oh! The quantities of cake! A batch of election cake was twelve loaves, but there had to be more than one batch, and plenty of sponge cake with it.

"Day before election!" That was a delightful occasion, the opening of the ceremonies. You didn't wear your white frock, but your new calico, best bonnet and red shoes; and you went down street to see the Governor come into town. . . . The streets were crowded; the bells rang: the principal citizens rode to meet His Excellency just out of town, and join in the parade. The horse guard came first, and I can hear now those first bugle notes, and the shout, "The troopers are coming!" Oh! How splendid it was to see them ride along on their prancing horses. . . . And, here's the foot guard, all in buff and scarlet. The Governor is in plain black, with only a cockade in his hat. "There he comes; that's the Governor, there with his hat off. Is he of mortal mold?" The [Governor's] council comes next, and all the militia companies, in gorgeous array, and then the citizens— up and down Main street and then to deposit the Governor at the hotel and salute him as he stands on the steps. But it was solid satisfaction to feel at night, that that was only the beginning, and that "tomorrow is 'lection.

The sun usually keeps 'lection and is up bright and early. The best clothes go on as soon as possible after breakfast, white frock to be sure, new bonnet, open work flat with a wreath of roses, pink sash and the red shoes. . . . Lots of money to spend—children could have a cent any time they asked for it 'lection day.

And cake! A big piece, not a slice, every time they run into the house; nobody dared refuse them. It stands ready, all day, for wagons full of country friends and acquaintances come to see the parade; all must eat loaf cake and tell what luck they had with theirs. If you go to the neighbors, you must eat a piece, of course. It is next in importance to the Governor and the stars and stripes; and wherever there is a Connecticut man or woman—man especially—there is one who will not refuse a piece of 'lection cake , for the sake of its associations, not to *say that it is about the best cake "for a steady diet", that can be made.*

'Lection day! As long as I live and wherever I go, I never shall see anything finer. Nothing can surpass the parade on election day. Who else will tell some more? All about making the cake; all the ceremonies attending it; the care and anxiety, the waiting and watching, sitting up at night.

The wonderful lady who wrote that piece two years after the Civil War ended was looking back wistfully from a world transformed. During the 1800s, as Connecticut industrialized, welcomed people from many new nations, broke its official ties to the old Puritan church, and experienced the sectional divide that led to the American Civil War, some of Connecticut's time-honored election day traditions—riding out to meet the new governor as he made his way into Hartford, and parading behind the state's ministers to hear an election sermon in the First Congregational Church—fell by the wayside. But the election cake remained a steady, and delicious, habit.

Connecticut continued to change, expand, and grow in size, economic strength, and manufacturing might. By the 1870s, it had become an industrial colossus. A new seat of government was needed, and in preparation for its upcoming move to a brand-new state capitol building, and to meet its increasingly demanding role in public affairs, the general assembly decided in 1876 to change the start of its sessions from May to early January, beginning in 1877.

People recognized right away that the new January date threatened one of the most venerable of Connecticut's election traditions—the election parade. A journalist lamenting the switch of Election Day to midwinter, said: "The coming election parade [of May 1876] is likely to be the last that will take place in Connecticut. The governor's guard are not armed with snow shovels, nor does the rubber boot at all approach the elegant calves [leather boots] of the Mayday march. In ordinary January weather people do not gather for . . . parades. And it is an old and very interesting custom that we are cutting loose from." The newspaperman went on to describe all the old Election Day traditions that had fallen by the wayside over time. He saw the decision to change the date of the legislative session opening as the final blow. But not one without at least a modicum of hope.

"Though the sermon has gone out, though the parade is going out, though the whole institution may become an element of the past, one feature of it will always remain, and that is the Election Cake.... Lovers of it when it is just right say no other cake equals it.... It is only necessary to add, that nobody can make it but an old Connecticut housekeeper, and that each housekeeper and her circle of adherents know that she can make it a deal better than any of her rivals."

Continue the Election Cake did, not just in Connecticut but elsewhere. In 1889, for example, a dozen years after Connecticut moved its state capitol, Ellen Terry Johnson of Holderness, New Hampshire, published *Hartford Election Cake and Other Receipts: Chiefly from Manuscript Sources*, in which she captured the personal election cake recipes of eleven of Hartford's most famous domestic homemakers and cake bakers. And while it shows there was still considerable interest in and practice of election cake baking, her election cake recipe book may have foreshadowed the cake's last hurrah. For since Johnson's time, Connecticut's greatest and most delicious election tradition has all but faded from memory.

But perhaps this is exactly the right time for the Connecticut Election Cake to make its comeback. At this moment when American politics seems so divisive and bitter, wouldn't it be great if a cohort of culinary Connecticans—men and women equally this time—joined together to use their ovens to remind people that democracy, the right to choose the people who rule your government, is a sweet privilege indeed. And what better way could there be to celebrate sweet democracy than to bring back the tradition of the Connecticut Election Cake?

Ideally, in every election in every one of our state's 169 towns, voters (and future voters) would be invited by friends, neighbors, and poll workers, too, to enjoy a slice of non-partisan Election Cake—maybe from some of the old recipes and from some brand-new ones, as well—as a reminder that the vote they cast is in many ways, the sweetest gift Connecticut and the United States of America offers its citizens. Maybe this is just a state historian's dream, but if so, it's a very, very sweet one indeed.

A MODERN ELECTION CAKE RECIPE

⅔ cup warm water (105°F to 115°F)

1 (¼ ounce) package active dry yeast

Pinch sugar

4 cups all-purpose flour

1 teaspoon baking powder

2 teaspoons cinnamon

½ teaspoon salt

½ teaspoon ground ginger

¼ teaspoon nutmeg

1 cup (2 sticks) unsalted butter, softened

2 cups firmly packed brown sugar

1 cup buttermilk

1 tablespoon vanilla

2 large eggs, slightly beaten

1 cup golden raisins

¼ cup finely chopped dried fruit (optional)

For the Glaze

1 cup confectioners' sugar

2 tablespoons of whiskey

½ teaspoon vanilla

DIRECTIONS

Butter and flour in a bundt pan

Put warm water in the bowl of a stand mixer. Add yeast, sprinkling it to cover the top of the water. Sprinkle a pinch of sugar on top of the yeast and allow it to stand for 5 minutes.

Mix the flour with the baking powder, cinnamon, salt, ginger, and nutmeg, then set aside.

After yeast has dissolved and is beginning to bubble, add 1 cup of flour mixture, stirring it in thoroughly. Add butter and mix well.

Next add sugar, buttermilk and vanilla and mix until well combined.

Add the eggs and mix until just combined.

Finally, mix in the flour, reserving 1 tablespoon. If desired, toss the dried fruits in tablespoon of flour and then fold them into the cake batter.

Put the batter into the prepared bundt pan. Loosely cover the pan with a towel and allow to rise for about 1½ hours.

Bake cake for 50 to 60 minutes or until a cake tester comes out clean. Place pans on wire rack to cool, then carefully remove from pan after a few minutes.

Glaze:
In a medium-sized bowl, whisk the confectioners' sugar, whiskey, and vanilla until smooth. Drizzle over the top of the cake when completely cool.

Adapted from a Serious Eats (Fannie Farmer) recipe (www.christinascucina.com/election-cake) Thanks to Dotti Dori and Harriet Wyse

GOVERNOR JOHN N. DEMPSEY, SON OF CAHIR

John Dempsey was one of Connecticut's most successful and popular governors. Thank a little Irish town called Cahir.

John Noel Dempsey may have been the best governor Connecticut ever had. He certainly was one of the most popular governors in our state's history, and one of the most unique. He served as governor for nine years, eleven months, and sixteen days, from January 21, 1961, to January 6, 1971. That was longer than any governor had stayed in office for nearly a century and a half. When he *did* retire from office, it was *his* choice to step down, not the decision of the people at the ballot box. Dempsey was that rarest of politicians, a man who even his opponents liked and admired. He possessed great charm and fast wit, was a gifted orator, a tireless worker for the causes he believed in, and he was an extraordinary manager. He was a family man, too. Not in the smile-for-the-cameras sense we get from many politicians today, but in the next-to-God-my-family-matters-most sense that reflected the deepest convictions of this remarkable man. He was a person, above all, with a great compassion for humanity and a sense that God put him on this earth to do good. At a time when public cynicism about all politicians and the political process is at unprecedented highs, such sentiments undoubtedly sound at best naïve and possibly even pandering. But I am a historian, trained to search out the motivations and complexities and self-serving characteristics of those in power. After months spent researching the life of Governor Dempsey, poring through his official archives and personal papers, and talking with those who knew and worked with him, it really does seem that John Noel Dempsey was

John Dempsey was the only foreign-born governor of Connecticut since the colonial period. Photo courtesy the Dempsey family. COURTESY ED DEMPSEY

the real deal, a good man, who cared deeply about the people, and became one of the state's best governors.

But he was also a son of the little Tipperary County town of Cahir, Ireland, through and through. Dempsey was the first immigrant elected governor of Connecticut since the colonial days of the 1600s, when almost all white Connecticans were immigrants, and he wore his Irish roots with extreme pride. Throughout his life, he traced the foundations of both his character and his political success to his boyhood in Cahir; not just to the faith, friends, community, and land that made Tipperary a good place for a boy to be raised, but also to specific experiences that were both profoundly personal and profoundly memorable and that helped a boy understand what mattered in a man's life. This story reviews the political life of John Noel Dempsey in Connecticut, reflecting on how specific experiences he had in Ireland shaped both the person and the politician he later became.

One of those experiences happened on the very day ten-year-old John and his parents, Ned and Nell Dempsey, left, or rather tried to leave, Ireland for America. After the final packing of suitcases, tearful farewells to friends and family, and more than a parting glance at the town none of them expected to ever see again, the Dempsey family made their way to Cork and boarded a White Star Line ship for passage to America. This was during the summer of 1925. In 1970, as he neared the end of his governorship, Dempsey described what happened that day.

> We were actually aboard ship, ready to sail, when a complication arose in the form of a demand for a much higher fee than we had been led to expect for the health certificates we were required to have.
>
> Convinced, and no doubt rightly so, that an attempt was being made to victimize him, my father, a veteran of many years of army service, refused to pay. Instead, we disembarked, returned to our County Tipperary home in Cahir, and the ship sailed without us.
>
> Back in Cahir, my father got in touch with a civic leader of his acquaintance. The difficulty about the health certificate fee dissolved like magic, and ten days later we were on our way again, this time for good.

Could it be that this experience gave me, a ten-year-old boy, his first inkling of the way in which a person in a position of responsibility can be of help to others? Quite possibly.

Certainly, throughout his life in office, Dempsey recognized both the ability and the responsibility of political leaders to use their influence to help meet people's needs, especially those who could not help themselves, or people who could not get responsive service elsewhere. Strikingly, one of his first acts in public life, and the one that launched his political career, was an act somewhat reminiscent of his father's that day in 1925, when he had disembarked the ship in Cork and brought his family back to Cahir to seek help in taking care of a difficulty.

As was true of many Irish immigrants, the Dempseys came in America to a place where they already had family, in this case the textile mill town of Putnam, Connecticut, where Nell Dempsey's sisters and a brother lived. There, his father found work in the Putnam Woolen Mills not unlike the supervisory work he had performed at the Going and Smith Flour mill in Cahir. Nell made the family home in a rented house from which they could walk to St. Mary's Catholic Church, and John, the future governor, settled easily into the Putnam school system. He was a natural athlete, and, in addition to excelling in debate and literature, he became captain of both the high school basketball and the track teams. After graduation he hitched a daily ride with other students to Providence College, where, as a freshman, he set an intercollegiate track record for the half-mile run that wasn't broken for a generation. His freshman year at Providence proved to be his only year there, though. His father became quite ill and, combined with the effects of the Great Depression, John found it necessary to take a job at the Woolen Mills, too—for $22.50 a week.

Then he encountered the streetlight that changed his life. As Bill Stanley, a fellow Irish-American state senator from Norwich who became a close friend of the governor's told it, "Twas the street light you know, that he couldn't get fixed that brought John Dempsey into politics." The streetlight near the Dempsey home had burned out, and calls and letters trying to get the bulb replaced didn't get any response. So, just as his father had done back in Cahir, young John took his case to the persons who could help with his difficulty. Not yet twenty-one, he appeared before the Putnam board of alderman and made a speech asking for help. The aldermen were so impressed with the young man's eloquence, they not only ordered the light fixed, they suggested that young Dempsey should run for alderman at the next election. And so, at just twenty-one years old, John Dempsey entered public service. As a person in power, he would be the catalyst to get things done for those who weren't for the next thirty-five years.

Over the years, Dempsey held every elective office the town of Putnam had, including serving as mayor for six terms. He was elected to the General Assembly of Connecticut three times, and in his third term he was chosen by his peers to be the party leader of his chamber. The reporters covering the General Assembly voted him "the most able lawmaker in the house." He became executive assistant to Connecticut Governor Abraham Ribicoff in 1955. Then, in the 1958 election, Ribicoff chose Dempsey to run as his lieutenant governor. Ribicoff knew then, that even if reelected, he would be deeply engaged in helping John F. Kennedy run for the presidency, and he told colleagues he "wanted someone as lieutenant governor who was close to him, someone he could leave the store in charge of . . . ." That is exactly what he did. When John F. Kennedy became America's first Irish Catholic President in 1960, his first cabinet appointment was Abraham Ribicoff, who resigned as governor and went to Washington as Secretary of Health, Education, and Welfare. He handed the keys to the store, as it were, to Lieutenant Governor John Noel Dempsey, who stepped into the governor's office on January 21, 1961. A political wag at the time described Dempsey as "the understudy with the big chance." This was to some extent true, but Dempsey knew it was his big chance and he made the very most of it. Described as coming into the office "a little unsure of himself," he had, by his reelection campaign twenty months later, transformed himself into a sure-footed political orator, a powerful speaker with a long list of accomplishments to his credit. He defeated a strong competitor to win the governorship in his own right in 1962, and four years later he won a resounding victory over another popular Republican opponent in a year Republicans swept the elections in all surrounding states. His accomplishments were measured in a lot more than ballot box numbers, too. By the time Dempsey announced he would step down from the governor's office in January 1971, he had presided over a complete transformation in the government of Connecticut. Whereas it had previously been a state known for its general frugal tightfistedness, under Dempsey, Connecticut became a state singularly known for its commitment to help those who could not help themselves.

If Dempsey's belief that those in power have a duty to help those who are not came from his boyhood shipboard experience with his father, it is equally likely that his *total* commitment to those in need came from his mother and another Cahir experience. Hers was a simple and spontaneous—if dangerous and character-defining—act. One high-water spring morning Ellen (Nell) Looby Dempsey—was walking beside the Suir (pronounced "sure") River, which flows through the center of Cahir, when a small child fell into the rushing water and was instantly swept into the fast-flowing current. The child couldn't swim and neither could Nell, but without a second's hesitation she waded out into the river to save the child, and succeeded, though she herself couldn't swim a stroke and might have died in the attempt.

Like his mother, John Dempsey launched out boldly to help those in need, and did so fearlessly throughout his career. As governor, he expanded facilities for the intellectually disabled, the handicapped, and the mentally ill; he set up new Departments of Children and Youth, and of the Aging. The existence of such governmental social service agencies are taken for granted today, but in the 1960s they represented radical innovations in ideas about the government's responsibilities toward the unfortunate. John Noel Dempsey was a great champion of that new approach, in both word and deed.

> *The physically and mentally ill, the disabled and the handicapped, the blind, the deaf, the mentally retarded, the helpless and the needy, are, even as we are, children of Almighty God," he told the General Assembly in his 1966 State of the State address. "The kind of Connecticut we have created and which we want to maintain and improve, will not permit them to suffer neglect.*

What greater reward can we know," he asked, "than the light which our help brings to the eyes of the crippled child? Will we measure their needs in the terms of cold budget figures? Or will we acknowledge that the enrichment which they bring into our lives far outweighs the cost?

Dempsey said it, and he meant it. One of the ways he showed the strength of his commitment to those with intellectual disabilities was through an event that made some of those around him at the time quite uncomfortable, at least initially. Alan Olmstead, a columnist for the Manchester, Connecticut, *Herald,* wrote about this event in words that reveal just how radical John Dempsey's commitment was, for the time, to those other people would have preferred to put out of sight and mind.

Olmsted had been invited to one of the traditional Christmas parties for the press held at the governor's mansion. "But this year," he noted, "something new had been added. There was on the walls . . . a new display of art. And the art display, in picture after picture, was art produced by inmates of state mental institutions. Some was perhaps elemental and hopeless, artistically speaking, and some seemed very impressive. . . [but] we wouldn't know from art standards," Olmsted wrote. The art, however, was not the thing that stood out at this event.

"What we did notice was the extraordinary interest and pride with which Governor Dempsey and his first lady Mary Dempsey display these paintings on their walls, not merely for their visual interest, but for the fact that they have been produced by lives which, in another day and age, might have been considered hopelessly blank and lost. This represents a breakout from the closed-door policy of other days."

The art exhibit was not the only break-out event that occurred that night. Still more surprises awaited the press corps. There was, Olmsted continued:

. . . at the Governor's parties, some of the expected food. And then there was dessert."

Dessert was the presentation of a Christmas pageant acted and sung by inmates of the Mansfield State Training School. Governor

*Dempsey must have anticipated and felt the sudden drop in tempera-
ture of his holiday audience as he announced what we were about
to encounter. . . . He must have understood, too, that some of us, not
zealous to see the less happy side of humanity, had great difficulty in
looking toward the performers then presented to us.*

*But we think the Governor knew also, that as the performance
and presence of these fellow human beings continued, some of us might
grow stronger, and be able to open our eyes and turn our heads, and
we would be better for it.*

*And certainly, he knew that to make us look at this, and . . . go
beyond our sense of shock to a sense of gratitude and shared humanity
was a fit and proper thing to do in a season named after Christmas.*

*It is in the intensity of his regard for these unfortunates, in the
passion of his determination . . . to promote every possible ounce of public responsibility for them and feeling with them, that John Dempsey,
as man and governor, is going to leave his own very special mark on
Connecticut.*

And leave his mark he did. Though he did not do it alone. If his
mother inspired him to take risks for the needy, John Dempsey's wife,
Connecticut First Lady Mary Frey Dempsey, nurtured that inspiration
throughout his life. John and Mary met during his senior year in high
school, when she was, as he had been, a newcomer to Putnam, where her
parents worked in the silk mill. Six years later, in 1940, they married, and
Mary Frey Dempsey became the anchor supporting him, not just in making a home and raising a family, but in helping accomplish much of the
radical goodness he tried to affect.

Once, at a national governor's conference meeting with New York
governor Nelson Rockefeller and Michigan Governor George Romney,
Rockefeller, who knew Dempsey's reputation for advocating for the rights
of the handicapped, leaned over and asked, almost in a whisper, whether
any of the Dempsey children were mentally retarded. "My first reaction,"
Dempsey said, was to say, "No." But Mary, before I had a chance to say
anything, answered, "Yes. Every youngster in the state of Connecticut
who is retarded is our kid."

"That was the best answer of all," confirmed Dempsey.

In their commitment to keep the needs of the less fortunate squarely before the public, the entire Dempsey family would participate in annual summer outings with groups of physically and mentally challenged and blind adults and children at state parks around Connecticut. Dempsey would play baseball and other sports events with them, and engage in swimming contests that the governor, unfortunately, always lost. What comes through in the reports of these encounters is that they were not what we today think of as photo-ops, though that indeed was part of it, but gatherings where genuine affection and warm fellow feeling were at the center of everything. If the governor was extraordinarily successful at selling the legislature on the need for new facilities and services for the less fortunate, it was in part because his conviction that *that* was the most important reason government existed was real, and he had the charisma to make it contagious.

It was also because John Dempsey possessed extraordinary political talent. People—even political opponents—liked him, and he could use relationships to make deals. One of his truly extraordinary gifts—one he possessed even in the early days at Cahir—was an absolutely uncanny ability to remember names. As friend Bill Stanley remembered, "If he met you once, he would remember your name forever. When he met you, if you told him your wife and children's names, the next time he saw you, he would remember your name, and he would ask you about the health of your wife and children, and he would call them all by name." That ability—so useful to a politician—was most evident on the day Dempsey returned to Cahir after a thirty-two-year absence in 1965. His return, as the son of Cahir who had gone to America and become the governor of one of its then most prosperous states, was a shutter-the-shops and close-the-schools event in Cahir, and the townspeople turned out and lined the streets to see what connection, if any, there might still be with this hometown boy. Imagine their surprise and elation when just as Dempsey's car reached the edge of town, he ordered the driver to stop, got out of the car, and waded into the crowd calling out to a remembered face. "Timmy Looney—see, I didn't forget." All those people whose names

John Dempsey remembered did not forget either, and in Connecticut as well as Ireland, people loved him for caring enough to remember them.

Of course, a likeable nature and a good memory for names alone don't account for John Dempsey's extraordinary success at transforming state government, which is what he did across so many fronts: human services, education, transportation, environmental protection, even the constitutional organization of government was restructured under his watch. A historian studying state government before Dempsey came into office and after he stepped down encounters two very different entities. So many of the agencies and programs that are essential to the operation and well-being of the people of Connecticut today came into existence on his watch. The reason he was able to do so much was because Dempsey as an executive was an extraordinary manager, and that, too, can be traced back to his roots in Cahir.

John's father Ned was a supervisor at the Going and Smith Flour mill by the town center bridge. From the top floor of the mill Ned had a very good view of the surrounding town, and he used that perch to keep an eye out for his young son John. "My father used to keep tabs on me from the top floor of that mill," Dempsey recalled, "and he would use his distinct and piercing whistle to stop me from mischief, such as stealing Black Tom's crabapples." As governor, John Dempsey managed people just the way his father had managed him. He was known for choosing people fit to the task he assigned them, and he'd let them run their own show, while keeping figurative watch over them from the top floor of the state capitol. When he saw things about to go amiss, he didn't hesitate to blow the whistle and set things straight. If he heard or read something that puzzled or rankled him about the operations of one of his departments, he would have the commissioner in charge of that agency in his office the same day to clarify the situation and, if necessary, address the problem. A long-time member of the governor's staff reported that "he only saw Dempsey angry once—when he found out there was a thirty-seven-million-dollar deficit in the welfare account and the welfare commissioner was on vacation for a month in Florida. Though he wouldn't hesitate to call appointees to account for their failings, he also was a fiercely loyal leader. A newspaper editorial reflecting on Dempsey's career stated, "Dempsey demanded accountability of himself and those who worked for him and in return he defended them against any charge from any critic." That was a management style whose roots could be found in an Irish flour mill along the River Suir.

Dempsey was an education governor, and that commitment to education also had its roots in Cahir. Dempsey supported a multi-year expansion of the University of Connecticut that transformed it from a good state college into a top national research university. He passed legislation to create the state's first schools of dentistry and medicine. Today, the University of Connecticut's primary medical education facility is named the John Dempsey Hospital. Dempsey also established a network of regional community and technical colleges that today provides affordable access to higher education for 67,000 students a year, and he simultaneously increased state aid to primary and secondary education in the state's 169 cities and towns.

Why was good education, affordable and available to all, such an important part of Dempsey's political agenda? As he himself said, "The sole reason my parents emigrated was to give me a good education and a good start in life. In those days [in Cahir] little or no secondary educational facilities were available to ordinary people."

Like many Irish-Americans, Dempsey was both an ardent American patriot and a committed Irish nationalist. The source of both, I think—and certainly the latter—was an event that happened in Cahir in the summer of 1921 that was, to a six-year-old boy, simply terrifying. In an effort to capture an Irish Republican Army leader named Dan Breen who was rumored to be hiding nearby, all the people of Cahir in the Dempseys' neighborhood, including the entire Dempsey family, were herded into an enclosed park as soldiers searched house to house for the fugitive. While Breen, disguised as a priest, made his way out of town, blessing the enemy searchers as he departed, young Dempsey got a taste of freedom-denied in the town of his birth, and it stuck with him.

As he prepared to leave the governor's office late in 1970, Dempsey was asked who his heroes had been. He mentioned Abraham Lincoln, who freed the enslaved and led America through its Civil War, and Franklin Roosevelt, the president who guided the nation through both the Depression and World War II. "I had other heroes, too," he said, "from earliest boyhood; men whose entire lives were a constant struggle for the cause of Irish independence. Those I particularly admired were Wolfe Tone, the rebel who died at age thirty-five while fighting the British almost two hundred years ago; Daniel Connell, called 'the Liberator' for his efforts to obtain justice for Ireland during the early nineteenth century; and Michael Collins, the patriotic leader whose untimely death at thirty-two occurred while I was living as a boy in Ireland."

The cause of Irish nationalism was important to Dempsey throughout his life. He often spoke of it in the talks he gave to the many Irish-American clubs and societies around the state. Sometimes, too, hints of it made their way into the broader American political arena, as happened during his 1958 campaign for Lieutenant Governor. His opponent that year was another Irish-American, a Republican named Stephen J. Sweeney from the industrial town of Naugatuck. The two met face to face at a special annual event called the meeting of the Crocodile Club, which takes place at Bristol's Lake Compounce amusement park. There, in the way of smiling crocodiles, politicians take good-natured satirical jabs at each other before a bipartisan crowd of onlookers. The Crocodile Club, in other words, is known for humor with a bite. At this gathering Sweeney was to speak before Dempsey, and he recognized that everyone would associate his opponent's name with that of the renowned prizefighter Jack Dempsey, who had lost a still-famous fight to Gene Tunny in 1926.

"Now in Ireland," Sweeney began, "there are kings, and the Sweeneys are descended from them. But unfortunately," he continued, "there are also sheep stealers there." He said a relative of one of the sheep stealers who had since come to Connecticut, had fought a prizefighter named Gene Tunney some years ago," and he warned people that if they saw this man, they should protect their sheep from being fleeced. The crowd roared as Sweeney took his seat.

A smiling Dempsey then rose and responded in kind. "We got rid of kings in Ireland in 1922," he dead-panned. "We also got rid of sheep stealers, except one family named Sweeney." He then said it had been ascertained that the Sweeney family was now living in Naugatuck, Connecticut (the politician Sweeney's home town), and that word was being sent to the Irish Republican Army about the discovery. By all accounts at the time, Dempsey won *this* match.

Both Dempsey's Irish and American patriotism were deeply connected to his Catholic faith, which was the anchor of all he did, throughout his life. To him, service to God and duty to country were part of the same Christian call to serve others that lay at the foundation of his beliefs, and his actions. His parents and he had become naturalized citizens as soon as the five-year waiting period for new immigrants was over, in 1930. As they left the chambers where they had just taken the oath of new citizens, Dempsey remembered his father saying, "We're Americans now, and, with the help of God, we'll see to it that America is never sorry. We must do what we can for this country." John Dempsey did much for his state and country through a career in public service that lasted thirty-five years, with an additional nineteen years of public engagement after that.

Dempsey was not hesitant to invoke the name of God in reminding his fellow citizens of their duty. And he did not do it in the half-embarrassed, all-inclusive efforts one finds many American politicians striving for today when they speak of a deity. Dempsey's faith was very real and very Catholic; it's Christian imperative to help others was just as real to him. Just as John F. Kennedy called on Americans to "ask not what their country can do for you, ask what you can do for your country," Dempsey never failed, in word or deed, to remind his fellow citizens that they had, in his opinion, a God-given duty to think beyond their own self-interest. "His devotion was to God, country, and certainly to the state." said his friend Bill Stanley. "He achieved all he achieved without ever losing his 'touch of the simple man, his love of God, of country, and of his fellow human beings'."

John Dempsey admired John Kennedy, and he knew him well, through his relationship with Connecticut party leader John Bailey, who was instrumental in Kennedy's election, and through Abraham Ribicoff, the Governor Dempsey served and subsequently succeeded. Dempsey shared all Irish Catholics' pride in Kennedy's election to the American Presidency, and it was lost on neither Kennedy nor Dempsey, that, but for a certain provision in the US Constitution, Dempsey had what it took to perhaps become another Irish Catholic President. That constitutional provision calls on all US Presidents to be born in the United States; Dempsey as an immigrant, was therefore disqualified. On one of his White House visits, though, Kennedy is reported to have told Dempsey, "Don't you worry. We're going to get that Constitutional provision changed." Then he paused and said, "But not till after I'm done."

Dempsey was on the highway between Boston and Hartford, returning from a meeting of the New England Governor's Conference on the afternoon of November 22, 1963, when a Massachusetts trooper stopped his car to tell him what had happened in Dallas. "I could not have been more affected had the news concerned a death in my own family," Dempsey said, "and I think most Americans felt the same way. I am wholly convinced," he continued "that no one had a greater love for his country, a greater desire to see the world at peace, or a greater concern for the well-being of his fellow man."

One source of Dempsey's dual-national patriotism was the belief—as true in Ireland as it is in America—that governments should be based on constitutions of the people and not the whims of monarchs. Just as Ireland in 1937 replaced the imperfect constitution it had implemented when Dempsey was a boy in Cahir, Dempsey oversaw the replacement of an imperfect constitution in Connecticut that was 147 years old. In early 1964, a federal court ruled Connecticut's constitutionally mandated way of creating legislative districts violated the fundamental principal that every person's vote should have equal influence. In similar cases, the federal courts had taken over the process of deciding how to rectify the error and imposed the new requirements by court order. Dempsey personally appeared before a three-judge federal panel to argue for Connecticut's ability to correct the problem without court intervention. The court assented, which led to the Connecticut Constitutional Convention of 1965, and its creation of a new state Constitution that Dempsey formally proclaimed as adopted in December. That document created the one-man, one-vote representation standards that will perpetually govern Connecticut districting, and marks one of the most distinctive moments in Dempsey's career in public service.

Governor Dempsey and the Irish salmon that helped clean Connecticut's rivers.

One of the most important programs of John Dempsey's administration, path-breaking then and transformative now, came about, at least in part, as a result of his 1965 return to his boyhood hometown. Dempsey was an avid fisherman, and on what was supposed to be the last day of his week-long visit, he went with a fishing-guide to the banks of the Suir, the river in which he used to fish and swim, in quest of one of those big salmon that were not so uncommon there, but which were by 1965 all but extinct along the polluted Connecticut River back home. A day of careful casting produced a lovely speckled trout, though a good-natured argument soon broke out over whether the diminutive fish weighed in at eight—or could it be nine—ounces. One of the guides refused to carry it to Dempsey's car, because, he said, "I might get a bloody hernia."

Undaunted, and intent on catching a salmon, the governor changed his travel plans to leave a day later, which gave him one more day for casting on the Suir. Sunday after Mass he was back at the water and—prayers answered—he got a salmon, and a fine, big one, on his hook. Even with all the remarkable memories that trip produced for Dempsey, he recalled years later that catching that salmon was one of the very best parts of a very best trip.

Now this joy of fishing for good big fish in his boyhood stream in his boyhood town may not have been the only reason, as the concept had been sitting around for a while, but shortly after his return to Connecticut, Governor Dempsey called together a committee of one hundred citizens from around the state to form a Clean Water Task Force. It's mission, he told them, was "not to be a committee to study the pollution problem" but rather to develop and present to the General Assembly "an action program" to control water pollution that had become so bad, Connecticut actress Katherine Hepburn had called the Connecticut River, "the world's most beautiful open sewer."

The result of Dempsey's action was America's first model pollution-control program, enacted before the nation's own clean water act, the start of a program that dramatically transformed New England's longest river—the Connecticut—as well as other streams, from open sewers to vibrant sources of natural beauty, wildlife habitat, and recreation. In 2012, the Connecticut River was designated the United States' First National

Blueway, "a model of how communities can integrate their land and water stewardship efforts with an emphasis on source to sea conservation." That designation was a tribute rooted in the work of John Dempsey, and a tribute to a salmon in Ireland.

John Noel Dempsey was proud to be Irish, and he was proud to be American. He was very proud of all the ways that the Irish in America had helped it become the nation it was. He saw his own life's work as part of that contribution, and he saw the source of his ability to make a difference as emanating from the town of his birth. Just a few months before he stepped down from office, Governor Dempsey made a speech at the twenty-fifth anniversary dinner of the Irish-American Home Society in Glastonbury, Connecticut. In that speech he talked about things that surely reflected his own experience, his own sense of self, and the importance of place.

"I think all reasonable men will agree," he told his audience, "that in virtually every conceivable field of endeavor, the Irish have made contributions of outstanding importance to making America into the most powerful nation in the world. There are many, many sources to prove they did this, and that they are doing it today.

"However," he continued, "When we ask how it was that the Irish, coming from a small and relatively obscure land, were able to do this, we find that question is more complex. One clue leading us to an answer may be found by going all the way back to the Old Testament—to the words spoken by Isaiah to the people of Israel.

'Look unto the rock whence you are hewn,' the prophet said, 'and to the hole of the pit from which you are dug out.'

Now I don't pretend to be a Biblical scholar," the governor said, "but it seems to me that Isaiah is saying here that man is like a piece of stone.

If you want to identify a particular piece of stone, you go back to the quarry from which it came. And in the same way, if you want to know what a particular individual is, you look back to his origins . . ."

Throughout his life, John Noel Dempsey looked back to his origins with pride, love, and thanksgiving to God that he had been placed on this earth as a son of Cahir, and that Cahir had formed him into the shape of the man he later became. When Dempsey returned to Ireland after a gap of thirty-two years and stood in the Cahir town square on a July day in 1965, he said, "My beloved people of my native town of Cahir, this is one of the happiest moments of my life. I came here today to say in some very small way how very grateful my family and I are to many people in this town. They have never permitted me to forget that if I was to go to a strange country and if I was to become part of it, then I should bring with me the traditions and the love and the faith of the Irish as my contribution to America."

And that he did. John Noel Dempsey became a great governor, perhaps the greatest, of a great American state. He made Connecticut better by far than it was before he arrived. One of the most significant reasons he was able to do this—and on this point those who knew him best all agree—was because long before John Dempsey was the Governor of Connecticut, he was a son of Cahir.

FURTHER READING
John Dempsey's official papers, photographs, and many of his personal papers as well are in the state archives in Hartford. The newspaper archives from the years of his administration are also a fine source of information on Dempsey.

For a view of Dempsey as primarily a subordinate of Democratic Party boss John Bailey, see *Joseph I. Lieberman, The Legacy: Connecticut Politics 1930–1980* (Hartford: Spoonwood Press, 1981).

There is a nice summary by Dempsey of his legislative achievements, and the shifting nature of gubernatorial power in *Public Administration Review,* Jan/Feb 1970, vol. 30, pp. 27–28.

WHY IS CONNECTICUT CALLED THE NUTMEG STATE?

Of all the nicknames used to describe Connecticut, none is more colorful, or controversial, than the "Nutmeg State." That slogan was born in the early days of the American republic, and it captured in two words much of what was both best and worst about the newly emerging Connecticut Yankee.

During the years surrounding 1800, Connecticut sea captains actively traded Wethersfield onions, which were used largely to feed Caribbean slaves, for the coveted spice called nutmeg. Nutmeg was grown only on the West Indian island of Grenada and in the Mollucas Islands of Indonesia. Also during this time, young Connecticut men ventured in ever-increasing numbers to the American South and Midwest to peddle the clocks, buttons, needles, and other sundries being produced by a host of small, new Connecticut manufacturers.

These Yankee peddlers loved having the hard-shelled nutmegs. They were durable, light, profitable, highly desired, and always easy to sell. So easy that, as the story goes, some of the craftier (and less ethical) of these Connecticut lads took to mixing wooden nutmegs in with the real ones, simultaneously increasing both their profits and their "nutmeg" supply. They, of course, counted on the fact that the purchaser wouldn't discover the difference until the trader himself was back in the Land of Steady Habits (or was that the Provision State?). As a result of these and similar trickster-like practices, Connecticut Yankees' reputation for clever-but-not-fully-principled trading spread widely and quickly, and the homeland of these likeable but shrewd hucksters became known as the Nutmeg State.

Just as their forefathers had done when they adopted as their own the song "Yankee Doodle"—a tune originally intended to ridicule Yankees for being crude rustics, Connecticans took to Nutmeg State the way snake oil took to salesman. At an early and quite formal dinner gathering of the Connecticut Historical Society, one of the dignitaries, following a numerous and extended series of toasts preceding his own, offered this salute to the assembled guests: "To the Nutmeg State," he said, lifting his glass yet again. "Where shall we find a grater?"

Throughout the nineteenth century, despite the sobriquet's pejorative connotations, most Connecticans remained pleased with their reputation for cleverness, and it was (and still is in some circles) common for men to wear a wooden nutmeg in their jacket lapels, identifying them as Connecticans. Such approbation was not universal, though, by any means. On several occasions, and especially in 1903, when it endorsed Emily G. Holcombe's efforts to officially name Connecticut the "Constitution State," the *Hartford Courant* urged citizens to reject the old nickname. "Do not yourself, and do not let others in your presence," it exhorted, "allude to Connecticut as the 'Nutmeg State.'" Continuing to use the phrase, they opined, was "an insult which we give ourselves." One hundred years later, Connecticans still, though with perhaps a bit less frequency, think of themselves as Nutmeggers, preferring, perhaps, a little spice to a lot of propriety.

WHAT MAKES CONNECTICUT, CONNECTICUT?

We all know there's something special and unique about Connecticut. Perhaps this is what it is.

Ancient trees of oak and maple and ash, taller than the steeple that makes the old church our town's tallest building, line walls of stone that frame the fields where my great-grandfather's grandfather plowed out his family's livelihood. I view those fields through rippled windowpanes of the house Eleazar Woodward built in 1780. It was, and is, a two-story, eight-room hilltop anchor of stability in a time of revolution. My old single-stack colonial farmhouse in Columbia, and the literally thousands of historic homes like it that are treasured parts of each of our 169 towns, are the story of Connecticut.

These Yankee farmsteads, whose owners answered Israel Putnam's call to defend embattled Boston after the shot heard 'round the world, are still real, still cared for by stewards who love their homes' connections to the past even as they tolerate their structural concessions to time and gravity. Culturally the old houses, walls, and trees of Connecticut are at the epicenter of who we tell ourselves we are: flinty, independent, freedom-minded folk, afraid neither of hard work nor of standing up for our rights. They call up a people at once both proud and restrained, eager to show in stone and clapboard that they had attained social standing but anxious to avoid ornamental excess or prideful display. It is a good story, and we like it, not just because the evidence for its basis in reality surrounds us, but also because it is aspirational, a call to the present to emulate former virtues.

217

Yet for all its reality, like all origin stories, this one is also part myth and, more important, only one chapter of Connecticut's story.

The Anglo-Puritan monopoly on the creation of Connecticut society lasted nearly two hundred years, etching its values deeply into our cultural heritage. After English Puritan migrants settled their first plantations of Windsor, Wethersfield, Hartford, and Saybrook along the Connecticut River in the 1630s, Connecticut became a vast cousinage. Almost the entire population consisted of descendants of the first twenty thousand Puritans who arrived in New England between 1620 and 1640. They prayed together, cleared forests together, built homes, plowed fields, and made walls together. They feared, friended, and then together fought the native inhabitants to take control over ever more land, all the while joining together in holy matrimony and vigorously obeying the Biblical injunction to be fruitful and multiply. The average Puritan family in Connecticut had eight children, and through those offsprings' repeated intermarriages, it is an exaggeration with more truth than lie in it to say that by 1750 every Anglo-Connectican was related.

But by 1818, when the state's first constitution disestablished the Puritan church as the official religion, other cultures, voices, ideas, and faiths had begun to add new colors, flavors, and influences. These augmented, and sometimes supplanted, the old Yankee ways. First came the Irish and the Germans, to build canals and railroads and to work in factory villages along Connecticut's fast-running streams and rivers. As the village factories were replaced by industrial cities, the immigrants from northern Europe were joined by southern and eastern Europeans, the largest groups consisting of Italians and Russian Jews. They were in turn followed by French-Canadians, African-Americans from the southern United States, and, more recently still, Puerto Ricans, Latinos, and Asians. All were responding to the push and pull of homeland misfortune and Connecticut opportunity. Each in their own way was shaped by and helped reshape the bedrock Connecticut Yankeedom into something still the same and yet different, and much more interesting.

Everyone who lives in Connecticut for any period of time is molded in subtle but powerful ways by the state's distinctively beautiful but challenging natural environment and the meteorological zones that give us four sharply different seasons and constantly changeable weather. Mark Twain, who wrote his greatest works while living in Hartford, once said he counted "one hundred and thirty-six different kinds of weather in four and twenty hours."

He was not the first Connectican to face the need to adapt to a changing climate. That privilege belonged to the Paleolithic bands who entered Connecticut more than twelve thousand years ago, as the Laurentian glaciers of the last ice age slowly retreated northward. These, the true first settlers, were nomadic hunters who followed mastodons, elk, giant beavers, and other animals into an arctic tundra. As the climate warmed, and the land began to host many of the trees, plants, and wildlife we associate with Connecticut today, natives settled into communities participating in seasonal rounds, changing locations several times a year to take advantage of the best hunting, fishing, or gathering opportunities.

By 1614, the year Dutchman Adriaen Block became the first European to explore the river that gives our state its name, Connecticut's indigenous people had evolved into tribal groups with recognized languages, pottery styles, and territorial distinctions. Some of them had been growing corn on the rich alluvial floodplains for many centuries. Today, in the shadows of the world's largest casinos, owned by the Pequot and Mohegan descendants of those tribes, are archaeological sites of their ancestors dating back more than ten millennia.

Indigenous peoples, the Puritan settlers, and all the immigrant groups who came after them have faced the challenge of making their way in a glacier-carved-and-scoured land. Connecticut has a rich and diverse geological history. The Appalachians, among the oldest mountains on Earth, make up the northwest hills of Litchfield County. The state's distinctive traprock ridges, such as the Hanging Hills of Meriden, were produced by lava flowing from rifts in the earth's crust, created when the super-continent Pangaea broke apart some two hundred million years ago. These rift valleys provided the foundation of the Connecticut River valley, the state's most fertile agricultural land. Southeast Connecticut, near New London, was formed from Avalonia, once part of the tectonic plate that is now West Africa, but which broke off and drifted north to merge with Pangaea

All these features were molded into the distinctive natural environment that is today's Connecticut by the intense glaciation of the past two million years, the most significant of which was the Laurentian ice sheet that began clawing its way through Connecticut only twenty-six thousand years ago. At its peak, the glacier covering Connecticut was more than a mile thick and extended to the far south shore of what is now Long Island. By the time it melted out of the state eleven thousand years later, it had completely transformed the land. The north-south grain of the landscape was accentuated, valleys were deepened, and hills rounded. The resulting pockets of lowland fertility surrounded by stony, hardscrabble hills help explain why the early settlers quickly hived off new settlements, sister towns four and five miles apart at sites where needed pockets of fertile soil could be found. Of Connecticut's 169 mostly small, mostly early towns, 144 of them still have fewer than twenty-five thousand residents.

The glaciers also carved out features that made ours a state of crystal lakes, vernal ponds, and long, straight rivers, which today, as ever, act as magnets for the people around them. Chief among all is the river the Indians called Quinnehtukqut, meaning "the long tidal river." Four hundred and ten miles from its source at the Canadian border to its outlet at Long Island Sound in Saybrook, the Connecticut River is New England's longest and most powerful river. With 148 tributaries and a watershed of more than eleven thousand square miles, it provides 70 percent of the fresh water that flows into Long Island Sound—a greater volume than the Hudson. Its daily tidal flows affect water levels sixty miles upstream, all the way to Enfield Falls, above Hartford.

Along with the river's outflow comes the sediment that saved much of the Connecticut's natural beauty. Silt deposits at the river's mouth created a massive sandbar that remained a barrier to deep-draft vessels until well into the twentieth century. In consequence, Connecticut never developed a major riverine port such as those in New York City or Boston, and the lower river valley remains so pristine that the Nature Conservancy has named it one of the Western Hemisphere's forty "last great places."

The Connecticut not only flows through the center of the state, it has also always been central to our economy, agriculture, politics, industry, and culture. The rich, alluvial terraces first attracted maize growers and then colonial settlers, followed by market farmers for New England's rising cities, and finally shade-tobacco producers. Visitors to the state were often surprised to see the (now disappearing) long, red tobacco barns next to gauze-covered fields near Windsor and beside the road to Bradley International Airport. But the Great River (the early English name for the Connecticut) offers a unique combination of soil, heat, and humidity that produces some of the finest cigar-wrapper tobacco in the world. For many years, shade tobacco was the state's largest single cash crop, although today's locavore food movement has brought a resurgence of small farms to the valley.

Shipbuilding, too, once flourished along the Connecticut. (Deeper-draft vessels had to be ox-hauled over the Saybrook bar.) During the age of sail, the state's then-abundant forests attracted shipwrights up and down the river. Most of what they constructed were the small, fast coastal vessels that plied the West Indian trade, taking food, barrel staves, and horses to be exchanged in the Caribbean for sugar, molasses, and slaves. In wartime, however, these same boats could be, and often were, converted into the armed privateers that preyed on enemy merchant ships. In 1814 a British raiding party attacked the town of Essex and destroyed twenty-seven vessels—the greatest single loss to American shipping in the entire War of 1812.

Hartford, sixty miles upriver from Saybrook, was the first capital of colonial Connecticut. Travel issues and intercity rivalry caused sessions of the general assembly to be held alternately at Hartford and New Haven after 1701, but Hartford became the sole capital in 1875. The decision came about as the result of a plan to build a new showcase capitol building overlooking the prospering city's other new civic showcase, scenic Bushnell Park. When, after seven years of construction, the building (designed by Richard M. Upjohn and built by James G. Batterson) was completed in 1878, all three branches of government moved from the 1796 Old State House near the river to the new Victorian edifice, where state government has been centered ever since.

In marked contrast to today, Hartford was one of America's wealthiest cities when the new capitol was built. Much of that wealth was generated by the great new industries made possible by the Connecticut

River valley's machine-tool revolution. Samuel Colt's onion-domed arms complex at Coltsville, the ax factory in Collinsville, the Cheney textile mill complex in Manchester, and the Pratt and Whitney aircraft engine operations in East Hartford all evolved from the brilliant innovations in machine-tool design that made the Connecticut Yankee a world-renowned symbol for technological innovation. From Putnam to Bridgeport, Waterbury to Norwich and points in between, Connecticut factories and the hundreds of thousands of Yankees and immigrants who worked in them turned our state into a manufacturing phenomenon of unprecedented proportions. This industrial greatness rose hand in hand with the insurance industry that remains synonymous with Connecticut and the publishing industry that attracted some of America's best and brightest authors, including Mark Twain, Harriet Beecher Stowe, and later the insurance executive-turned-poet Wallace Stevens.

If the Connecticut River centers us, it also divides us. From the beginning, the settlers of the eastern part of the state felt a natural orientation toward, and affinity with, the metropolis of Boston, while those west of the river have had interests more closely aligned with metropolitan New York. The differences that today are most clearly seen in the friendly rivalries between Yankee fans (west of the river) and Red Sox fans (east of the river) were expressed two centuries ago in the violent exchanges between Tories loyal to the Crown (west) and the Patriots (east) during the American Revolution. Of course, such predispositions are and were far from universal—there were plenty of patriots west of the river and vice versa. Still, those who know Connecticut well sense the very real differences between the Quiet Corner and the Gold Coast, the Litchfield Hills and the Last Green Valley.

All Connecticans, wherever they live, share a soul-deep appreciation for two things our state has in absolute abundance and in unusually close proximity: nature and culture. Even though we are the fourth-most densely populated state (742.6 people per square mile), Connecticut's original dispersed settlement patterns combined with widespread reforestation let almost all of us live surrounded by, or with nearby access to, great natural beauty of immense variety. Ours is a state of sun-drenched summer beaches, achingly beautiful red- and gold-leaved forests, rail beds

The Goodspeed Opera House, along the Connecticut River in East Haddam. Connecticans love culture, because it's in our nature. CAROL M. HIGHSMITH COLLECTION, LIBRARY OF CONGRESS

turned into ski trails, bubbling trout streams, steep mountain paths with stunning vistas, sculpted parks, beaver ponds, and signature stone-walled fields and byways that let one and all know they really are in New England. It is astonishing how close all of these are to interstate highways that sometimes resemble parking lots.

Within, among, and around Connecticut's profusion of natural wonders are the cultural treasures of a people who value ideas, find inspiration in art and theatre, are moved profoundly by music and dance, and who center themselves in the present by immersing themselves in the past. Connecticans built the nation's first public art museum, the Wadsworth Atheneum in 1843, and its first publicly funded park, Hartford's Bushnell Park, in the 1850s. It established the third-oldest university in 1701, and Yale continues to rank as one of the world's leading educational institutions. The 1877 Goodspeed Opera House still introduces the world to classics of musical theatre, such as *Annie, Shenandoah,* and *Man of La Mancha,* all of which first came to life on its stage. The Connecticut Historical Society, founded in 1825 as one of America's first historical societies, helps ensure that those charged with creating Connecticut's future are informed by the ideas and artifacts of our past. It might be said that each of the above-named institutions has been parent to the hundreds of museums, galleries, theaters, and concert halls across our small state that together have created one of the richest cultural environments in America. As Connecticans, we love culture, because it is in our nature.

Whenever you wonder what it is that connects you so deeply to Connecticut—this land, its culture, and its people—pause in your reflection, and go immerse yourself in all the beauty, talent, and inspiration that is everywhere around you. Take a walk in the woods, a drive through the countryside, a paddle around the lake, a walk through that exhibit. Ask yourself, "What makes Connecticut, Connecticut?" It will all become clear to you, clearer than words can say.

A HISTORIAN COMES HOME

How it feels to buy the family home your sixth great grandfather built 260 years ago.

This is a story about a house. Not just any house, but a house with long, deep roots—roots that wind through time, cross through space, and wrap themselves around my consciousness. It is a house that affects, in the most primary way, my own sense of who I am and where I belong.

I first encountered this house as a child visiting Columbia, Connecticut (the town where my father was born), from Europe (where I was born, and where my father was fighting the Cold War as a military attaché to the Department of State).

I loved Columbia—it's colonial green, crystal lake, white-steepled church, and the three cottages where my grandfather supported his later years by renting summer to tourists. Columbia was my America; and my

Woodward Hill Farm, Columbia Connecticut. CAROL M. HIGHSMITH, LIBRARY OF CONGRESS

love for this state and country was born on my grandfather's screened-porch and beside the evening campfires. There I became a historian, listening to tales of my family's long-time connection to Columbia, stories that reached all the way to the early 1700s when it was called Lebanon Crank. Many of those stories centered around the house on Woodward Hill, a three-story colonial built by my many-times-great grandfather Eleazar and his father Israel during the American Revolution, and in which succeeding generations of my family lived until 1875. Then, the accidental death of my great-great grandfather Madison led to a distress sale outside the family. The place was still called the Woodward Hill Farm, though, and whenever we drove by it on those childhood visits, I looked with longing and wonder at this house that bore witness to so much of my family's past.

In my thirties, as a successful songwriter and music producer, I heard that the Woodward Hill house was for sale. I flew in from Ohio to offer the then-owner their asking price. Seeing the name Woodward on the offer, the owners instantly increased the price by $20,000, which at the time, was a considerable amount. Angered, I flew home. I didn't buy the house then, but I never got over my longing for it.

A few years ago, thirty-years after the sale-that-wasn't, I indulged myself and took the long route through Columbia on my way to give a Sunday talk in Groton. As always, I slowed when I came to the top of Woodward Hill to look with regret at the house I had so wanted. When I saw the "For Sale" sign, I literally slammed on the brakes, pulled to the side of the road, and just stared. I could not believe that the dream deferred so long ago might yet be realized.

My immediate reaction was that this was truly providential. That's the old Puritan idea that there are no coincidences in life, but rather, that God (or Fate) intervenes in our affairs to make things happen when and the way they do. Here I was, at a time of great change in my own life (an ended marriage and a just sold house) presented with an opportunity to reclaim my own history, and a childhood dream, by, literally, coming home.

I am a history professor these days. The glory days and income of my music career are long behind me. And without the cooperation of sellers who understood the importance of history and the meaning of family, my dream deferred might have ended for good. Today though, thanks in no small part to them, the Woodward Hill Farm in Columbia, Connecticut, is once again back in the family, and my wife Marie and I are its stewards. My sense that I am where I was always meant to be has never, ever been stronger.

As Robert Frost said in his poem, "Directive"

Here are your waters and your watering place,
Drink and be whole beyond confusion.

ACKNOWLEDGMENTS

People are basically generous – this book is the proof. It exists because so many people offered so many things to its creation—ideas, insights, encouragement, time, resources, friendship, and more—I fear it is impossible to thank all of them. So, in humility, I offer this recognition of *some* of this book's midwives. Those I have unintentionally overlooked, please rest assured I will remember you in the middle of the night—curse my oversight—and give heartfelt thanks that you were there to help.

First, are the hundreds—over the years, in fact, thousands—of people who have taken the time to attend the lectures, talks, performances, conferences, and symposia where many of these stories had their first-draft hearings. Your questions, reactions, additions, and critiques helped make each of them better than they began—I hope you can see your reflections in the final product.

Next are friends and colleagues in both the academic and public history communities who sometimes read, sometimes listened, sometimes praised, sometimes criticized, but always inspired me with their ideas and by their examples: Karen Kupperman, Bruce Fraser, Joan Hill, Tim Breen, Sally Whipple, Jason Mancini, Briann Greenfield, Ed Dempsey, Tim Oliver, Ken Wiggin, Elizabeth Normen, Matt Warshauer, Ann Plane, Nick Bellantoni, Faith Damon Davison, Mark Healey, Charles Lyell, Dean Nelson, Meg Harper, Brian Jones, Donna Baron, Brian Cofrancesco, Anne Raymond, Todd Levine, Brenda Miller, Kerry Marsh, Cary Carson, Sue Haverstock, Rebecca Taber Conover, P J O'Meara, Catherine Fields, Melissa Tantaquidgeon Zobel, Don Rogers, Fiona Vernal, Michael Jehle, Dave Corrigan, Linda Hocking, Brian Cofrancesco, Sara Nelson, Brendan Kane, Greg Mangan, Cathy Fields, Peter Hinks, Melanie Newport, Liz Shapiro, Gail Hurley, Sally Nyhan, Dean Nelson, Alan Marcus, Richard DeLuca, Brenda Milkovsky, Kate Grandjean, Jim Moran, Tracey Wilson, Mary Donohue, Kip Bergstrom, Beth Regan, Scott Wands, Kathy Maher, Stephen Shaw, Shirley Roe, Steve Armstrong, Carolyn Ivanoff, Lizette Pelletier, Nina Dayton, Barbara Austen, Kevin McBride, Helen Rozwadowski, Dick Tomlinson, Kate Steinway, Susan Orred, Chris Clark,

Acknowledgments

Bill Hosley, Andrea Stannard, Beverly Lucas, Christine Ermenc, Helen Higgins, Allen Ramsay, Amy Trout, Betsy Golden Kellem, Lisa Wilson, Christine Pittsley, Richard Pickering, Bob Thorsen, Beth Rose, Wick Griswold, Christian Ayne Crouch, Steve Bullock, David Naumec, Anna Mae Duane, Mark Overmeyer-Valezquez, Helen Rozwadowski, Ingrid Wood, Bill Keegan, Jenny Anderson, Brenda Miller, Dick Brown, and Bruce Clouette, and many others.

A very helpful group of archivists and archives helped me secure permissions for the use of images. These include: Lizette Pelletier, Barbara Austin, Allen Ramsay and Christine Pittsley at the Connecticut State Library; Major John Bainbridge, USA Ret; Ashley Cataldo and Jim Moran at the American Antiquarian Society; Meredith L. Steinfels at the Hood Museum of Art, Dartmouth; Tim Burt at Lyman Orchards; Lauren Chen at Boston Public Library; Meg Ryan & Ross Harper at PAST, Inc.; Michelle Henning at the Bowdoin College Museum of Art; David K. Leff; Ruth Shapleigh Brown; Andrea Felder at the New York Public Library; Katie Randall at Oxford University Press.

Some people offered extraordinary assistance, for which I am extraordinarily grateful. Meredith Petersons meticulously proofed and formatted the final draft that went to the publisher—words can't express. The Band of Steady Habits (Rachel Smith, Teagan Smith, Jeremy Teitelbaum, Duke York, and sometimes Rick Spencer, too) helped put the words to music, the place where I often found the deeper meaning of the story. Bill Keegan served as mapmaker extraordinaire. My assistant Kathy Foley kept the trains running on time and is the Queen of the Morning Nag List.

Family came through in wonderful ways. Sue Hart, who is family in all but DNA, has supported my work as State Historian in more ways that I can count. My brother Charles Dean Madison Woodward provided the quiet place in the Berkshires where the last lap of the writing was completed. My sister Sharon Jackson loved this book without reservation before she'd read a page. My brother-in-law Jim encouraged her to do so. My children (Peter, Thomas, Michael and Halley) showed me the continuum of history, and my grandchildren (Beebe, Lily, Abby, Zoe, Henry and Claire) reminded me why getting it down on paper matters.

230

I have also been blessed during the long process of book-making with five four-legged family pals, only two of whom are still on this side of the bridge: Gracie the Wonder Dog, who wagged her way into my soul and never left; Spencer, the Cavie who liked to fish; Simon, all heart, and he still has mine; and Jasper and Callie, the new twins who make every day a happy adventure.

Finally, and most importantly, there's Marie: smart, talented, creative, and a tireless worker, baker of cakes, and master of gardens, she is the home this historian comes home to.

This book is dedicated to her.

INDEX

ABOUT THE AUTHOR

WALT WOODWARD is the State Historian of Connecticut and an Associate Professor of History at the University of Connecticut. He is the narrator and producer of *Today in Connecticut History* (with CT Humanities) and *Grating the Nutmeg: The Podcast of Connecticut History* (with *Connecticut Explored* magazine). His book *Prospero's America: John Winthrop, Jr., Alchemy and the Creation of New England Culture 1606–1676* won the Homer D. Babbidge Award for Best Book on Connecticut History from the Association for Connecticut History. He also writes the "From the State Historian" column in *Connecticut Explored*. A widely sought after public speaker and historian, he lives in Columbia, CT.